The Iranian Christian Diaspora

The Iranian Christian Diaspora

Religion and Nationhood in Exile

Benedikt Römer

I.B. TAURIS
LONDON • NEW YORK • OXFORD • NEW DELHI • SYDNEY

I.B. TAURIS
Bloomsbury Publishing Plc, 50 Bedford Square, London, WC1B 3DP, UK
Bloomsbury Publishing Inc, 1359 Broadway, 12th Floor, New York, NY 10018, USA
Bloomsbury Publishing Ireland, 29 Earlsfort Terrace, Dublin 2, D02 AY28, Ireland

BLOOMSBURY, I.B. TAURIS and the I.B. Tauris logo
are trademarks of Bloomsbury Publishing Plc

First published in Great Britain 2024
This paperback edition published 2026

Copyright © Benedikt Römer, 2024

Benedikt Römer has asserted his right under the Copyright,
Designs and Patents Act, 1988, to be identified as Author of this work.

For legal purposes the Acknowledgements on pp. vii–viii constitute
an extension of this copyright page.

Series design by Adriana Brioso
Cover image courtesy of the author

All rights reserved. No part of this publication may be: i) reproduced or transmitted in any form, electronic or mechanical, including photocopying, recording or by means of any information storage or retrieval system without prior permission in writing from the publishers; or ii) used or reproduced in any way for the training, development or operation of artificial intelligence (AI) technologies, including generative AI technologies. The rights holders expressly reserve this publication from the text and data mining exception as per Article 4(3) of the Digital Single Market Directive (EU) 2019/790.

Bloomsbury Publishing Inc does not have any control over, or responsibility for, any third-party websites referred to or in this book. All internet addresses given in this book were correct at the time of going to press. The author and publisher regret any inconvenience caused if addresses have changed or sites have ceased to exist, but can accept no responsibility for any such changes.

A catalogue record for this book is available from the British Library.

Library of Congress Cataloging-in-Publication Data
Names: Römer, Benedikt, author.
Title: The Iranian Christian diaspora : religion and nationhood in exile / Benedikt Römer.
Description: London, UK ; New York, NY, USA : I.B Tauris, 2024. | Revised version of a PhD thesis, originally published under the title: Elam in exile : religion and nature among Iranian Christians in the diaspora, and submitted to the Faculty of Humanities and Social Sciences, University of Bayreuth, 2022. | Includes bibliographical references and index.
Identifiers: LCCN 2023039116 (print) | LCCN 2023039117 (ebook) |
ISBN 9780755651689 (hardback) | ISBN 9780755651726 (paperback) |
ISBN 9780755651696 (pdf) | ISBN 9780755651696 (epub) | ISBN 9780755651719
Subjects: LCSH: Christianity–Iran. | Christians–Iran. | Iranian diaspora. |
Iranians–Foreign countries–Religion. | Nationalism–Religious aspects–Christianity.
Classification: LCC BR1115.I7 R66 2024 (print) | LCC BR1115.I7 (ebook) |
DDC 275.5–dc23/eng/20240129
LC record available at https://lccn.loc.gov/2023039116
LC ebook record available at https://lccn.loc.gov/2023039117

ISBN: HB: 978-0-7556-5168-9
PB: 978-0-7556-5172-6
ePDF: 978-0-7556-5169-6
eBook: 978-0-7556-5170-2

Typeset by Newgen KnowledgeWorks Pvt. Ltd., Chennai, India

For product safety related questions contact productsafety@bloomsbury.com.

To find out more about our authors and books visit www.bloomsbury.com
and sign up for our newsletters.

Contents

List of figures		vi
Acknowledgements		vii
Note on transliteration		ix
Notes on citation		x
Introduction		1
1	Historical overview: Iranian Christians and their journey into exile	9
2	Theoretical perspectives on religion, the nation and diaspora	37
3	Naturalizing Christianity (I): Introduction and the festivals of Nowruz and Yaldā	55
4	Naturalizing Christianity (II): Persian poets and poetry, Iranians in the Bible and the Iranian Christian martyrs	97
5	Critical engagement with Islam between expatriation, non-Islamiosity and Islamophobia	137
6	Diasporic religion among Iranian Christians: Meanings of exile, visions of return and the Elam Prophecy	161
Conclusion		189
Notes		195
Bibliography		211
Index		233

Figures

1	A 'Persian National Hymn', composed by Hassan Dehqāni-Tafti	61
2	A *Haft Sin* table with a Bible	76
3	The '*Haft Sin* of the Titles of Christ' (*Haft Sin-e Alqāb-e Masih*)	81
4	A poem entitled *Jahān-e Zibā*, 'Beautiful World', by Qarācheh-Dāghi	111
5	Scenes from a children's book narrating the story of a 'martyr' killed during the Iran-Iraq War	130
6	Portraits of the 'Martyrs of the Iranian Church'	131
7	Film poster of *The Tune of Nostalgia*	162
8	A 2015 issue of the magazine *Rāh-e Salib* seemingly arbitrarily features the Hebrew name of the Feast of the Ascension of Christ (*Khag ha-Aliyah*)	175
9	A video screened during a worship session at Elam Alive Ministries in Essen, Germany	177

Acknowledgements

This book is a thoroughly revised version of a PhD thesis with the title *Elam in Exile: Religion and Nation among Iranian Christians in the Diaspora* that I submitted to the Faculty of Humanities and Social Sciences at the University of Bayreuth on 5 May 2022 and successfully defended in a viva voce examination on 28 July of the same year. First and foremost, I am indebted to my supervisors, Paula Schrode and Benjamin Weineck, who throughout the project provided me with thorough guidance and allowed me to follow my personal curiosities, and to Robert Langer, who kindly agreed to serve as a third examiner for the viva voce examination.

A number of colleagues, both former and current, supported me by reading parts of my material and discussing it during lunch or coffee breaks. I am particularly grateful to Muhadj Adnan, Sebastian Ambros, Ibrahim Bachir, Loïc Bawidamann, Hanni Bezem, Christoph Bochinger, Benedikt Erb, Sophie Faulstich, Andrea Göcer, Benjamin Kirby, Jakob Krais, Hakan Mertcan, Lisa Mohrat, Hanna Nieber, Maria Papenfuss, Stefan Schröder and Eva Spies. My Persian language skills owe a great deal to Christian Funke and Nima Mina who both also taught me much about Iran. Julian Schmeißner volunteered to read an earlier draft of this book and made valuable comments. Chris Hitchcock was always available to answer any question I had on the intricacies of the English language. Daniel Grün discussed my ideas with ruthless candour during hours-long phone calls. Other friends and colleagues who contributed to this project preferred to not be mentioned by name. I would like to hereby thank them as well.

Much gratitude is due to the Iranian Christians who most kindly agreed to share their experiences and perspectives with me. While many of them as well opted to remain anonymous, I would like to specifically mention the faculty members of PARS Theological Centre (Hampshire, UK) who kindly welcomed me at their institute and introduced me to their work. I would also like to thank Kathrin Weiss and Johannes Hägel who helped me get in touch with most of my personal interlocutors.

Since my undergraduate studies, I have benefited extensively from two scholarships by the German Academic Scholarship Foundation that, among other things, enabled me to spend two formative years at SOAS University of London. For my PhD research, I could moreover rely on the funding provided by the German Federal Ministry of Education and Research. This project would not have been possible without this financial support.

I would like to thank Yasmin Garcha, Faiza Zakaria and especially Nayiri Kendir at I.B. Tauris, who patiently accompanied the publishing process and were there to answer the many questions I had. Gratitude is moreover due to Elam Ministries, CAS Bayreuth and the Rt Revd Dr Guli Francis-Dehqani for granting permission for the usage of scans and images under their copyright. All other third-party copyrighted material displayed in the pages of this book is done so on the basis of 'fair use for the purposes of teaching, criticism, scholarship or research' only in accordance with international copyright law and is not intended to infringe upon the ownership rights of the original owners.

Finally, given that most of the research for this book took place during the Covid-19 pandemic lockdowns, I would like to thank my friends who made those difficult times more bearable, particularly Awda, Daniel, Hanni, Jonas and Sophie. I am thankful to my parents, Friederike and Norbert Römer, who have tirelessly supported me over the years. I dedicate the book to my late grandmother, Berni Sommermann, who passed away as I was finishing off the manuscript and who was excited that I am writing a book.

Note on transliteration

This book follows the guidelines suggested by the journal *Iranian Studies* for transliterating terms and quotes from Modern Persian. For terms familiar in English the conventional spelling is preferred over a transliteration (i.e. Tehran instead of *Tehrān*). In the transliteration of personal names, those names common in English are likewise spelled the familiar English way rather than following the transliteration scheme (i.e. *Joseph* instead of *Zhuzef*, or *Thomas* instead of *Tumās*). This is most relevant for names of Iranian Armenians and Assyrians. For individuals' names in this book that occur both in Persian-language and in English-language sources, I use their transliterated Persian spelling to refer to their Persian-language work and their self-chosen English spelling to refer to their English-language work in citations and bibliography (e.g. Shari'at and Shariat).

Since this book to a large extent relies on audiovisual sources, the question of how to transliterate spoken Persian became a pressing issue. I have decided to maintain the transliteration system suggested by *Iranian Studies* and transliterate episodes in spoken Persian, imagining how they would be written out in a casual setting, for instance, an online chat. Accordingly, I have refrained from rewriting, for instance, *mano* as *man rā*, *khubeh* as *khub ast* or *midunan* as *midānand*. Persian speakers are thus enabled to gain a sense of the tone and register of the cited quotes. Lastly, while I have indicated the *nim-fāseleh* with a hyphen when transliterating texts, I have used a hyphen only to indicate the plural suffix *-hā* and *ezāfeh* constructions for audiovisual sources.

Notes on citation

When using video sources in this book, the in-text citation indicates the main individual(s) involved, for instance, the pastor delivering a recorded sermon (e.g. 'Navā'i 2015'). This appeared more reasonable than labelling video sources according to, for example, the name of the YouTube channel they have been uploaded to (e.g. to use the same example, '*kelisa Iranian*'), which can be quite arbitrary. In cases in which a video source has not been dominated by one or several identifiable individuals, I have indicated the institution behind the video (e.g. 'Kelisā-ye 222 Kāyseri 2019'). I have sorted the bibliography by the same principle.

Introduction

First of all, I want you to know that, as Christians, we have come to love Iran even more. We have become more Iranian (Irāni-tar shodim)! The reason for this is that, where the Arabs used to be our heroes [in the Quran], we in the Bible see Iranians as heroes. … Read the Bible and you will come to be even more in love with Iran, because you will see the love of God for Iran and Iranians! You will become more devoted to Iranian culture. Yes, whoever becomes a Christian will love Iran more than before, because when they are reading the Bible, they will see that God has a wonderful plan for Iran.

(Shariʿat and Ebrāhimiān 2016: m. 48:08–48:45)

With this statement, the US-based Iranian Christian televangelist Hormoz Shariʿat began his 2016 address on the occasion of the Iranian new year festival of Nowruz. Speaking to an imaginary interlocutor who asked him why Muslim-born Iranian converts to Christianity, once they left Islam, continued to cherish Iranian national traditions, Shariʿat's assertive reply almost comes across as a counterattack. His reference to the 'Arab heroes' of the Quran suggests that Shariʿat deemed it more reasonable to ask Iranian *Muslims* why they cared about Iranian national traditions, thus insinuating that Islam was an 'Arab religion'. According to Shariʿat, the conversion of an Iranian Muslim to Christianity by no means constituted a step away from true Iranian-ness but the exact opposite: a conscious reaffirmation of their Iranian national identity.

Religious and national identities are intimately connected. This book will demonstrate how this connectedness becomes particularly pronounced among first-generation emigrants who are unable to return to their homeland because of their religious affiliation. During the past few decades, a steadily growing diasporic community of Iranian Christians has come into being that has its main centres in Turkey, Germany, the Netherlands, Scandinavia, the UK and North America. While, in 2004, Kathryn Spellman estimated that there were 20,000 Evangelical and Pentecostal Iranian Christians living outside Iran (Spellman 2004: 169), this number is likely to have markedly increased by the early 2020s. Some Iranian Christians have joined existing Christian congregations using the language of their new country of residence. Others, however, have joined or founded Persian-speaking exile churches. The material discussed in this book stems from these communities.

Episodes like the one mentioned previously illustrate just how vibrant discourses on Iranian nationhood are in Iranian Christian exile churches. Exploring the triangular connection of religion, the nation and diaspora, this book focusses on the following questions: What narratives and practices do Iranian Christians in exile use to construct an explicitly Iranian Christian national-religious identity? Why, at all, do they see a necessity to make their Iranian national identity a constant topic in their services and media productions? How does their dwelling in exile interrelate with their national self-perception and their religious ideas? What visions of a future Iran do they entertain and how are these visions different from those of other Iranians in the diaspora? Among the existing scholarly literature on Iranian Christians, which includes works in diverse academic fields including anthropology, sociology, psychology, history, theology and the study of religions, these questions have so far only been raised to a very limited degree. Moreover, previous pertaining works have suffered from three concrete shortcomings that this book seeks to address.

Academic research on Iranian Christians: Three shortcomings

The first and most obvious shortcoming is a lack of proficiency in the Persian language among researchers.[1] The root of this problem arguably lies in the status quo of academic curricula: the prevalent branding of Persian as an 'Islamic language' predetermines *who* will learn the language in the first place, namely students at departments for Islamic Studies, and *what* researchers possessing or attaining proficiency will end up researching, namely matters relating to Islam. Conversely, students of the study of religions rarely learn a language like Persian to a level that enables them to fully use it for research. Because of this unfortunate deadlock, a large amount of highly interesting and relevant material has so far remained unstudied. A secondary aim of this book is therefore to detach the Persian language from its 'Islamic(ate)' branding.

The second shortcoming is that many of the existing works, especially those dealing with historical aspects of Iranian Christianities, adopt an implicitly or even overtly (Evangelical) Christian theological or missionary perspective.[2] Depending on one's personal point of view, this may not necessarily be deemed objectionable. In this book, however, I am explicitly writing as a sociologist of religion with expertise in Iranian studies and not as a (non-)religious individual. Questions of whether Iranian Christians practice a 'correct' form of Christianity or whether there *actually* is a 'spiritual awakening' happening in Iran are consequently of absolutely no concern to this book. My perspective aims to be descriptive in nature, not normative. This criticism notwithstanding, the works in question contain valuable accounts of the history of the Iranian Christian movement that have greatly helped me in the writing of this book.

The third and final shortcoming in the existing literature on Iranian Christians primarily concerns sociological studies dealing with the conversions of Muslim-born Iranians to Christianity. Alongside the mentioned issue of language that has also prevented researchers from conducting interviews in their interlocutors' native/national language, researchers have tended to treat such conversions as merely the results of religious individualism. Darwish, for example, highlights a 'religious quest for personal spiritual fulfilment, a universal expression of human spirituality' (Darwish 2018: 5) as a driving force behind such conversions, while Kéri and Sleiman, who also took into account conversions beyond the Iranian case, foreground 'intraindividual processes dominated either by intellectual-experimental orientation or emotiondriven mystical experiences' (Kéri and Sleiman 2017: 12). Conversions of Muslim-born Iranians to Christianity may thus appear as if they evolve in a de territorialized vacuum.

In this book, I treat the Iranian Christian movement as one result of an ongoing religious and social transformation in Iran. A recent quantitative study suggests that the official population census of Iran, which records religious affiliation through family descendancy and identifies 99.6 per cent of Iranians as Muslims (Markaz-e Āmār-e Irān 2018: 99), strikingly differs from the religious self-image of Iranians.[3] As attachment to Islam is dwindling,[4] many Iranians abandon religion altogether and consider themselves as areligious or atheist, while others embark on a quest for religious alternatives. One of these alternatives is Evangelical Christianity. Academic research therefore runs the risk of being reductionist if it only analyses post-conversion narratives and disregards wider developments in contemporary Iran. By pointing to the saliency of discourses on Iranian nationhood in Iranian Christian diaspora communities, this book aims to offer a new contextualization that is informed by an area studies perspective.

There are, of course, other ways to contextualize and explain conversions of Muslim-born Iranians to Christianity, such as their description as a 'migration strategy' (Akcapar 2006) and their discussion in the context of asylum trials.[5] One may also approach the Iranian Christian movement as a product of global Evangelicalism or study it within the field of World Christianities. In this book, however, I am more concerned with local, national dimensions, rather than global or universal ones.

Terminologies: Why 'Iranian Christians'?

The designation 'Iranian Christians' is not as straightforward as it may seem at first glance. There are alternative terms used to describe the individuals I will collectively refer to as 'Iranian Christians' in this book. For terminological clarity, they require a brief discussion.

Although commonly used, the terms 'Christian converts' (cf. Chehabi 2013) and 'non-ethnic Christians' (cf. Sanasarian 2004) would not be accurate designations because they do not include members of the Iranian Armenian and Assyrian ethno-religious minorities. As we shall see in Chapter 1 and throughout this book, Iranian Armenians and Assyrians who founded or joined Persian-speaking churches have played a major role at the early stages of the Iranian Christian movement and partially today. Moreover, the term 'Christian converts' excludes the children of Muslim-born Iranian converts to Christianity who are playing an increasingly significant role in Iranian Christian exile churches.

A second option is to highlight the denominational identity of Iranian Christians and call them 'Iranian Protestants', 'Iranian Evangelicals' and/or 'Iranian Pentecostals'. Certainly, it is important to highlight the Evangelical and Pentecostal character of the bulk of Iranian Christian exile churches; likewise, the historical relevance of the Western Protestant missions to Iran should be acknowledged as they constitute one of the multiple roots of the Iranian Christian movement. That said, denomination plays virtually no role in the religious self-perception of Iranian Christians. Likewise, Iranian diaspora churches in their names almost never indicate their denominational affiliation (if they have one at all). Instead, they use epithets highlighting their Iranian character by using terms like *Irāni* (Iranian) or *fārsi-zabān* (Persian-speaking). I will expand on this phenomenon in Chapter 1.

Unless they are explicitly relevant, I will therefore refrain from using denominational terms in this book. One may object to this approach and accuse me that, by doing this, I unjustifiably equate Christianity and Evangelicalism in my analytical language. At the same time, it appears patronizing to impose denominational labels when they are completely irrelevant to the individuals described. More importantly, however, this book describes the Iranian Christian movement as a *national* movement. It therefore seems justified to de-emphasize matters of denomination when looking for a succinct collective designation for the communities studied.

Thirdly, the term 'Persian-speaking Christians' has historically emerged as a collective label for Iranian Protestant Christians using the Persian language in their services.[6] Indeed, the use of the Persian language is *the* crucial identity-marker for Iranian Christians, not least because it is the main factor leading to their legal persecution within Iran. This book, however, is mainly concerned with the Iranian Christian *diaspora*. To use the epithet 'Persian-speaking' for churches in Turkey, Germany or the UK implies that Persian speakers from Afghanistan and Tajikistan are equally relevant attendants of the communities studied in this book. Although there may be a small number of non-Iranian Persian speakers active in these churches, their Iranian character is taken for granted by its members and leaders. Pastors in diaspora churches using the Persian language as a rule preach *as Iranians to fellow Iranians*. In their sermons, they self-evidently reference current events in Iran, not Afghanistan or Tajikistan. Thus, although many churches operate under the potentially transnational label 'Persian-speaking', it seems reasonable to not adopt this designation to the analytical level and use the term 'Iranian Christians' instead.

Taken all together, this book uses the term 'Iranian Christians' to designate attendants of Persian-speaking Christian communities, usually Evangelical and Pentecostal in denominational leaning, which are located outside of Iran. Iranian Christians may be Muslim-born converts or Christian-born Iranian Armenians and Assyrians.[7] Notably, those Iranian Armenians and Assyrians who have moved abroad and attend churches using the Armenian or Neo-Aramaic languages are not covered by the term. Although they, too, are Christians from Iran, their communities do not make references to Iran as a homeland in the way Persian-speaking churches do.

Sources used and methodology

Like many academic works composed between the years 2020 and 2022, this book and especially its methodology are also a product of the Covid-19 pandemic. Due to the global travel restrictions, I had to largely cancel the planned field research I was going to conduct. Online sources, especially video recordings of sermons delivered in Iranian Christian exile churches, consequently feature more centrally in this book than they might have without the pandemic. Regrettable though this may be, the digital media productions of Iranian Christian exile churches constitute a key source that so far has remained virtually unstudied. For almost two decades, Iranian Christians have made ample use of the internet to achieve a transnational integration of their communities and concomitantly reach out to potential converts back in Iran. It is for this reason that Marcin Rzepka already pointed out much before the Covid-19 pandemic:

> Research on Iranian Christian cyberspace seems to be unavoidable today even when we take into account the revolutionary era. The new websites, social networks, blogs, and other forms of the new media offer the opportunity to create archives with very rich and diverse sources: audio-visual, visual, oral, and written, containing the personal testimonies of converts, pictures, films, and recorded sermons. They are collected by Iranian Christian organisations and by local Iranian churches and appear on the official sites and on the private blogs, which helps to memorialise the Iranian Christian martyrs, believers, and thinkers from the time of the revolution. (Rzepka 2017: 205–6)

Overall, this book is based on the analysis of seventy videos with an added length of sixty hours, uploaded on the video platform YouTube by Iranian Christian exile churches as well as Iranian Christian TV channels. With two minor exceptions, all videos were uploaded between the years 2010 and 2020. While some videos are only a few minutes long, others last up to three hours. When citing these videos, a brief contextualization will be given to clarify whether the specific excerpt stems from, for example, a sermon, a conversation on stage, a personal testimony of faith or a prayer.

Given the abundant availability of video material, I decided to take videos recorded on the occasion of the Iranian new year festival of Nowruz as a starting point. It seemed reasonable to assume that matters of Iranian national identity are put centre stage on this occasion. As more and more relevant topics started to crystallize, I later enlarged the body of video sources by specifically searching for videos relating to, among other aspects, the figure of King Cyrus the Great and Persian poetry. It bears highlighting that, by and large, the discourses touched upon emanate primarily from pastors and ministers, rather than from regular attendants of Iranian Christian exile churches. Applying also to the non-visual sources used for this book, this circumstance is not necessarily disadvantageous as it is arguably the church leaders who shape the thoughts of the 'wider masses' of Iranian Christians.

A second major source that has equally remained unstudied in existing works are Persian-language magazines published by Iranian Christian exile churches and organizations. Back in Iran, some of the Protestant Churches were publishing magazines and newsletters in the Persian language.[8] As for exile magazines, some can be accessed online while others are only available in print and can be ordered from the publishers. Nevertheless, there are some limitations in availability. This book draws upon the following publications:

- *Kalameh: Majalleh-ye Imān o Farhang-e Irāni-ye Masihi* – 'The Word: A Magazine for Faith and Iranian Christian Culture'. Thirty-two issues published between 2003 and 2012 in London, UK.[9]
- *Māhnāmeh-ye Tabdil* – 'Transformation Monthly'. Forty-six issues published between 2006 and 2013 in Los Angeles, CA, USA.
- *Rāh-e Salib: Avvalin Faslnāmeh-ye Irāniān-e Masihi-ye Holand* – 'The Path of the Cross: The First Quarterly of Christian Iranians in the Netherlands'. Twenty-five issues published between 2012 and 2019 in Doorn, The Netherlands.
- *Shāgerd: Faslnāmeh-ye Jahānbini-ye Masihi* – 'The Disciple: Quarterly of the Christian Worldview'. Six issues published between 2015 and 2018 in London, UK.
- *Esmirnā: Majalleh ye Farhang o Honar e Masihi* – 'Smyrna: A Magazine of Christian Culture and Art'. Fifty issues published between 2016 and 2020 in İzmir, Turkey.

A further type of printed sources are English and German-language books written by Iranian pastors residing abroad. This source has been particularly relevant for the study of discourses on Islam which I will treat at detail in Chapter 5. Finally, I have conducted seven semi-structured interviews with Iranian Christian pastors and ministers active in Germany, Switzerland and the UK. Most of them have in the past been active in leading positions in Iranian Christian churches within Iran and were eventually forced to go into exile. They thus could also function as eyewitnesses to the situation of Persian-speaking communities within Iran. Six interviews were conducted in Persian and one in German. I will use pseudonyms for my interviewees.

Chapter overview

Following this introductory note, Chapter 1 will illustrate the historical genesis of a Persian-speaking Christianity and describe the current situation of Persian-speaking Christians in Iran. It will also provide a rough mapping of Iranian Christian exile churches and institutions. Chapter 2 offers a theoretical discussion of the intersection between religion, nationhood and diaspora. It will further clarify key terms used in this book and derive a framework helpful to the study of Iranian Christians in exile from previous works in similar settings. Chapters 3 and 4 will present the main narratives and practices that Iranian Christians in exile use to construct an Iranian Christian national-religious identity. Alongside celebrations of the Iranian festivals of Nowruz and Yaldā in a Christian idiom, the usage of Persian poetry, references to biblical figures identified as Iranian and the commemoration of Iranian Christian martyrs are the main narratives and practices to achieve what I shall metaphorically term the naturalization of Christianity to the Iranian nation. Chapter 5 analyses discourses on Islam in Iranian Christian exile churches. Given that the vast majority of Iranian Christians today are Muslim-born converts, a portrayal of the Iranian Christian exilic milieu which disregards these discourses would be incomplete. Finally, Chapter 6 engages with visions of a future return to their homeland among Iranian Christians in exile. Most prominently, Iranian Christian exiles point to an episode from the book of Jeremiah in the Bible, the Elam Prophecy, to argue that their forced displacement is a necessary step in a divine plan, at the end of which stands a Christianized Iran.

1

Historical overview: Iranian Christians and their journey into exile

Introduction

Iran is home to Christians of different backgrounds and histories. Only in the twentieth century did the Persian language – the national language of multi-ethnic and multilingual Iran – come to be systematically used in a Christian context. This chapter will historicize the emergence of a Persian-speaking Christianity, unearth its multiple roots and highlight critical moments in its gradual genesis. Moving towards the present, the chapter will moreover retrace the journey of Persian-speaking Christians into exile. Since the 1979 Revolution and the triumph of Islamism in Iran, Persian-speaking Christian communities have experienced oppression and violence, culminating in the killing of a number of prominent pastors in the 1990s. Thus, Iranian Christian exile churches came into being and continue to grow in number today.

For the discussion of the historical overview, beginning with the Western Protestant missions of the nineteenth century, I will draw upon the existing secondary literature. Primary sources, among them interviews with pastors active in the early Persian-speaking movement in Iran published in the magazine *Kalameh*, the memoirs of Anglican bishop Hassan Dehqāni-Tafti and my own interviews with exiled Iranian Christian leaders, are more relevant for the years following the 1950s. These sources require critical assessment, given that they are all accounts by individuals actively involved with the Iranian Christian movement. In the present chapter, I have focused on specific historical claims and filtered out theological narratives. These narratives will be relevant in the later chapters of this book.

Regarding the post-revolutionary era and especially the past two decades, reports by NGOs and human rights organizations based outside Iran constitute the most valuable source providing insights into the situation of Persian-speaking

Christian communities in Iran.¹ Field research in these communities is impossible as it would put both attendants of house churches and researchers at substantial risk. Diaspora communities, conversely, are usually open to research, although a certain suspicion may persist. At the end of this chapter, I will provide a vague mapping of the Iranian Christian exilic landscape and introduce some central Iranian Christian exile institutions.

The ethnic Christian minorities of Iran

Before the nineteenth century, the Christian populations of Iran comprised Assyrians, who after an early nineteenth-century schism were divided between the Assyrian Church of the East and the Chaldean Catholic Church, and Armenians, mainly belonging to the Armenian Apostolic Church. While the history of the Assyrians living in today's Iran goes back to the first centuries CE, the Armenian presence dates only to the rule of the Safavid Shah 'Abbās (r. 1587–1629) who in the early seventeenth century forcefully resettled a significant Armenian population from the Safavid Empire's northern frontiers to the area around Isfahan.

Over the centuries, both Iranian Assyrians and Iranian Armenians developed into an integral part of Iranian society, while maintaining their ethnic, linguistic and religious distinctness. More recently, Assyrians and Armenians have emigrated from Iran at a staggering speed. While, according to Eliz Sanasarian, 250,000 Armenians lived in Iran by the mid-1970s, their number had decreased to between 150,000 and 200,000 in the 1990s (Sanasarian 2004: 36). According to Barry's recent study, a mere 30,000 Armenians are likely to have remained inside Iran by the mid-2010s (Barry 2020: 248). As for Assyrians, Sanasarian estimates their number to have plummeted from 30,000 by the mid-1970s to 16,000–18,000 by the mid-1990s (Sanasarian 2004: 36). However, considering the massive emigration of Armenians since that time, the current number of Assyrians may be much lower today. Both Iranian Assyrians and Armenians are constitutionally recognized minorities in the Islamic Republic of Iran and possess the right to cultural and religious autonomy to a certain degree.²

One may reasonably refer to the Assyrians and Armenians of Iran as ethno-religious minorities, or as *ethnic Christians*, insofar as their religious identity is inextricably tied to their membership of an ethnic minority with a distinct culture and language. Nowadays, Iranian Assyrians and Armenians can usually be recognized by their names; moreover, they have maintained a high level of fluency in their native languages – a fact that certainly owes much to almost complete endogamy. However, one realm in which the internal unity of Assyrians and Armenians has been less unshakeable is religion. This brings us to the early nineteenth century and the arrival of Western Protestant missionaries to the Iranian Qajar Empire.

The Western Protestant missions to Iran: Anglicans and American Presbyterians

Catholic missionaries first established their presence in Iran in the sixteenth century, hundreds of years before the arrival of the Protestant missions (cf. Waterfield 1973: 57–86). Their efforts, however, largely failed to bear fruit: Bradley rightfully remarks that 'Roman Catholic missionaries were never able to make any serious headway in Iran' (Bradley 2008: 144). According to Robin E. Waterfield, many of the Armenians who were the primary targets of the Catholic missions feared that the Catholics wanted 'to make them "Portuguese" or *Farangis* of some kind' (Waterfield 1973: 64). Nevertheless, a small Catholic Armenian community persists in Iran today.

Like their Catholic predecessors, the Protestant missionaries directed most of their energies towards the ethnic Christian minorities.[3] The American Presbyterian mission to the Assyrians of Urmia, for example, aimed to 'purify' and 'revive' (i.e. de facto, protestantize) the Christianity of the locals, which the missionaries felt to have undergone a period of drastic spiritual decay (cf. Becker 2015).[4] Accordingly, the Assyrian Evangelical Church came into being in the second half of the nineteenth century. The second major Protestant missionary project in Iran was led by the Anglican Church Missionary Society (CMS) which, unlike the American Presbyterians, focused more on the southern side of the country.[5] One of its early faces, the missionary Henry Martyn (1781–1812), rose to fame as an avid translator of the New Testament. During his stay in Iran, Martyn actively sought to engage in theological disputes with Shi'ite clerics (cf. Amanat 2005). Today, he is commemorated favourably in Iranian Christian exile publications.[6]

At the official level, the missionaries pledged to the authorities that they would abstain from proselytizing among Muslims (Rzepka 2017: 48; Spellman 2004: 157). That said, there is no doubt that, sooner or later, Protestant missionaries were hoping to also gain converts from Islam. Rzepka cites a 1905 letter by the Archbishop of Canterbury in which he reminds a missionary to Iran that conversions from Islam to Christianity were the ultimate goal of the Anglican undertakings in the country (Rzepka 2017: 68).[7] One strategy to achieve this goal was to have converted Protestant Assyrians and Armenians missionize among their Muslim compatriots (Hopkins 2020: 70; Waterfield 1973: 103). However, the number of Iranian Muslims who converted to Christianity remained extremely low until well into the twentieth century.

The two realms in which the Protestant missions had their most significant impact on Iranian society were their educational and medical facilities. Schools and hospitals were opened throughout the country and a special emphasis put on the education of girls.[8] In 1895, the Presbyterian Mission alone was running 117 schools in north-western Iran (Rostam-Kolayi 2008: 219). Most notably, the Presbyterian Alborz College of Tehran, founded as the American School for Boys in 1873, became a prestigious institution, the graduates of which featured prominently in Iran's modernizing movement of the 1920s (cf. Ricks 2011: 631). The educational work of Protestant missionaries certainly served as a means of proselytizing pupils; after all, biblical studies constituted a major component of the schools' curricula. Especially when Muslim pupils came to outnumber their Armenian peers by the 1920s (Rostam-Kolayi 2008: 225), the 'proselytization question' became a major bone of contention and ushered in a 1928 agreement demanding the Presbyterians to cease their missionary endeavours (cf. Zirinsky 1993: 348).

Matters nevertheless seem to have been more complex on the individual level. Jasamin Rostam-Kolayi points out that the Presbyterian schools' staff members were always dependent on the goodwill of their donors in the United States and therefore may have exaggerated the role religious conversions played in their daily work (Rostam-Kolayi 2008: 221). In any event, Protestant missionaries, next to their religious mission, also functioned as 'missionaries of Western modernity'. Thomas M. Ricks writes: 'It may be more accurate to say that the American missionaries were themselves slowly "being converted" to pursuing social service work, and to serving as "models" of modern men and women rather than "converting" Iranians to the religious and spiritual practices of nineteenth-century America' (Ricks 2011: 632). In this regard, the missionary schools' work chimed well with the political climate of Iran in the 1920s. This, however, did not save the schools from their forced closure in 1939, when Rezā Shah, as part of his broader political agenda, nationalized all foreign-led educational institutions.

The quest for indigenization and mission beyond ethnic borders

Until the first half of the twentieth century, missionaries tended to impose a strong and unfiltered denominational identity upon converts, no matter their background. Leading positions were exclusively staffed by Western clerics as 'the period of indigenisation had not yet begun' (Waterfield 1973: 162). Thus, when in 1913 the fully independent Anglican Diocese of Persia[9] was called into being, the Englishman Charles Harvey Stileman became its first bishop. Similarly, the American missions were clinging on to what Philip O. Hopkins called the 'traditional model', emphasizing 'the missionary as a paternal figure, as the one who knew best' (Hopkins 2020: 92).

Hopkins acknowledges the 'racist overtones' of this approach (ibid.). Indeed, some of the missionaries saw Iranians, in racialized terms, as 'Aryans'. While harbouring a negative attitude towards non-Iranian Muslims, missionaries thus vindicated Iranian Muslims by viewing them as their own racial peers. An early example of this propensity is a 1927 treatise by missionary Henry C. Schuler.[10] He insinuated that Islam 'is not suited to the Persian character and never was'; ever since it was 'forced on them', Persians 'have been trying … to get rid of some of [Islam's] teachings, against which the Aryan mind rebels' (cited in Zirinsky 1993: 338). Schuler's view certainly owed much to discourses on race and the Iranian nation prevalent at the time. Described by historian Reza Zia-Ebrahimi as 'dislocative nationalism' (Zia-Ebrahimi 2016), I shall later in this book return to this intellectual strand that still features prominently in the collective self-image of many Iranians.

Among missionaries, racializing discourses of this kind have prevailed in the second half of the twentieth century. Both Rzepka and Hopkins refer to a 1959 conference held in Princeton, NJ, during which the Presbyterian missionary Cady Allen presented an analysis of Muslim responses to Western missionary endeavours in Iran. Hopkins explains:

> Allen supposed that Iranians would convert to Christianity because their Aryan heritage enabled them to have closer connections with missionaries. According to Allen's understanding, he believed Persians were of Indo-European origin and that Iranians desired to purge Arabic words from their language; the outflow of increased nationalism would weaken Islam in Iran and lead educated Iranians to wander from the religion of their forefathers. (Hopkins 2020: 93)

Whether the positive racial bias discernible among missionaries like Allen played a part in their decision to make another 'leap of faith' in the 1960s by granting the Iranian churches self-government is a matter for speculation. What is beyond doubt, however, is that the year 1961 constituted a watershed in the genesis of the Iranian Christian movement. The American Presbyterians, as Hopkins points out 'perhaps out of necessity' (ibid.: 94), then decided to decouple the Iranian Evangelical Church from the Presbyterian mission and allow for its independence. By 1 September 1961, much of the Presbyterian ministry was transferred to the Iranian Evangelical Church (ibid.: 95). In the same year, the Anglican Diocese of Iran consecrated its first native Iranian bishop: Hassan Dehqāni-Tafti (1920–2008). Dehqāni-Tafti, whose father was a Muslim and mother a Muslim-born convert to Christianity, became a pioneer of Persian-speaking Christianity.

Another question becoming more and more pressing at the time was how to deal with the ethnic diversity of the congregations. By the mid-twentieth century, converts from the ethnic Christian minorities still constituted the majority in most Protestant churches. Gradually, however, the number of converted Muslims was increasing. Moreover, especially in the Anglican parishes, Western expatriates living in Iran formed a major part of the flock. Bishop Dehqāni-Tafti stressed the Anglican Diocese's independence and Persian character, which, he insisted, also embraced the numerous foreign doctors, teachers and clergy attending Anglican churches in Iran (Dehqāni-Tafti 2000: 153).

Another interesting example of how ethnic and linguistic diversity was dealt with stems from the early Pentecostal *Jamā'at-e Rabbāni* Church. Pioneered by Iranian Armenians, the attendance of Iranian Assyrians and other Iranians soon challenged the hegemonic status the Armenian language had during the church's early stages. Dāvud Thomas, himself an Iranian Assyrian and an early leader of the church, reminisces in a 2010 interview:

> One of the problems that I myself was faced with in the beginning of my cooperation with the brothers [other leaders of the church] ... was the issue of language. While I was trying to speak in Persian, my Armenian friends insisted on using their own language and, since I did not know Armenian, a problem was created. Gradually, the brothers understood that it was necessary to speak Persian in the presence of a person who does not understand Armenian. Of course, as time went on, I also picked up some Armenian, and enjoyed the ministry (*khedmat*) with the Armenian-speaking brothers and sisters a lot. (Thomas and Dibāj 2010: 12)

While here the usage of the Persian language served the pragmatic purpose of mutual communication among early Iranian Pentecostal leaders, Thomas also reports that, during missionary outreach, Persian was consciously used to reach as many people as possible, including, of course, Iranian Muslims (ibid.: 12–13).[11] This approach is a key trait of the Iranian Pentecostal movement, which since the 1979 Revolution has evolved into the main denominational group among Iranian Christians.

Pentecostalism in Iran

While the conventional view in academic works locates the origins of Pentecostalism at the 1906 Azusa Street Mission in Los Angeles, more recently the multiple origins and the global history of the movement have been emphasized (cf. Bergunder et al. 2010). Pentecostalism evades a clear-cut definition; accordingly, Allan Anderson suggests that 'it is probably more correct to speak of Pentecostalisms in the contemporary global context' (2010: 15). Generally, Pentecostal Christians emphasize the relevance of the Holy Spirit and its gifts, the so-called 'charismata', which account for the common alternative designation of Pentecostal Christians as *Charismatic* Christians. Services of Pentecostal Christians tend to be characterized by a high emotionality, foregrounding healing, speaking in tongues and extensive episodes of worship.

The historical roots of Pentecostalism in Iran can be traced relatively clearly to several pioneering individuals. Unlike its Anglican and Presbyterian counterparts, the Pentecostal presence in Iran does not originate from a large-scale Western missionary enterprise in Iran. Until 1959, virtually all Iranian Pentecostals were of an Assyrian background and remained in churches using the Neo-Aramaic language (cf. Rzepka 2017: 59). A key individual in the spread of Pentecostalism among Iranian Assyrians was the Iranian Assyrian Andrew David Urshan (1884–1967) who, educated at a Presbyterian college in Urmia, had emigrated to the United States as a young man and embraced Pentecostalism in Chicago (cf. Schmidt 2016). Having returned to Qajar Iran in 1913, he started preaching in the Urmia region. Iran is thus immediately embedded in the early global history of Pentecostalism. Notably, Urshan's biography resembles the biographies of some of his Iranian Assyrian contemporaries. My interlocutor Martin, an exiled Iranian Assyrian pastor in his mid-sixties, told me that his grandfather as well had embraced the 'Pentecostal faith' (*imān-e Pentikāsti*) during a stay in the United States (interview with Martin 2022). After his return home, he passed it on to other Iranian Assyrians, first in the Urmia region and later elsewhere in Iran; sporadically, non-Assyrians converted during the latter missionary ventures (ibid.).

In the second half of the twentieth century, Pentecostalism started to spread among Iranians of different backgrounds, though Iranian Armenians featured most prominently. Seth Yeqnazar (1911–2010) in this regard is a most noteworthy individual; he today is commemorated as 'the father of many Iranian believers (*imāndārān*)' in Iranian Christian publications (Dibāj 2011). In the 1930s, he attended the Pentecostal Brethren Church founded by the Iranian Kurdish physician and convert to Christianity Sa'id Kordestāni (1863–1942) (Bradley 2008: 155; Van Gorder 2010: 145),[12] where he 'accepted the good news (*mozhdeh*) of salvation' in 1937 (Dibāj 2011).[13] Beginning in January 1956, Yeqnazar organized Bible studies and worship gatherings in his private flat in Tehran (ibid.). In 1957, his cousin Leon Hāyrāpetiān (1917–2011) joined the meetings (Hāyrāpetiān and Dibāj 2010: 13). He too became an important early leader of Iranian Pentecostal Christians.

Yeqnazar's house church also became a nucleus of leading Iranian pastors of the post-revolutionary era, among them the brothers Hāyk (1945–1994) and Edward Hovsepiān (b. 1950) who in the late 1950s were neighbours of Leon Hāyrāpetiān (ibid.: 15). At the same time, the private gatherings were met with hostility by some Armenian Orthodox neighbours who, according to Hāyrāpetiān, actively aspired to sabotage (*beh ham zadan*) them (ibid.: 14). This notwithstanding, Yeqnazar and his fellow Iranian Armenians decided to widen their ministry in other Armenian quarters of Tehran. In 1959, the group was joined by the brothers Hrānt and Hāykāz Khāchāturiān who, while studying in London, had become Evangelical Christians in a service led by the American awakening preacher Billy Graham (1918–2018) (Thomas and Dibāj 2010: 11). Together, they decided to move their ministry to its own building and started the Philadelphia Pentecostal Church in Tehran. The Khāchāturiān brothers, who died in a car accident in 1961, started their work with the concrete vision of missionizing in Persian and among Muslims (Bradley 2008: 155; Rzepka 2017: 59). Thus, the early 1960s constitutes a critical moment not only among Iranian Anglicans and Presbyterians who, as I have pointed out, shifted to a conscious agenda of indigenization during this time, but also for Iranian Pentecostals.

In 1965, the Philadelphia Church became affiliated with the American Assemblies of God Pentecostal churches (Rzepka 2017: 59). Upon the request of Iranian pastors, the missionaries Mark and Gladys Bliss came to Iran and assisted Seth Yeqnazar in the establishment of a Bible school (Hopkins 2020: 123). Although an agreement was signed, the Iranian Assemblies of God, which soon began operating numerous churches throughout Iran, maintained a high degree of independence. Throughout this book, the Iranian Assemblies of God churches will be referred to by their Persian name *Jamā'at-e Rabbāni*.

Conducting extensive research in the Assemblies of God archives in Springfield, Hopkins has documented the church's development through to the late 1970s. In 1970, Hāyk Hovsepiān founded a church in the north Iranian city of Gorgān, which 'became a place of emphasis for the Assemblies of God' (Hopkins 2020: 124). Hovsepiān proselytized extensively among Iranian Muslims. He occasionally also was given the opportunity to preach on Iranian radio (Rzepka 2017: 100). By April 1972, the *Jamā'at-e Rabbāni* was running eleven churches throughout the country (Hopkins 2020: 125). Its main branch, the Central Church (*Kelisā-ye Markazi*), was located on Takht-e Jamshid Avenue (Tāleqāni Street after 1979) in Tehran. By 2013, when the Central Church was closed and confiscated by the Iranian state (see the section 'Closure of public churches and the current status quo'), only a small percentage of the congregation were ethnic Christians; Muslim-born Iranians were now dominant. This reflects the overall development of Persian-speaking Christianity in Iran after the 1979 Revolution.

Iranian Christians since the 1979 Revolution

Pentecostals and the first Islamist decade: Ambiguity and growing discrimination

Before I provide an overview on the post-revolutionary violence against Persian-speaking Christians of different denominations, two excerpts from interviews I conducted with exiled Iranian Christian leaders shall illustrate the ambiguous experiences of Iranian Pentecostal Christians during the first decade of the Islamic Republic. Accounts of the everyday experiences made by members of Persian-speaking churches during the early days of the 1979 Revolution have so far been absent in the existing literature.

My interlocutor Peymān spent his childhood in Northern Iran during the late 1960s and in the age of fourteen moved to Tehran with his family. His father was a Muslim-born convert to Christianity. Because his father was an avid evangelist, Peymān's schoolmates knew that he and his family were Christians. Moreover, he was exempt from Islamic religious education. When I asked Peymān how his peers reacted to his Christian faith, he explained to me that they usually expressed great astonishment (*ta'ajjob*) and refused to believe him. Before the 1979 Revolution, however, he never experienced outright hostility. After the revolution, many of his friends became very religious and started to regularly debate his Christian beliefs. Yet, Peymān emphasized, such debates were always done in a friendly manner (*dustāneh*). At university, Peymān even was friends with many members of Islamic student organizations, colloquially referred to as *Hezbollāhi*s. He remembers about the early 1980s:

> As a matter of fact, I was good friends with the *Hezbollāhis*! I also used to debate the Communists frequently as I had read a lot of philosophy. I really was an avid debater. But I remember well that, at this time, everyone was respectful and not yet … well, sometimes they made fun of me. But overall, there was respect and discussion. This is what I can say. (Interview with Peymān 2021)

As a young man in the 1980s, Peymān held various positions in the Tehran *Jamā'at-e Rabbāni* Church. In 1991, he moved to the UK to pursue his studies in theology. After the 1994 murders of leading Iranian Pentecostal pastors, Peymān decided that it was not safe for him to return to Iran, given his Muslim background and his leading position in the church. He has lived in exile in the UK ever since.

My interlocutor Amir, born into a secular Muslim family, who by the time of the 1979 Revolution was a young adult, converted to Christianity in the 1970s and attended the *Jamā'at-e Rabbāni* Central Church in Tehran. He worked for a company whose employees prior to the revolution included both Americans and Iranians. After the revolution, the American employees had to leave Iran. An Islamic Society (*Anjoman-e Eslāmi*) was established in the company and pious Muslim Iranians loyal to the government staffed the leading positions. The ritual Islamic prayer, though not compulsory, was performed by most of his co-workers during the working hours. Amir occasionally shared his Christian faith with his close friends at work. One day, one of his friends told the Islamic Society's head about Amir. He then was called to the society's office:

> He [the society's head] was not at all a bad guy. He called me and asked 'What imperfection did you see in Islam?' *(az Eslām cheh badi didi?)* I said 'None. It is rather that I have seen many good things on *that* side [Christianity].' So we engaged in a conversation and I explained my faith to him. Later, I shared the good news with some of my personal friends and this came to the attention of the company's bosses. The boss at the time did not react; he was religious but not particularly touchy regarding my case. But then the company's management

changed and new bosses came in who had a much stricter approach. They called me in and said 'We have heard that you are a convert to Christianity?' (*Masihi shodi?*) I said 'Yes.' They answered 'Unfortunately, we can no longer keep you in this company.' We talked for a moment and they said 'You need to go.' When I then went to the company's administration to ask for the rest of my salary, they threatened me and said 'You are endangering yourself.' (Interview with Amir 2021)

Both Peymān's and Amir's testimonies suggest that, shortly after the 1979 Revolution, the nature of the encounters faced by Iranian Christians was very individualized. Accordingly, Peymān stresses the respectful character of the debates he engaged in with Islamist and Communist students; likewise, Amir emphasizes the fair treatment of the company's head of the Islamic Society. At the same time, their accounts as well as their overall biographies illustrate that, as time went on, discriminatory structures gained the upper hand and became the norm. Discrimination in the workplace, for example, is commonly experienced by members of Persian-speaking Christian communities within Iran.

My interlocutors were aware that I was informed about the ordeals experienced by Iranian Christians especially in the 1990s and until the present. Moreover, the simple fact that our conversations took place in the UK, the involuntary new home of Peymān and Amir for over three decades, rather than, for example, a Tehran café, speaks for itself. Our conversations did therefore not focus on the post-revolutionary violence experienced first by Iranian Anglicans and then Iranian Pentecostals.

Post-revolutionary violence

Until the unfolding of the 1979 Revolution in Iran, the different Iranian Protestant communities were by and large able to operate in an unimpeded manner. Occasional harassment was notably experienced by the Anglican Church, both from non-governmental Islamist organizations and from the Shah's secret service (SAVAK). Bishop Dehqāni-Tafti recounts in his autobiography:

> We would often have trouble from the Tablighat-i-Islami, or 'Islamic propagation' group, whose members posted themselves at the door of the church and took stock of who was coming and going. These people they might later threaten or attack. Alternatively these activists would come inside and try to disrupt the meeting. (Dehqani-Tafti 2000: 142)

Dehqāni-Tafti further explains that his Muslim background, easily discernible because of his name, meant that 'certain mullahs urged the fanatical people to get rid of me' (ibid.). As for governmental interference, Van Gorder remarks that SAVAK, the ill-famed secret service of Mohammad Rezā Shah's government, became more heavy-handed: 'At times, church property was vandalized, and some evangelistic publications were forbidden to be published by the government because they were seen to be divisive' (Van Gorder 2010: 135).[14]

But such episodes by no means compare to the post-revolutionary violence against Iranian Protestants, first Anglicans and later Pentecostals. Most of the available secondary literature on Iranian Christians treats this violence in great detail (Bradley 2008: 164–74; Rzepka 2017: 137–41; Sanasarian 2004: 123–7; Van Gorder 2010: 180–2, 219–36). On the discrimination and violence against Iranian Anglicans in the early 1980s, Dehqāni-Tafti wrote a first-hand account entitled *The Hard Awakening* (Dehqani-Tafti 1981).

On 19 February 1979, eighteen days after the Ayatollah Ruhollāh Khomeini's return from exile to Iran heralded the victory of the Revolution, the Anglican pastor Arastu Sayyāh (1928–1979) was murdered in his office in Shiraz. His family went to live in the UK shortly after the event. During the following months, several institutions belonging to the Anglican Diocese of Iran were confiscated, shut down or raided. During a ransack of Hassan Dehqāni-Tafti's personal office in Isfahan, personal belongings like family albums as well as addresses of the church members were stolen. Later, clerical and administrative staff members of the Anglican Diocese were temporarily imprisoned and physically attacked. On 26 October 1979, Bishop Dehqāni-Tafti and his wife Margaret (1931–2016) survived an assassination attempt in their bedroom. On 6 May 1980, their son Bahrām (1955–1980) was murdered while returning from his workplace, Damavand College in Northern Tehran. At the time, Hassan Dehqāni-Tafti was attending a conference outside Iran; unable to return, he could not attend his son's funeral at St. Luke's Church in Isfahan. Soon after, he was joined abroad by his family who decided to settle in the UK. Dehqāni-Tafti's daughter Guli (b. 1966) today serves as the Anglican Bishop of Chelmsford and since 2021 is a member of the House of Lords.

That specifically the Anglican Church of Iran was hit this heavily during the early days of the 1979 Revolution was most likely a consequence of its political association with the UK in the eyes of many revolutionaries. Newspapers of the time published vilifying articles attacking Bishop Dehqāni-Tafti and the Anglican Church, accused the murdered Arastu Sayyāh of having been a CIA agent and printed the facsimile of a letter supposedly proofing that the Anglicans active in Isfahan were spies (Dehqani-Tafti 1981: 65–7). According to Dehqāni-Tafti, the attacks were the work of fanatical individuals, such as members of the aforementioned Tablighāt-e Eslāmi, rather than the result of a governmental order (Dehqani-Tafti 2000: 191).

Meanwhile, the Pentecostal *Jamāʿat-e Rabbāni* churches were able to continue their activities without major complications throughout the 1980s. During the 1979–81 hostage crisis in the American Embassy in Tehran, *Jamāʿat-e Rabbāni* pastor Lazarus Yeqnazar (b. 1949) was invited twice to conduct services for the American hostages. The Iranian Bible Society, headed by the Iranian Armenian Tateos Mikāʾeliān (1932–1994), was likewise able to continue its work and print and sell the Bible in Persian until 1990. However, as the number of Muslim-born Iranians attending Pentecostal churches was increasing steadily – with some receiving baptism – the Iranian authorities started to curtail the Pentecostals' activities from the late 1980s onwards. In 1988, the brothers Hāyk and Edward Hovsepiān were summoned by the Ministry of Intelligence. They were demanded to halt admissions of further members and stop holding services in Persian (Hovsepiān and Hovsepiān 2007). Such conditions were unacceptable to the Iranian Pentecostal leaders who continued their activities unwaveringly. From 1988 to 1992, *Jamāʿat-e Rabbāni* churches in Mashhad, Sāri, Gorgān and Kermān were shut down by the government (Rzepka 2017: 134).

Between 1990 and 1996, four leading pastors of the *Jamāʿat-e Rabbāni* churches as well as one Presbyterian pastor with close personal contacts to Iranian Pentecostals were killed. Their killings coincided with the chain murders of prominent Iranian dissidents, both inside Iran and abroad.[15] In 1990, Pastor Hoseyn Sudmand of the *Jamāʿat-e Rabbāni* church in Mashhad was executed on the charge of 'apostasy' (*ertedād*). As of today, he remains the only Iranian Christian against whom the death penalty on the grounds of 'apostasy' was implemented. Another leading pastor of the *Jamāʿat-e Rabbāni*, Mehdi Dibāj (1935–1994), was also sentenced to death after more than a decade in prison between 1983 and 1994. In early 1994, however, Dibāj was acquitted after Hāyk Hovsepiān had mobilized international protest. Only a few days later, Hāyk Hovsepiān became the victim of a brutal extrajudicial killing. In summer 1994, Dibāj himself was also murdered, along with Tateos Mikāʾeliān, Hovsepiān's successor as chairman of the Iranian Council of Protestant Churches. The Iranian government later blamed the killings on three young women supposedly affiliated with the Islamist-Marxist opposition group *Mojāhedin-e Khalq*. Finally, in 1996, Pastor Mohammad Bāqer 'Ravānbakhsh' Yusefi (1964–1996) was found dead. While the Iranian authorities claimed that Yusefi had committed suicide, his family believe that he was murdered: Yusefi had ignored government warnings to cease his missionary activities in the northern province of Māzandarān (cf. Dibāj 2004b).

The 1990 killings of Iranian Protestant pastors have had a profound effect on the Iranian Christian movement. On the one hand, they further galvanized a sense of collective identity: the murdered pastors are commemorated today as 'Martyrs of the Iranian Church' (see Chapter 4). On the other hand, the assassinations caused an exodus of many leading Iranian pastors understandably worried that they would face the same fate as Sayyāh, B. Dehqāni-Tafti, Sudmand, Hovsepiān, Mikā'eliān, Dibāj and Yusefi. In the long view, Iranian Christians – and especially Iranian Christian leaders – after the 1990s were presented with three options: to accept the considerable risk and continue serving in one of the remaining public Persian-speaking churches (*kelisā-hā-ye sākhtemāni*); to move their activities into the private sphere and found so-called 'house churches' (*kelisā-hā-ye khānegi*) or to go into exile. The first of these three options ceased to be viable by the early 2010s because governmental forces shut down all remaining churches offering Persian-language services.

Recent developments

The 2000s: Heightened pressure and early house churches

After the killings of the 1990s, the remaining churches offering services in Persian continued to be subject to major pressure from the Iranian government. In 2004, security forces raided a church council meeting of the *Jamā'at-e Rabbāni* and arrested all eighty of those attending (Bradley 2014: 175). Edward Hovsepiān, who was the leading pastor of the Tehran *Jamā'at-e Rabbāni Central Church* until his emigration to the UK in 2003, described the restrictions pushed for by the government after the raid in his 2004 testimony to the British government:

> For four nights they kept them [the 80 members of the church council] in solitary confinement and released them only with this condition: you have no right to evangelise or accept new members, you have no right to conduct any conferences outside the church building. Inside the church also if you want to have a conference we should be informed and we should know about the subject of the conference. You have to report all the journeys you are making and you have to submit regular reports to us. (Cited in Bradley 2014: 175)

As is apparent from the latter demand, the Iranian authorities at the time already had been aware that Iranian Christians were building an international network organizing occasional leadership trainings abroad. Due to the forced emigration of many leading Iranian pastors, Persian-speaking churches inside Iran have faced a lack of trained theologians and ministers. This continues to be a challenge in the present. Especially in Turkey and Armenia – two countries easily accessible for Iranian passport holders – Iranian Christian organizations based outside of Iran organize meetings to provide interested individuals from Iran with information and training. To a lesser extent, they use these occasions to perform baptisms. In some instances, the Iranian authorities have actively prevented Iranian Christians travelling to such conferences from leaving the country (ICHRI 2013: 57).

In the early 2000s, house churches started to become more prevalent as a consequence of the increasing clamp down on public churches offering services in Persian. Concomitantly, interest in Christianity seems to have spiked among Muslim-born Iranians to such a degree that the few Persian-speaking churches could not accommodate the number of interested congregants (ibid.: 21–2). It is important to point out that house churches, although the term is certainly apt, vary greatly in size and have very individual stories. As, in the words of Bradley, 'It is not really possible to talk about a homogenous movement as if all these churches are the same' (Bradley 2014: 118), one may heuristically think of house churches as worship gatherings in the private sphere relying on the initiative of devoted individuals who have converted to Christianity without a formal process. Some of them may actively proselytize among friends and colleagues and invite them to join their private meetings; others may consciously abstain from missionary activities out of fear of potential repercussions. While some house church leaders may be in touch with more experienced pastors abroad (facilitated through social media), others may be 'self-made theologians'.

Khāmene'i's 2010 speech and the post-2010 period

Around the year 2010, the measures taken by the Iranian government to thwart the Iranian Christian movement became harsher yet. There are several possible reasons for this shift: firstly, the presidency of hardliner Mahmud Ahmadinezhād (in office between 2005 and 2013) is often cited as an exacerbating factor (cf. Bradley 2014: 48–74; ICHRI 2013: 7; IHRDC 2021: 16). Secondly, it appears that, around the year 2009, the supervision of Persian-speaking churches, previously under the purview of the Ministry of Intelligence, came under the direct auspices of the Iranian Revolutionary Guard Corps (IRGC) (IHRDC 2021: 11). Thirdly, the Supreme Leader of the Islamic Republic of Iran, 'Ali Khāmene'i, in a 2010 speech directly targeted house churches and mentioned them in one breath with other shunned groups, among them the Bahais. He stated:

> There are two fundamental aspects [sustaining the revolutionary system]: religion and the people. Therefore, the enemy has consciously chosen these two as the targets of his attacks. ... Whether it is exterior enemies or their shameless hirelings and servants (*mozdurān yā nowkarān-e bi-mozd o mennat*) inside our country – they have discredited and denied the sacred realities (*moqaddasāt*), the religious truths and the clear proofs of Islam. This is not a coincidence. They have done this consciously. The Salman Rushdie affair to anti-Islamic Hollywood movies, the [Muhammad] cartoons, the Quran burnings, the manifold other anti-Islamic incidents that have unfolded at different places – their purpose has been to diminish the faith of the people in Islam and its sacred truths. Inside the country, they use several means to unsettle the foundations of the people's faith and especially of the young generation: the dissemination of moral permissiveness and religious indifference, the promotion of false mysticism – a fake version (*jens-e badali*) of real mysticism – the promotion of Bahaism *and the house church network*. All these are things that today are unfolding with the elaborate and conscious foreseeing of the enemies of Islam. Its purpose is to weaken religion [Islam] in society. (Khāmene'i 2010; italics added)

It is worth quoting Khāmene'i's reference to house churches within its wider context as it is illustrative of two important aspects. On the one hand, Khāmene'i places the house church movement in the context of other groups, the undertakings of which he ultimately identifies as a foreign conspiracy. Individuals gathering at private worship meetings and Bible studies accordingly become 'hirelings' and 'servants' of Iran's exterior enemies. Secondly, house churches (and 'the like') become a matter of national security. They weaken the two pillars of the revolutionary cause, named by Khāmene'i as the Islamic religion and the Iranian people.

Khāmene'i's derogatory statement is immediately reflected in the sort of legal persecution levelled against Iranian Christians, especially since the year 2010. According to the IHRDC, 'During subsequent years, religious charges, such as apostasy, gave way to charges related to acting against national security' (2021: 16). This includes the charge of 'acting against national security by spreading Zionist Christianity' (cf. Article18 2022b) – 'the Zionists' being a regularly invoked exterior enemy in Iranian state discourse. The charge of apostasy, it should be noted, is not part of the penal code of the Islamic Republic of Iran; however, Article 167 allows a judge to refer to 'authoritative Islamic sources' or an 'authentic fatwa' in case the codified law does not provide a suitable frame for an individual case (cf. IHRDC 2014: 10). Historically, it has been primarily Muslim dissidents or reformers who have been accused of apostasy in the Islamic Republic (ibid.: 15–26).[16] The shift from apostasy as a legal charge to accusations relating to national security may moreover be expedient to the Iranian government's public image, given that they are less likely to spark an international controversy than a blunt violation of the freedom of religion. Through this strategy, the term 'apostasy' disappears from official state discourse while, according to the testimony of Iranian Christian journalist Shahāb Ebrāhimi, during the actual interrogations 'the interrogators mostly focus on the issue of apostasy and leaving Islam (IHRDC 2014: 50).

Ultimately, the Iranian authorities punish what Bradley calls 'Christian activism' (Bradley 2014: 174). Using the Persian language in a Christian context in the Iranian state's view immediately amounts to proselytism and thus a subversive act. Consequently, Iranian Armenians and Assyrians, who can hardly be accused of 'apostasy', may just as well be subject to harsh treatment as Muslim-born Iranian converts if they are active members or, worse still, leaders of Persian-speaking churches. As will be explored later in this book, the notion that Persian is an *Islamic* language and therefore ought not to be used in a Christian context has dominated discourses on Iranian nationhood – already since before the 1979 Revolution.

At the same time, non-leading members of house churches, even if they technically may be labelled 'apostates', as a rule do not experience repercussions, provided they are willing to give up their right to religious freedom and keep silent about their religious identity. Similarly, the few Muslim-born Iranian converts to Christianity who converted before the 1979 Revolution seem to have been treated with a certain pragmatism and were recognized as Christians in the Islamic Republic (cf. IHRDC 2021: 3). Regarding the present, my interlocutor Martin recounted the curious case of two Muslim-born converts attending his Persian-speaking church who, after a protracted correspondence with their local town administration, acquired passports indicating 'Pentecostal Christian' (*Masihi-ye Pentikāsti*) as their religion (interview with Martin 2022). Concessions of this sort, however, are an absolute exception. Overall, the approach of the Islamic Republic to Persian-speaking Christian communities is ruthless.

Closure of public churches and the current status quo

Between 2009 and 2013, the remaining public churches offering services in Persian were forced to close by the Iranian authorities. The closures included churches which, although nominally belonging to the ethnic Christian minorities, offered services in Persian alongside those in Armenian or Neo-Aramaic to anyone willing to attend. Among them were the Assyrian Pentecostal churches in Tehran, Urmia and Kermānshāh, shut down between March and December 2009 (Bradley 2014: 155).[17] The *Jamāʿat-e Rabbāni* churches in Shāhinshahr, Urmia, Ahvāz and Jannat-Ābād in Tehran were closed between 2009 and 2012 (IHRDC 2021: 20). In 2013, the *Jamāʿat-e Rabbāni* Central Church in Tehran had to close as well. In most instances, the leading pastors of the churches were at least intermittently imprisoned, many of them in solitary confinement.[18] The few Anglican churches in Iran were likewise targeted: in 2012, Hekmat Salimi, pastor at the St. Paul's Church in Isfahan, was arrested and later released on bail. He, as well as his colleague at the Church of St. Simon the Zealot in Shiraz, was then urged to release the membership list of their congregations (ibid.: 17–18). More recently, the Iranian government also has increasingly refused to renew the visa of non-Iranian clerics working for churches inside Iran, among them the Anglican Albert Sundararaj Walters who served as the vicar general of Iran (ibid.: 11).[19]

As a result of this new wave of governmental measures, by 2013 no Christian services and worship gatherings in the Persian language were available in Iran beyond the private sphere. Security forces are monitoring the entrances of church buildings to make sure no one apart from the recognized members of the respective communities, that is, usually ethnic Christians, will enter. Those congregations previously able to gather in public churches now had to move to house churches as well. Even there, however, regular raids continue to disrupt worship meetings. House church leaders are frequently imprisoned (cf. Article18 2022a). They usually are released only on cash payment of extortionate bail sums;[20] this often does not save them from renewed arrests. Some Muslim-born Iranian Christians have been flogged for their consumption of communion wine (IHRDC 2021: 26).[21]

Iranian Christians also face severe discrimination in other realms of daily life. Because Iranians, when interacting with governmental bodies or entering a new job, are required to indicate their religion, individuals who identify as Christian while having a non-Armenian or Assyrian name easily evoke suspicion. Iranian Christians from a Muslim background, whether they are converts themselves or the children of converts, thus can easily be singled out. They may be denied employment. Even if their employer personally may not favour such discrimination, they practically have no choice due to the consequences they as well could face (cf. ICHRI 2013: 64–7). Another area of discrimination is the right to education which 'typically involves expulsion from or denial of admissions to secondary school or universities, or refusal to grant a diploma despite completing course work' (ibid.: 68) as well as, of course, the denial of the right to Christian religious education.

On the legal level, the situation of Iranian Christians can be said to resemble that of Iranian Bahais who lack legal recognition and have experienced harrowing violence as well as severe discrimination and social ostracism (cf. Vahman 2019). Accordingly, Houchang Chehabi in a 2013 lecture on the legal aspects of religious diversity in Iran allocated what he called 'Christian converts' to the same category as Bahais, namely 'unrecognised non-Muslim minorities' (Chehabi 2013: m. 7:45).[22] Following the account of my interlocutor Martin, there are nevertheless subtleties that distinguish the situation of Persian-speaking Christians from that of Bahais. While he by no means denied the brutal treatment of Iranian Bahais, he suggested that because of their now over 150 years-long presence in Iran, a limited degree of accommodation has evolved for Bahais in some areas that was yet absent for Persian-speaking Christians. He explained:

> The Persian-speaking Church is not recognized and accepted as such. The Bahai community, for instance, is recognized *as a community*. They have the 'Bahai Society', they have their own cemeteries and their own meetings and rituals, during which they may be arrested. But they are known as the 'Bahai community'. The Persian-speaking Christian community, on the other hand, is not known as such. This is why the Persian-speaking [Christian] community inside Iran is facing massive problems. (Interview with Martin 2022)

It is important to point out that Martin here does not talk about *legal* recognition; Chehabi's classificatory scheme of religious minorities in Iran is therefore valid. What is at stake in Martin's statement is that Bahais are thought of as a distinct entity, the existence of which is not denied. Persian-speaking Christians, on the other hand, still find themselves at a stage where they need to campaign for the very *concept* of 'Persian-speaking Christians'. Campaigns to establish such a category and, by extension, achieve legal recognition have so far failed.[23]

Martin then went on to describe the ramifications of this total lack of recognition, some of which we are already familiar with by now:

> First of all, they [Persian-speaking Christians] cannot get together and if they do so not more than four or five people who then are accused of 'activities against national security', or of building a 'proselytizing Zionist church' ('*kelisā-ye sahyunisti-ye tabshiri*' behesh migand). … Moreover, [Persian-speaking]

Christians cannot have a Christian marriage; they may have a Christian wedding ceremony but they cannot legally register their marriage as such. A [Persian-speaking] Christian individual also cannot be buried at a Christian cemetery. Neither the Assyrians and Armenians nor the state will allow that. Thus, they are buried at Muslim cemeteries. Their children at school cannot say that they are Christians and are obliged to attend Islamic religious education. … Meanwhile, they also face problems at universities. … An Assyrian brother who was studying for his master's degree in the final term was told 'We are sorry, you can't continue.' He then had to emigrate from Iran. (Interview with Martin 2022)

It is telling that Martin's description of the current status quo ends with an emigration. Leaving Iran is something that is taken into consideration by a great number of Iranian Christians. Factors unrelated to their Christian identity may play a big role in these considerations as well. By the early 2020s, Iran continues to be in a desolate economic state and to deprive its citizens of fundamental freedoms. Especially young people – no matter their religious background – are disillusioned regarding their personal futures in the country and inform themselves about their prospects of moving abroad. Some may be content with moving to neighbouring Turkey and Armenia while others are willing to undergo the lengthy process of applying for a visa in Central Europe or North America. Still others may try to irregularly cross the borders and claim asylum once they have arrived in the country in which they hope to build a better future for themselves.

Mapping Iranian Christian exile churches

The number of Iranian exile churches has been increasing steadily during the past two decades. Their respective locations have often been dictated by the international politics of migration. Accordingly, one finds that older Iranian churches abroad, founded in the 1980s and 1990s, tend to be located in the UK and North America, then a popular destination for Iranian emigrants. More recently, these countries have become more difficult to access for Iranian passport holders. Therefore, newer Iranian exile churches are often located in Turkey, Germany, the Netherlands or Scandinavia.

Because this book had to greatly rely on online video sources, Iranian exile churches that are not active on YouTube or on social media lack representation. However, it appears that most Iranian exile churches are very active on the internet. As mentioned in the introduction, the cyberspace has proven expedient for the establishment of a transnational Iranian Christian network and enables potential converts as well as fellow Christians inside Iran to follow the services of exile churches online. The organization 222 Ministries, for instance, founded by former *Jamāʿat-e Rabbāni* pastor Lazarus Yeqnazar in 1991, has consciously used the internet to carry out what they call 'media ministry'.[24] Through their umbrella association Persian Christian Community Church, which encompasses Iranian exile churches from at least eight countries,[25] they regularly convene online services on the platform Zoom – and notably have done so since before the Covid-19 pandemic.

The video material analysed for this book originates from churches in Apeldoorn, Almere, Amsterdam, Venlo (Netherlands); Bremen, Essen, Hamburg (Germany); Dallas, Dickinson, Los Angeles, Sunnyvale, West Hills (United States); Goteborg, Stockholm (Sweden); Afyon, Denizli, Kayseri (Turkey); London (UK); Toronto (Canada) and Sydney (Australia). It thus covers a geographical range typical of the current international map of Iranian Christian exile churches. It is important to point out that these churches are always only representative of themselves; while some may maintain friendly relations, others consciously or without a specific reason may be completely independent. Moreover, not all attendants of these churches are Iranians who already *before* their emigration to Iran have converted to Christianity. Iran is a country with a large expat community. Accordingly, some Iranians have only started to attend Iranian churches while living abroad. Spellman's three-fold model which distinguishes between converts inside Iran, converts in transit (especially in Turkey) and converts in the UK (or other destination countries) seems accurate (Spellman 2004: 181).

Despite this geographic width, the UK has in a way evolved as an intellectual centre of Persian-speaking Christianity abroad. The reason for this is that the UK was the primary destination as the exile of leading Iranian Christian pastors pressured to leave Iran in the 1990s. Founded in 1990, Elam Ministries is a key institution; one of its central goals has been the training of Iranian Christian leaders and the publication of Iranian Christian literature in the Persian language.[26] The lack of trained theologians ready to serve both in Persian-speaking churches inside Iran and abroad has been lamented by most of my personal interlocutors.

In 2010, a group of senior Iranian pastors, many of whom were affiliated with Elam Ministries, founded the UK-based PARS Theological Centre. During a visit to the centre in autumn 2021, I was able to gather information on the institution's current activities. Offering a full BA program in Persian, the courses of which are offered online, PARS at the time had over 500 students who were enrolled and actively studying. Half of them were based in Iran, and the other half abroad. During interactions with students based inside Iran, staff members of PARS have to exercise great caution to keep the level of endangerment at a minimum. In the past, individuals with contacts to UK-based Iranian Christian organizations have been intimidated and arrested inside Iran (cf. ICHRI 2013: 50). Of the 500 students, only 5 per cent belonged to the ethnic Christian minorities. PARS pursues an interdenominational approach. Next to PARS, there are a few other institutions devoted to the training of Persian-speaking Christian pastors and ministers, all of which are based in North America.[27]

A mapping of the Iranian Christian exile milieu would not be complete without a mentioning of Iranian Christian satellite TV channels. In fact, these channels have been a chief medium for Iranian Christian pastors and missionaries abroad to reach potential converts inside Iran and establish contacts with them. Officially forbidden but practically condoned, Iranian homes use satellite dishes to gain access to Persian-language TV programmes broadcasting from abroad, first and foremost the United States. Iranians thus are enabled to consume media beyond the strongly censored Iranian state media. Exiled Iranian Christians as well have discovered this opportunity for their goals. A pioneer in this regard is the US-based pastor Hormoz Shariʻat (b. 1955) who first broadcasted to Iran in 2001 and since 2006 is involved with a 24/7 satellite TV channel which today is called *Shabakeh7* (Network7) (cf. Shariat 2020). Just as I have started this book with a quotation by Shariʻat, he and his colleagues will frequently feature throughout the following chapters. Likewise in the year 2006, *MohabatTV* under the supervision of Fariborz 'Mike' Ansāri and *TBN Nejat TV* (Rezā Safā) started their full-time broadcasts. Other channels include *KelisaTV*, *SamaTV* and *ICnetTV*. The Iranian state has tried to jam these channels and block their internet live streams (ICHRI 2013: 60).

Iranian Christian satellite TV channels offer a wide range of programmes that aim to promote their respective producers' understanding of Christianity. Some channels also broadcast Persian-language dubbings of prominent American televangelists. What should be highlighted is the interactive nature of many shows on Iranian Christian satellite TV channels: viewers are constantly given the opportunity to get in personal touch with staff members of the TV stations if they have questions about the Christian faith or wish to engage in a discussion. In many shows, phone numbers and contact details of other social media are constantly indicated at the bottom of the screen. Many channels, moreover, offer call-in shows in which the wider viewership can directly partake in the TV hosts' on-air discussions with callers. Fariborz Ansāri of *MohabatTV* has anecdotally collected interactions with callers to his channel in a book called *The Forbidden Stories* (cf. Ansari 2016).

Because of their interactive nature and the frequent emphasis on the 'unity' of TV hosts and viewers, some Iranian Christian satellite TV channels have a self-understanding as churches. Following this metaphor, the congregation sits at home in front of their TV or PC screens and takes part in services they, at least if they live inside Iran, could not attend physically. Throughout this book we will see how TV producers endeavour to broadcasts programmes that de-emphasize the spatial gap between the US-based hosts and the Iran-based viewership, for instance, through Nowruz programmes screened according to the Iranian rather than the American time zone. For matters of simplification, when mentioning 'Iranian exile churches' in this book, this may include Iranian satellite TV stations.

Summary: Pentecostalization and nationalization as two overarching trends

This chapter has traced back the historical genesis of a Persian-speaking Christianity in Iran and followed Persian-speaking Christians on their path into exile. Starting with the Western Protestant missions which were initially directed to the religious minorities of Iran, it has highlighted the gradual indigenization of mission churches as well as the ministry of Iranian Assyrians and Armenians returning from sojourns in the United States as critical episodes in this genesis. It was in the early 1960s when particularly Iranian Pentecostals began to actively use the Persian language to reach potential converts beyond ethnic and religious borders. After the 1979 Revolution, a growing number of Muslim-born Iranians started to attend churches offering services in Persian. Following governmental violence and ongoing discrimination against Persian-speaking Christian communities, a house church movement as well as a sizable and continuously growing exile community of Iranian Christians have come into being.

Especially the post-revolutionary period has witnessed both a 'pentecostalization' and a 'nationalization' of Persian-speaking Christianity as two overarching parallel trends that are also characteristic of the Iranian Christian exile milieu. As alluded to in the introduction, however, denominational identity does not play a role in the religious self-image of most Iranian Christians. Several reasons can be cited for the emphasis of Iranian national identity at the expense of a denominational identity. The marginalization of Persian-speaking Christians inside Iran *because of their language* and their stigmatization as 'foreign agents' may be one factor contributing to their active emphasis of an Iranian identity. I will further expand on this aspect in the following chapters. In line with the historical perspective of the present chapter, I will close by retracing discussions of (inter)denominationalism among Persian-speaking Christians in lieu of a conclusion.

Already in the early twentieth century, Iranian Protestants belonging to different churches were calling for an interdenominational national church transcending the boundaries of the Western mission churches (Rzepka 2019: 215). Rzepka cites the emergence of Iranian nationalism and its adoption into state policies in the 1920s as evoking the desire for 'one united Iranian church without confessional borders and division along doctrinal lines' among Iranian converts (Rzepka 2017: 84). Representatives of the Presbyterian and Anglican Churches appear to have been amenable to such suggestions. The Anglican Bishop James Linton, for instance, who functioned as bishop of the Diocese of Persia between 1917 and 1935, spoke out against the Anglican-Presbyterian division and for the training of a 'national ministry' (cf. Rzepka 2017: 70; Waterfield 1973: 165). During his tenure, three interdenominational conferences were convened (Rzepka 2017: 84).

An amicable relationship with other Protestant churches, specifically with the Anglican Diocese, was also sought for by the Presbyterians and further realized in the 1960s and 1970s (Hopkins 2020: 134–43). While Iranian Anglicans were welcoming the establishment of ties with Iranian Presbyterians, they viewed the early activities of Pentecostals in the mid-twentieth century with scepticism or even outright disapprobation. Rzepka cites the Anglican bishop William Thompson, head of the Iranian Diocese between 1935 and 1960 (and Hassan Dehqāni-Tafti's father-in-law), who as early as 1951 reported:

> We are unfortunately finding that Adventists, Jehovah's Witnesses and other sects of the extreme Pentecostal type are becoming much more in evidence out here. I look back to the happy days when we were largely free from such complications, but the tares are being sown today and we cannot hope to uproot them; but it does emphasise the importance of our following up our own members wherever they are otherwise they drift off into such sects. (Cited in Rzepka 2017: 87–8)

It perhaps is therefore not a coincidence that Iranian Pentecostals remain completely unmentioned in the Anglican bishop Dehqāni-Tafti's detailed autobiography, published in the year 2000.[28] Later in his life, however,

Dehqāni-Tafti, who was exiled from Iran in 1980, was in touch with exiled Pentecostals through the UK-based organization Elam Ministries which even filmed a documentary about the Anglican bishop's life (cf. Dibāj and Shirvāniān 2005). Dehqāni-Tafti, moreover, became a contributor to *Kalameh* magazine, published by Elam Ministries.

After the 1979 Revolution, the Pentecostal *Jamāʿat-e Rabbāni* churches evolved as the most vibrant Protestant community in Iran. This has led Rzepka speak of 'the "Pentecostalisation" of the Protestant tradition in Iran itself' (Rzepka 2017: 174). In 1982, Hāyk Hovsepiān became the superintendent (*nāzer*) of the Iranian *Jamāʿat-e Rabbāni* churches; in this position, he actively strived for the cooperation and unity of the different Protestant churches in the country (Dibāj 2004b). During this time, the different Protestant churches cooperated actively and invited each other's pastors to preach. Appointed as the chairman of the newly founded Iranian Council of Protestant Churches in 1986, Hovsepiān at the time functioned as the main spokesman of Iranian Protestants. Murdered in 1994, Hovsepiān's funeral, attended by over 2000 people, further 'integrated Iran's Protestants' (Rzepka 2017: 197).

The emergence of the house church movement has rendered matters of denomination even less palpable and relevant. One of my interlocutors, the exiled Iranian Armenian pastor Henrik, who held a leading position in one of the *Jamāʿat-e Rabbāni* churches until its closure in the early 2010s and since has maintained close contacts with Iranian house churches, explains:

> These days, especially because the church has gone underground (*zirzamini shodeh*) and turned into a house church movement, many believers completely lack an understanding of these things. They don't have any concept of what 'denomination' (*denomination*) means. They come to faith and start a house church. There they come together, pray and worship. All they know is that they are Protestants. Some may not even know this. Ninety percent are like this. (Interview with Henrik 2021)

Henrik then specified that there yet was a minority among Iranians active in the house church movement, who, because they were actively cooperating with a Western missionary society or church, had a strong sense of denomination. He seemed to find this regrettable as he himself favoured an interdenominational approach. Generally, however, Henrik pointed out:

> The truth is that, let's say, the DNA of the majority of underground churches is charismatic. ... Of course, without them having actively decided this. It's not

that they sat down and discussed 'what is this, what is that?', no (*naneshestand began 'In chieh, in chieh', na*). From the first day on, they thought: 'Ok, this is what it is (*Khob, ineh digeh*). There is healing, there is speaking in tongues, there is the Holy Spirit.' (Interview with Henrik 2021)

According to this observation, the trend for a 'pentecostalization' of Persian-speaking Christianity has reached an extent where practitioners subconsciously equate Christianity and Pentecostal Christianity. Iranian Christian exile churches equally reflect this trend – in fact, this tendency may well be a general feature of global Pentecostal Christianity.

A final instructive reflection on the denomination question can be found in the story of my interlocutor Daryā. Born into a Muslim family, Daryā in 1985 converted in the Presbyterian Evangelical Church of St. Peter in Tehran (*Kelisā-ye Enjili-ye Hazrat-e Petros*). During our interview, she described her arrival to Germany in 1994. As at that point there was no Persian-speaking church in her city, she ended up attending a German-speaking Baptist church. She remembers with amusement:

> I was completely unaware that all these denominations (*ferqeh*) existed. When I came here, I was flabbergasted! I just went to a church to feel better – then I understood how many denominations exist. At the time, I didn't even know what Baptists were. I said 'Wow, in Iran we had one Persian-speaking Church, the Evangelical Persian-speaking Church!' I didn't even know I was Presbyterian. When I came to Germany, they asked me 'What denomination are you? (*Cheh ferqeh'i?*)' I said 'Denomination? I am *Enjili* (Evangelical)!' [laughs] Later on, I understood 'Oh, I am Presbyterian!' (Interview with Daryā 2021)

Still later, Daryā founded a Persian-speaking congregation in the same Baptist church. In this congregation, she refrains from stressing a denominational Baptist identity. This is despite the fact that Baptists in Germany tend to have a strong sense of denomination and, as Daryā recounted from several personal encounters, occasionally like to proudly mention the number of generations their family had been Baptist. For Daryā's Persian-speaking congregation, however, the Iranian national identity played a bigger role, especially as she believed in an eventual return of Iranian Christians to Iran. Whether attendants were individuals who already were active in Persian-speaking communities inside Iran or who converted after their emigration, their sense of being *Iranian* Christians outweighed their sense of belonging to a particular church or denomination.

The emphasis of national identity among Iranian Christians in exile frequently surfaces in their religious services and media productions. The later chapters of this book will in detail describe the narratives and practices used by Iranian Christians to draw connections between Christianity and Iran and illustrate the specific meanings Iranian Christians ascribe to their national-religious identity by relating it to their exilic dwelling. Before entering the discussion of the primary material analysed for this book, it is necessary to discuss the concepts of religion, nationhood and diaspora on the theoretical level, considering that existing literature has used them in diverse and differing ways. By looking at how the interplay between religious and national identities in diasporic settings has been analysed before, we can arrive at a deeper understanding of the issue regarding the Iranian Christian case.

2

Theoretical perspectives on religion, the nation and diaspora

Introduction

Religion, the nation and diaspora are the three conceptual terms that frame this book. All three terms today appear as universal phenomena that can be found across cultures and throughout history. Classic scholarship and the broader public perception alike consider religion a primordial feature of human life, something that has existed from time immemorial. Similarly, nations appear as the self-evident and natural unit to structure the human populations. Diasporas tend to be thought of as a derivation of nations. In fact, the term today does not seem to make sense unless it is related to a nation state.

For all the three terms, however, critical scholarship has emerged during the past decades, which highlights their specific histories. Consequently, to freewheelingly use 'religion', 'nation' and 'diaspora' as ostensibly neutral analytical categories across time and space has become increasingly problematic. Much of the analytical vocabulary dominating the humanities today carries a heavy epistemological baggage. Scholars with a postmodern approach have unearthed the implicit biases that favour the distinct experiences of post-Enlightenment Europe and unjustifiably universalize them as a lens through which, supposedly, the entire world could be studied. In its most radical variant, this criticism ultimately advocates the abandonment of existing analytical tools. Only then, it is argued, scholarly work can free itself from previous patronizing tendencies.

This book takes the postmodern critique seriously without jettisoning the terms religion, nation and diaspora. A replacement of, for example, 'religion' by the coinage 'cosmographic formations', as suggested by Daniel Dubuisson (cf. Dubuisson 2007: 189–215), would arguably render a disservice to the study of religions. Instead, scholars should familiarize themselves with the histories of specific terms and, subsequently, be careful and transparent in how they apply them. This chapter aims to fulfil these two goals.

Although religion, the nation and diaspora are connected in certain ways, three separate fields of the study of religions, nationalism studies and diaspora studies have emerged that have their own respective debates. Accordingly, this chapter will first engage with the nexus of religion and nationalism, then move on to the concept of 'diasporic religion' and finally draw the three concepts together to provide a framework for the subsequent chapters.

Religion and nationalism

Nationalism versus nationhood

Having its roots in the late eighteenth century, nationalism in our day and age continues to be a hegemonic ideology of global relevance. While the term in its daily usage conjures up notions of radicalism, violent wars and ethnic supremacism, the academic field of nationalism studies has approached the phenomenon in a much broader way. Gellner's classic definition of nationalism, for instance, simply assumes that 'nationalism is primarily a political principle, which holds that the political and the national unit should be congruent' (Gellner 1983: 1). Likewise focussing on the political aspects of nationalism, Breuilly suggests that

> a nationalist argument is a political doctrine built upon three basic assertions: (a) There exists a nation with an explicit and peculiar character. (b) The interests and values of this nation take priority over all other interests and values. (c) The nation must be as independent as possible. This usually requires at least the attainment of political sovereignty. (Breuilly 1993: 2)

Rather than the political dimensions foreseen by points (b) and (c), this book is primarily concerned with point (a): the explicit and peculiar character ascribed to nations. I use the term *nationhood* to refer to the main features defining authentic belonging to a particular nation. Simply put, nationhood is what is mentioned in response to questions like 'What makes a true Iranian?' or 'What characterizes true Iranian-ness?' These questions are subject to constant negotiation. Different people may answer them differently today, and the same people would answer them differently tomorrow. Nationhood is constructed and thus always open to change.

My approach aligns with a specific strand in nationalism studies that was initiated by Michael Billig's 1995 book *Banal Nationalism*. Billig argued that the reproduction of nations is 'not removed from everyday life' (1995: 6) and called upon scholars to 'look for the reasons why people in the contemporary world do not forget their nationality' (ibid.: 7). 'Banal nationalism' developed into an impulse for later studies in 'everyday nationhood' (cf. Fox and Miller-Idriss 2008; cf. Skey and Antonsich 2017). With this shift in perspective, scholars of nationalism necessarily need not to be concerned with big politics, wars of independence or genocides, but may as well look at seeming 'banalities' like food, cinema, name giving practices, banknotes, football, music or language.

This book argues that religion – or at least *religious affiliation* – constitutes an inherent component of nationhood. I will expand on this argument later. This theoretical assumption is somewhat at odds with classic scholarship in nationalism studies that considered religion and nationalism adverse phenomena. More recently, the academic study of the intersection of the two has become more nuanced and diverse.

Studying religion and nationalism: From modernist secularism to the ethno-symbolist rediscovery of religion

The early 1980s mark a critical watershed in nationalism studies with the publication of theoretical works by Benedict Anderson (1983), Ernest Gellner (1983), Eric Hobsbawm and Terence Ranger (1983) and others. Arguing for an approach that considers the nation a uniquely modern and invented/imagined phenomenon, the mentioned authors have provided scholars of multiple disciplines with concepts and theoretical paradigms of unabated popularity. That said, although they firmly established a constructionist turn in the field, not each and every aspect of their modernist approach and its concomitant presumptions has remained uncontested. Religion as a factor in the genesis and persistence of the national idea is a case in point. Be it due to Marxist convictions, a consequence of blind trust in the then widely unchallenged secularization thesis or simply due to them being 'men of their time', the mentioned scholars in their otherwise pioneering work have greatly marginalized, ignored and underestimated the role of religion in nationalisms. Dismissing religion as a mere remnant of the pre-national past, nationalism in their works appears as the inexorable modern replacement of religion.

A corrective to the modernist school, the so-called 'perennialist' approach constitutes a second major strand in nationalism studies. As suggested by its name, its proponents hold that nations by no means are a merely modern phenomenon. By highlighting the *longue durée* of nations and ethnicity, the perennialist intervention has enabled scholars to embark on a quest for 'nations before nationalism', as the title of an early pertaining work put it (Armstrong 1982). A key point of criticism perennialists level against modernists is that the latter supposedly lacked knowledge of medieval history – or even history as a whole. Accordingly, one finds historian Adrian Hastings attacking Eric Hobsbawm's take on the history of nations and nationalism by claiming Hobsbawm denied the 'first half of the story' and thus 'inevitably skewed the whole' (Hastings 1997: 11). Historical sociologist Anthony D. Smith is to be credited with the striking of a sophisticated balance in the field. He refrained from naïvely applying the concept of the nation across time and space and nevertheless acknowledged the pre-modern roots of many nations. Shifting the perspective to the symbolical repertoire drawn upon by modern nationalists, Smith called his approach 'ethno-symbolism' (Smith 1986, 2009).

Religion is one of the central symbolical resources acknowledged by Smith who devoted a whole book to the search for 'sacred sources of national identity and nationalism' (Smith 2003: 18). Smith emphasizes the structural similarity of religion and nationalism, at the heart of both of which were 'the cult and the faith' (ibid.: 28). A similar argument, albeit in a less sophisticated fashion, was already advanced by sociologist Carlton Hayes who in his 1960 treatise *Nationalism: A Religion* posited a complete equation of the two (Hayes 1960). Smith cites notions of chosen-ness, references to 'golden ages' and the veneration for deceased heroes as realms in which parallels between religion and nationalism surface (cf. Smith 2003).

Ultimately, Smith and other scholars adhering to the perennialist and ethno-symbolist schools, such as the aforementioned Adrian Hastings or John Hutchinson, succeeded in freeing nationalism studies from its secularist bias.[1] Their pioneering work paved the way for new impulses in the field, one of them being the coinage of the term 'religious nationalism' (Friedland 2001; Juergensmeyer 1993; Van der Veer 1994) – itself an oxymoron in the modernist view of the matter. Nevertheless, several theoretical shortcomings persist in their writings, particularly regarding their conceptualizations of religion.

Firstly, authors like Smith and Hastings approached religion under a certain Judeo-Christian bias. In his book *The Construction of Nationhood: Ethnicity, Religion and Nationalism*, Hastings at great length extolls Christianity as a productive force in the genesis of nationalism (Hastings 1997). Without Christianity and the biblical tradition, Hastings avers that 'it is arguable that nations and nationalism, as we know them, could never have existed' (ibid.: 4). Later in his book, Hastings awkwardly contrasts Christianity with Islam, proposing that the latter was corrosive to nation-building given its supposedly fierce attachment to Arabic as a sacred language. Within the Christian tradition, conversely, 'only a sort of fundamentalism can make language sacred ... but to do so goes against the whole nature of the religion' (ibid.: 194). In agreement with this argument, Hastings uses the term nationalism only in quotation marks when mentioned in the context of Islam, which he ascribes with a 'culture of assimilation' (ibid.: 200). Hastings's argument leaves the reader with the impression that any further inquiry into the relationship of nationalism and Islam was a vain endeavour.

Secondly, adherents to the perennialist and ethno-symbolist schools, while being very cognizant of the historicity of the nation, have generally refrained from critically assessing the concept of religion. It appears that religion, in their works, is held to be 'simply there' and a primordial given (cf. Nongbri 2013: 15; cf. Sharpe 1986: 318). Van der Veer and Lehmann observed this tendency and remarked that the modernity of religion was much less of a 'truism' than the modernity of the nation (Van der Veer and Lehmann 1999: 4). Along the same lines, sociologist of religion Markus Dressler points out that 'it is not convincing, within a study of the relationship between religion and nationalism, to critically theorize nationalism and approach it as a historical concept while at the same time presupposing a static concept of religion that lacks such historicization' (Dressler 2015: 84).

Critical scholarship in the study of religions can attune us to the problems which result from an unhistoricized and essentialist approach to religion. Commencing in the 1990s, scholars like Talal Asad (1993), Jonathan Z. Smith (1998), David Chidester (1996), Russell T. McCutcheon (1997), Timothy Fitzgerald (2003), Tomoko Masuzawa (2007), Richard King (2009) and Brent Nongbri (2013) have demonstrated how one particular notion of 'Religion' (with a capital *R*) evolved into a universal category of 'religion'. This notion takes the premises of liberal Protestantism as a normative frame in the global search for 'world religions'. Accordingly, faith was emphasized over practice, individualism over communalism, scriptural traditions over oral traditions and, most importantly, religion conceived as a distinct sphere, clearly separable from realms like science, politics and common sense.

One aspect of this emerging knowledge regime was also a dichotomy between 'religion' and 'the secular'. The nation entered the latter category and, as envisioned by the modernist narrative, came to be thought of as a secular 'other' to religion. This assumption disregards, however, that religious and national belonging have only gradually disengaged from each other. The history of this disengagement in different geographical context (and particularly in post-colonial settings) has become a new area of interest by scholars operating at the intersection between the critical study of religions and nationalism studies.

Religious affiliation as a component of nationhood

Historians and historical sociologists, informed by critical works with a post-modernist and post-colonialist thrust, have in recent years described the codependent emergence of the categories 'religion' and 'nation' in different geographical contexts. It is crucial to emphasize this codependency. Adrian H. Becker, who studied the encounter of 'Nestorian' Christians in the borderlands of nineteenth-century Qajar Iran and the Ottoman Empire with Presbyterian missionaries from the United States, observed that 'religion and nationalism are not discontinuous from each other nor inherently linked as reductive equivalents, but two related instances of the reifications of modernity' (Becker 2015: 12). Other scholars espousing a similar approach are Monica Ringer (2011), Peter van der Veer (2013) and Markus Dressler (2015, 2022).

Presently, religion and the nation have become global categories that, at least on the surface, are considered distinct from each other. This is also the case for post-colonial contexts where colonial officers, Western missionaries, Orientalist scholars and local elites, often in acts of epistemic violence, restructured local knowledge regimes through the imposition of Western categories. Given that the nation state has become a global norm, few people would now disagree that national belonging – at least in theory – is decoupled from religious belonging, a circumstance becoming most graspable in passports that indicate the passport holder's religion. However, this does not mean that matters of religion are not discussed in the context of national belonging. To a certain degree, the historical disengagement of the nation from religion, or vice versa, has remained incomplete. This circumstance, I argue, can best be grasped if we consider religious affiliation a central component of nationhood. This argument requires further explanations on two levels.

Firstly, I specifically speak of religious *affiliation*. To recapitulate my conceptualization of nationhood, endeavours to define true belonging to a particular nation usually content themselves with the *mentioning* of a particular religious tradition supposedly intertwined with particular nations. Accordingly, one may find claims like 'to truly be Turkish means to be Muslim', 'to be a real American means to be a Protestant Christian', 'to be Polish means to be a Catholic', 'to be Israeli means to be Jewish', 'to be Indian means to be a Hindu' and so forth. Conversely, discussions of nationhood are unlikely to engage with, for example, matters of theology as they are perceived as belonging to a different realm, namely that of religion.

Secondly, my argument is based on the observation that it is unjustifiable to speak of a specific 'religious nationalism' as an exception to the supposed rule of a 'secular nationalism' – even more so if the former is presented as 'non-Western' and the latter as 'Western'. In his 1993 book *The New Cold War? Religious Nationalism Confronts the Secular State*, Mark Juergensmeyer hypothesized that it is 'difficult for Westerners to comprehend' that 'in many parts of the world … religious and ethnic identities are intertwined' (Juergensmeyer 1993: 4). The underlying assumption here appears to be that Western nationalisms were radically secular and tolerantly disregarded religious identities. In times where a 'Muslim ban' has become at least an intermittent reality in the United States and political parties hammering on the supposedly Judeo-Christian (and thus non-Muslim) nature of Europe have entered parliaments and even governments across the continent, this claim is no longer tenable. No doubt, religious affiliation as a component of nationhood can be less or more pronounced. That said, the degree of emphasis on a particular religious identity can change and a secular-seeming state suddenly reveal its exclusionary potential.

Discourses of exclusion and their subversion

If nationalisms, as a rule rather than exception, are not indifferent to religious identities, they are prone to marginalize the respective religious other. Individuals and groups that do not conform with the hegemonic conception of nationhood in a particular context run the risk of being labelled subversive by members of the favoured religious group. Unusual combinations of national and religious identities, for instance that of a 'Turkish Christian' or a 'German Muslim', create tensions and challenge accepted notions of nationhood. Depending on the political setting, non-conformation to the hegemonic national-religious identity may result in repercussions.

Marginalized religious groups and individuals, however, are by no means in a merely passive position. They may react to their marginalization by emphasizing their patriotism and connectedness with the nation in question. This book describes the discourses resulting from the exclusion of Iranian Christians from Iranian nationhood. It aims to illustrate how Iranian Christians in exile use specific narratives and practices to argue that one indeed can be authentically Iranian *and* Christian at the same time. Accordingly, it will use the term 'narratives and practices of authentication'.

This framework is equally applicable to other contexts, including the ones mentioned earlier. Özyürek in a 2012 article refers to a Muslim-born Turkish convert to Christianity who, having declared 'I am a Christian – and I am still a true Turk', added that much of the Bible was in fact written in the territory of contemporary Turkey (Özyürek 2012: 95). Similarly, Muslims in Europe may react to claims of a supposedly Judeo-Christian character of 'the West' by pointing to the long history of intellectual exchange between Muslims, Christians and Jews on European territory, for instance, in Muslim Spain, Muslim Sicily or the Ottoman Balkans.[2] Such narratives can also be specific to particular nations; in the German context, for example, Muslims may point to the penchant for Islam and the 'Orient' of famed national poet Johann Wolfgang von Goethe. The promotion of these narratives ultimately aims for a thorough acceptance of a hyphenated 'German-Muslim' identity. Metaphorically speaking, narratives and practices of authentication endeavour to achieve the 'naturalization' of a marginalized religious group to a particular nation. This book, and specifically Chapters 3 and 4, describes the case of Iranian Christians and their struggle in naturalizing Christianity to the Iranian nation.

Religion and diaspora

Given its importance in Judaism, the concept of diaspora appears to possess an immediate connection with religion. And yet, the discovery of diaspora as a field of study for scholars of religion came relatively late. Moreover, as we shall see, the Jewish conceptualization of diaspora is quite distinct from the way the term came to be used after it underwent a process of universalization. Only through this universalization could an academic field of diaspora studies come into being. Endeavours to formulate a satisfying definition of diaspora continue to oscillate between the avoidance of essentialisms and the will to maintain the term as a meaningful, clear-cut analytical category. For the purpose of this book, the following section will first trace back the changing conceptualizations of diaspora and then discuss how to arrive at a helpful framework of diasporic religion – a concept that, so far, has been used in different ways and thus created conceptual confusion.

The universalization of a very Jewish term

The forceful dispersion of Jews both after the destruction of the Temple in the sixth century BCE and in many later instances generally serves as the paradigmatic diaspora and is the most common venture point for theoretical discussions of the concept. Despite the long-standing interest in the word's origins, a certain degree of confusion regarding the etymological roots of diaspora persists. Two specific issues can be named here: the origins of the term as a designation for the Ancient Greek colonization of Asia Minor and, later, the congruence of Greek *diaspora* with the Hebrew word *galut*.

Deriving from the Greek verb *diaspeirein* (to scatter, to spread, to disperse), scholars like Robin Cohen and Manuel A. Vásquez write that the term before entering the Jewish context was used to describe the colonization process of Asia Minor by Ancient Greeks (Cohen 1997: 2; Vásquez 2010: 129). According to an article by Martin Baumann in the year 2000, this claim is not correct. Baumann suggests that the verb *diaspeirein* and its derivative *diaspora* bore thoroughly negative connotations in classical Greek writing, implying 'processes of dispersion and decomposition' or 'a dissolution into various parts (e.g. atoms) without any further relation to each other' (Baumann 2000: 316). Moreover, he points out that *diaspora* was not the Greek term used by Alexandrian Jews to translate Hebrew *galut* in the composition of the Septuagint (ibid.), as suggested, for example, by Tölölyan (1996: 11). On the contrary, the translators of the Septuagint consciously sought to maintain a semantic difference between *galut* and the diverse Hebrew terms translated as *diaspora* (Baumann 2000: 316–17; Dufoix 2008: 4). They used *diaspora* as a soteriological concept, described by Baumann as follows:

> It was understood, an intermediate situation until the final divine gathering in Jerusalem. Fundamentally, the term took on spiritual and soteriological meanings pointing to the 'gathering of the scattered' by God's grace at the end of time. 'Diaspora' turns out to be an integral part of a pattern constituted by the fourfold course of sin or disobedience, scattering and exile as punishment, repentance, and finally return and gathering. (Baumann 2000: 317)

Two aspects of this conceptualization are noteworthy here. Firstly, it is a conceptualization seemingly specific to the context of Judaism and Jewish history. Had diaspora remained in this narrow frame, it could not have possibly undergone its later popularization. Secondly, to conceptualize diaspora as a soteriological pattern is interesting and relevant for the discussion of 'diasporic religion', to which I will return later in this chapter.

Baumann and Dufoix cite examples for later usages of the term 'diaspora' beyond the Greek language, among them being the designation of Christian denominational islands in geographical areas otherwise dominated by a different denomination in the post-Reformation era (Baumann 2003: 60–3; Dufoix 2008: 16–17). Regarding the twentieth century, Tölölyan consulted French and English-language encyclopaedias published before the term's 'breakthrough' in the century's last decades: while the *Encyclopaedia Britannica* of 1910–11 does not contain the lemma 'diaspora', the 1958 edition astonishingly locates the term in chemistry, identifying it as an aluminium oxide (Tölölyan 1996: 9). Even the *Encyclopaedia of Social Sciences* of 1968 lacks a respective entry (ibid.). This is despite its earlier 1931 version not only introducing the term 'diaspora' focussing on its paradigmatic Jewish type, but also mentioning the Armenian and Greek diasporas (ibid.). Following Dufoix, this very entry written by the Russian-Jewish historian Simon Dubnov 'played a major role in the diffusion of the term "diaspora" itself, and in both its progressive secularization in general and its gradual separation from the historic experience of the Jewish people in particular' (Dufoix 2008: 17–18).

Finally, by the 1960s, diaspora began to experience a massive revival, as an academic analytical concept as well as in journalism (cf. Dufoix 2016: 406–13) and as a self-designating category of practice. It was the beginning of what later was termed a 'diaspora explosion' (Brubaker 2005: 1) and even a 'diaspora craze' (Cohen 2008: 8). The term had now been dissociated from its historical roots so that other diasporas could be found, among them the African diaspora.[3] The emergent field of diaspora studies flourished at the latest during the early 1990s, with the launching of the journal *Diaspora: A Journal of Transnational Studies* under the auspices of the Armenian-American Khachig Tölölyan in 1991 as its most visible embodiment.

Changing concepts of diaspora

Migrant, expatriate, expellee, refugee, alien resident, minority, guest worker, exile community, overseas community and ethnic community – all these terms had somehow been absorbed into the ill-defined realm of diaspora by the early 1990s. Scholars in the emergent field of diaspora studies therefore became occupied with the task of delineating the term in a satisfying way. The proposed definitions can be allocated to different larger strands in the field: while Vertovec distinguishes between diaspora as a social form, as a type of consciousness and as a mode of cultural production (Vertovec 1997), Johnson divides the field into definitions by etymology, typological features and relation (Johnson 2012). Dufoix as well proposes a threefold classification, comprised by open, categorical, and oxymoronic definitions (Dufoix 2008, 2016: 386). Robin Cohen, author of the influential book *Global Diasporas*, presents a chronological review of diaspora studies, which includes four stages: classical uses of diaspora, diaspora as a metaphorical designation, the social constructionist intervention and, finally, the phase of consolidation (Cohen 2008: 1–20).[4]

Classical uses of diaspora in Cohen's typology mean notions of diaspora before its universalization. As discussed in the previous section, diaspora here was strictly bound to particular historical circumstances, especially the Jewish narrative of dispersion and return. Re-conceived as a metaphorical designation, diaspora became open for application in any context. Definitions of this time continue to be influential, among them the 1991 polythetic definition by William Safran (Safran 1991: 83). He proposed six characteristics, 'several' of which should be fulfilled by an 'expatriate minority community' to qualify as a diaspora:

> 1) They [the members of the community in question], or their ancestors, have been dispersed from a specific original 'center' to two or more 'peripheral', or foreign, regions; 2) they retain a collective memory, vision, or myth about their original homeland – its physical location, history, and achievements; 3) they believe that they are not – and perhaps cannot be – fully accepted by their host society and therefore feel partly alienated and insulated from it; 4) they regard their ancestral homeland as their true, ideal home and as the place to which they or their descendants would (or should) eventually return – when conditions are appropriate; 5) they believe that they should, collectively, be committed to the maintenance or restoration of their original homeland and to its safety and prosperity; and 6) they continue to relate, personally or vicariously, to that homeland in one way or another, and their ethnocommunal consciousness and solidarity are importantly defined by the existence of such a relationship. (ibid.: 83–4)

Almost all criteria listed by Safran refer to an 'original homeland'. The pioneers of the third stage in diaspora studies, the social constructionist intervention, found this fixation on a point of origin suffocating and patronizing. Post-colonial thinkers like Paul Gilroy, James Clifford, Stuart Hall, Avtar Brah and Homi Bhaba were working to adjust the meaning of diaspora and rebrand it as a more positive, optimistic concept – a concept standing for and celebrating diversity and hybridity, not being occupied with some remote geographical territory which 'members' of diasporas often were identified with. Their ideas can also be loosely associated with a wider trend in the early 1990s triggered by a 'methodological nationalism' – the tendency of scholars to allow the borders of nation states to dictate their perspectives in research, thus ignoring 'transnational' phenomena (Glick Schiller, Basch and Blanc-Szanton 1992).

Diaspora here becomes a decentred *type of consciousness* rather than a *social form* (cf. Vertovec 1997). Proponents of this approach often focussed on the creative potential arising from diasporic identities. They usually rejected specific notions of diaspora but did not give up the concept as a whole. That said, more critical voices surfaced at the very end of the 1990s, with Floya Anthias and Yasemin Soysal's contributions ultimately suggesting that diaspora as an analytical tool was irretrievably flawed (Anthias 1998; Soysal 2000). Anthias indicted diaspora and accused it of emphasizing an approach to ethnicity which privileged a supposed 'origin' in constructing identity and solidarity, thus maintaining a 'notion of primordial bonding ... at the heart' of the concept (Anthias 1998: 563). She also disapproved of the uncritical assumption of monolithic diasporic communities and pointed to the intersectional nature of identities, including the relevance of factors like class and gender (ibid.: 570).

The opening of diaspora by scholars with a post-colonial impetus was a reaction to earlier conceptualizations of the term which, in their view, were too narrow and expressive of 'the old, the imperialising, the hegemonising, form of "ethnicity"' (Hall 1990: 235). By redefining diaspora as a type of consciousness, however, they concerned other scholars who feared that the term could become *too broad* and blurry. Cohen calls the resulting criticism the 'phase of consolidation' in diaspora studies (cf. Cohen 2008: 11–15); Dufoix referred to it as the 'critical turn' in the field (cf. Dufoix 2016: 392–443). One of the turn's proponents, Rogers Brubaker, coined the witty phrase '"diaspora" diaspora' and warned scholars that 'if everyone is diasporic, then no one is distinctively so. The term loses its discriminating power – its ability to pick out phenomena, to make distinctions. The universalization of diaspora, paradoxically, means the disappearance of diaspora' (Brubaker 2005: 3).

To preserve the analytical value of diaspora, Brubaker proposed dispersion, homeland orientation and boundary maintenance as three indispensable characteristics at the core of the term. Moreover, Brubaker focussed on the functionalist aspects of diaspora 'as an idiom, a stance, a claim' (ibid.: 12). By approaching diaspora as a category of practice, Brubaker's approach, though providing a useful narrowing of the term, raises the question of how to deal with discourses in languages that do not possess a direct translation of the term. Persian is a case in point.[5]

Definitions of diaspora should take notice of the diverse voices in the field and may yet favour a particular approach over another. Different case studies are likely to prompt scholars to emphasize one specific approach: while Safran's foregrounding of the homeland factor fits the case of Armenian references to Armenia or Jewish references to Eretz Israel, scholars like Hall and Gilroy were more concerned with the Black diaspora – a case in which diasporic imagining is less territorialized. Moreover, temporality is an important factor impacting the (de-)emphasis of attachment to a particular territory.[6] Descendants of emigrants, sometimes in the second generation already, may assimilate into their environment, and their attachment to the country of origin of their parents or ancestors consequently dwindle. For first-generation emigrants, much differently, this attachment is generally very pronounced. It would therefore be inadequate to draw upon a de-territorialized notion of diaspora when discussing the displacement of, for instance, Palestinians, Iranians, Afghans, Syrians or Ukrainians. Finally, exile – the inability of an individual or a collective group to permanently return to their country of origin – constitutes another factor which influences their diasporic experience. Like temporality, this aspect is equally relevant for conceptualizations of diasporic religion.

What is diasporic religion?

In the words of Susanne Rudolph, religious communities are 'among the oldest of the transnationals' (Rudolph 2018: 1). In recent years, scholars like Peggy Levitt, Steven Vertovec and Manuel Vásquez, among others, have proposed a number of analytical terms to account for transnational aspects of religious life. Mobile religion, travelling faiths, global religion, migrant religion, transnational religion and diasporic religion are examples for such concepts; not surprisingly, they have been understood differently by different scholars. Regarding the term 'diasporic religion', two distinct usages can be found in the existing literature.

Perhaps the earliest usage of the term 'diasporic religion' is found in the work of scholar of religion Jonathan Z. Smith. In his 1978 monograph *Map Is Not Territory*, Smith pointed to the reconstruction of religious space after an uprooting from its previous, accustomed locality; an instance in which deities gain meanings transcending their dependence on a specific place and turn 'into a divine protector who was tied to no land' (Smith 1978: xiv). Nine years later,

Smith pointed to the ramifications of exile for the changing nature of Judaism (cf. Smith 1987: 94–5). Ninian Smart, another leading scholar of religion in the latter half of the twentieth century, further theorized diasporic religion in his 1987 article 'The Importance of Diasporas' (Smart 1987). He likewise referred to the de-territorializing effect of migration, especially to religious traditions strongly tied to a particular locality or ethnicity, concluding:

> The lesson seems to be that you can only deal with the universalist intruder by adopting a universal-type defence. It is thus a natural thing for diaspora religions, even if they have no great missionary pretensions, to evolve universal-type explanations of their teachings and practices. Often they may follow the lead of Western traditions and publish translations and editions of their scriptures, or adopt other external models of operation borrowed on the whole from the West. (ibid.: 295)

Smart's observation bears striking similarities to the postmodernist and postcolonial critique of 'religion' which I have referred to earlier: to qualify for anything as religion – or a 'world religion' – Western expectations of what defines a religion, for example, universalism and the possession of sacred scriptures, must be fulfilled. Paul C. Johnson describes the resulting process as the re-evaluation, conscious selection and allotting of 'formerly "natural" or unspoken parts of the social environs and its quotidian routine' (Johnson 2012: 107). In other words, emigration and diaspora lead to the religionization of previously undefined aspects in the life of emigrants.

This, the first prevalent conceptualization of diasporic religion in existing literature, resembles what Markus Dressler and Arvind-Pal Mandair, though not specifically writing about migratory contexts, have termed 'religion-making' (Dressler and Mandair 2011b). To promote one's self-representation as a 'religion' possessing the features expected by the new country of residence's society can also serve practical interests, especially legal recognition. Dressler and Mandair term this process 'religion-making *from below*', defined as 'politics where particular social groups in a subordinate position draw on a religionist discourse to re-establish their identities as legitimate social formations distinguishable from other social formations through tropes of religious difference and/or claims for certain rights' (Dressler and Mandair 2011a: 21). Alongside migratory contexts, religion-making from below can become necessary in the context of the establishment of a new political order, for instance, a secular nation state. It includes the delineation of 'religion' from (secular) 'culture' – a process also referred to as the 'compartmentalization' of religion (Vertovec 2004: 296) or the 'religion versus culture discourse' (cf. Liberatore 2017: 109–46; Liberatore and Fesenmeyer 2019: 236). Remaining ties to the homeland do not play a central role here.

The second conceptualization of diasporic religion in existing works was largely developed by Thomas Tweed in his 1997 study among Cuban Catholic exiles in Miami (Tweed 1997). It is this conceptualization that the present book will emphasize. Tweed conducted extensive fieldwork in the shrine of Our Lady of Charity in Miami. The shrine was built centring around a statue of the Virgin Mary that was smuggled from Havana to Miami in September 1961, after it had become a sign of disagreement with the Cuban Revolution among anti-communist Catholics. In the early 1960s, around 80,000 anti-Castro Catholics had left the country, many of them settling in Miami. Here, the shrine and the Virgin became a sphere of national commemoration, a space of reconnection with Cuba by exercising devotion to the Virgin, and a way to 're-create the Cuban community – those on the island and in the diaspora – as an imagined nation' (ibid.: 83).

The national imagining of Cuban Catholic exiles is guided by what Tweed refers to as 'diasporic nationalism' (ibid.). It is more directed to a truly utopian idea of Cuba – a Cuba that for those imagining it is the only true rendition of their land but in the eye of a constructionist observer may in many ways only have been made possible by the, according to the exiles, catastrophic event of the Castro Revolution (ibid.: 85).

Tweed offers a detailed framework for the study of 'the religion of the displaced' (ibid.: 5). He establishes the theoretical premise that, alongside the obvious significance of spatial separation in exile, a disruption of time is equally meaningful (cf. ibid.: 85). Exilic history is about the 'before' and the 'after' of displacement. Subsequently, religion becomes a measure to express and attribute meaning to both the spatial and temporal disruption – it is *transtemporal* and *translocative* (ibid.: 94). In Tweed's own words:

> These translocative and transtemporal impulses are expressed religiously in a variety of ways in diasporic religion. In religious narratives, diasporas remember and compose tales that express attachment to the natal land, sacralize the new land, or form bridges between the two. The people and the clergy compose stories about the suffering and disorientation of displacement. (ibid.: 95)

Moreover, diasporic religion is concerned with the *future* and informs visions for the fate of the land of origin (ibid.: 84). Tweed also recognizes the importance of temporality, as discussed earlier. While the translocative aspect of diasporic religion described here proves particularly relevant to the first and maybe second generations, religion becomes *supralocative* among subsequent generations (ibid.: 94). In this latter instance, the meaning of both home and 'host' land is played down, and religion, as foreseen by the first conceptualization of diasporic religion, universalized and de-territorialized.

Before diasporic religion enters this supralocative stage, the importance of the homeland is crucial. Diasporic religion according to Tweed denotes the imagination of this homeland as well as its past and future through religious narratives (cf. ibid.: 95). It also entails the development of visions of return to the homeland. Tweed uses the Jewish Passover dictum of 'Next Year in Jerusalem!' and reformulates it as a general plea in the religion of the displaced:

> For now, however, Cubans at the Miami shrine still ask, 'Hasta cuando?' How long must we wait? If the future mirrors the past, when the national patroness does guide Cuban migrants home, another group elsewhere will be displaced and count themselves among diasporic peoples. That new diaspora, then, will join others in offering the familiar plea and prediction of the displaced: Next year in Jerusalem! Next year in Havana! Next year in Saigon, Palestine, and Llasa! (ibid.: 142)

In Chapter 6 of this book, we will observe how Iranian Christians in exile join this plea and long for 'Next Year in Persepolis!'. Tweed's conceptualization reconnects with the soteriological making of diaspora in the Jewish tradition, as described by Baumann. Generalized beyond the Jewish context, diaspora as a soteriological scheme becomes a theoretical framework in the study of the religion of the displaced. Its 'fourfold course of sin or disobedience, scattering and exile as punishment, repentance, and finally return and gathering' (Baumann 2000: 317) will therefore serve this book to frame how Iranian Christians in exile make religious sense of their forced displacement and formulate religious visions of a future return to Iran.

Conclusion

In Chapter 1, I illustrated the historical aspects that have contributed to the emphasis of national belonging over denominational belonging among Iranian Christians inside Iran and in exile. The theoretical discussion of this chapter has added further, more generalizable factors that cause religious communities to foreground issues of nationhood. Religious affiliation plays a role in the negotiation of authentic national belonging. Communities and individuals not conforming with the hegemonic idea of what religion a 'true' member of a particular nation ought to be affiliated with may react by emphasizing their patriotism and develop narratives linking their religious identity with the nation in question.

The freedom to promote these dissenting narratives, however, is not always given. Exile, as tragic as its experience may be, can serve as a sphere from which dissenting visions for the homeland can be freely promoted. Hence, diaspora does not appear as a de-territorialized, de-centralized notion in this book. Much like Tweed in his 1997 study, this book describes a group of (vastly) first-generation emigrants with a vivid memory of life in the homeland. Their forced displacement is immediately tied to their religious identity; Iranian Christians in exile are a 'religious diaspora' (cf. Johnson 2012: 104) or 'religious refugees' (cf. Lachenicht 2007). This aspect constitutes a connecting element in the triangular relationship of religion, the nation and diaspora; their connectivity results in a 'diasporic nationalism' in a religious idiom.

The following two chapters will describe in detail the narratives and practices used by Iranian Christians in exile to construct an, in their view, authentic Iranian-Christian national-religious identity. Due to the lack of religious freedom in the Islamic Republic of Iran, as described in Chapter 1, the open promotion of these narratives and practices is solely possible in exile. After a brief digression to discussions of Islam in Iranian Christian exile churches in Chapter 5, Chapter 6 will use the framework illustrated in the latter part of this chapter to discuss diasporic religion among Iranian Christians in exile.

3

Naturalizing Christianity (I): Introduction and the festivals of Nowruz and Yaldā

Introduction: Iranian nationhood and the double foreignness of Christianity

When Hassan Dehqāni-Tafti, later the Anglican Bishop of Iran, in the early 1940s requested the approval for the publication of a monthly Christian magazine in the Persian language, he received the following reply: 'Persian is the language of Muslims, Armenian is the language of Christians' (Dehqāni-Tafti 1994: 7). His request was subsequently denied. The answer of the governmental clerk responding to Dehqāni-Tafti's request succinctly illustrates how the Christian religion in the Iranian context has come to be discursively conflated with Armenian ethnicity. Rooted in pre-modern epistemologies of 'nationality' and 'religion', the usage of the term *Armani* (Armenian) in the Persian language resembles pre-modern European usages of the term 'Turk':

> In practice, 'Turk' was employed by Europeans quite differently, as an indiscriminate blanket term for a Muslim of any ethnic origin. Even Western Europeans who converted to Islam could be referred to as 'Turks' – as in the English phrase 'to turn Turk', meaning 'to convert to Islam' – though such converts were obviously neither natives of Anatolia nor native speakers of Turkish. (Casale 2007: 124)

Along analogous lines, the term *Armani* in Persian has evolved as a catchall label for *all* Christians, irrespective of their origins, and the verb 'to turn Armenian' (*Armani shodan*) as a synonym for 'to convert to Christianity'. Accordingly, one finds that the historian Mohamad Tavakoli-Targhi refers to a nineteenth-century Iranian Sheykhi author who, in his discussion of the dangers resulting from a blind imitation of European modernity, raises the risk of conversions to 'Armenianism' (Tavakoli-Targhi 2001: 72). Even members of the smaller Iranian Assyrian Christian community have been subsumed under the label *Armani*. Writing about the late 1930s, Ervand Abrahamian mentions a political prisoner referred to as 'Yousef "The Armenian"', adding: '(in fact, he was Assyrian)' (Abrahamian 1999: 47). Similarly, Mehdi Dibāj, who later served as a pastor for the *Jamā'at-e Rabbāni* churches, upon confiding his conversion to Christianity to his parents, heard the following response: 'No way! You went and turned Armenian?!'[1] (Dibāj 2003a: 14).

The 1979 Revolution has further buttressed the hegemonic discourse of a Persian Islam and an Armenian Christianity. The Iranian nation (*mellat*) was reconceived as an Iranian *ommat* – a religious, Islamic community (Amanat 2017: 785). This renewed turn has made self-identification as Iranian very difficult for Iranian Armenian Christians who suddenly found themselves living in an 'Islamic Republic', the public sphere of which is governed by Islamic principles, to be adhered to by Muslims and non-Muslims alike.[2] While Iranian Armenians and Assyrians resorted to increasing self-segregation in minority-only gated compounds, Persian-speaking Christians were left behind as an ultimate religious 'other'. Falling through the established cracks, they seemed not to belong anywhere. A 1979 article in the Anglican newsletter *Message of Love* (*Payām-e Mohabat*) used the Persian word *gomnāmi* to describe the situation of Persian-speaking Christians (cited in Dehqāni-Tafti 1994: 411) – a term one Persian-English dictionary tellingly translates as 'the state of being unknown' (Emami 2006: 742).

It bears mentioning that many Iranian Armenians likewise endorse the dichotomy of a Persian-speaking, Iranian Islam and an Armenian-speaking, non-Iranian Christianity, mainly to avoid assimilation. Episodes from the interviews I conducted with Iranian Armenians who attended public Persian-speaking churches in Iran (when they still existed) suggest that the existence of these churches angered other members of their ethnic community. One of my Iranian Armenian interlocutors poignantly described this tendency by telling me how his mother, after she heard that her son now attended the Persian-speaking *Jamā'at-e Rabbāni* church, reacted by incredulously asking him: 'So you are going there and praying next to some 'Abbās?' (interview with Henrik, 2021). The name 'Abbās here, of course, serves as a paradigmatic Muslim name. I asked my Iranian Assyrian interlocutor Martin whether, in his perception, Iranian Assyrians possessed a similar sensitivity towards the issue as Armenians. He averred that the sensitivity was markedly more pronounced among Iranian Armenians for whom the affiliation with the Armenian Orthodox Church was a primary marker of their national identity (interview with Martin, 2022). Nonetheless, later in the interview, Martin mentioned that the decision to conduct Persian-language services in his Assyrian Pentecostal church was met with resistance – also out of a fear of assimilation (ibid.). Notably, both Martin and my Iranian Armenian interviewees suggested that matters today were more relaxed and the formerly hardened fronts loosened (interviews with Ānāis and Henrik, 2021; interview with Martin, 2022).

Apart from Barry's illustrative 2019 book, few sources describe contemporary aspects of Iranian Armenian life in Iran. A 2019 episode of the Iranian podcast *Radiomarz*, however, provides further insights regarding Iranian perceptions of their Armenian compatriots. The podcast's host invited a number of Iranian Armenians of different generations to speak about the clichés and misconceptions they were faced with when interacting with Iranian Muslims. One respondent, 23-year-old Nārineh, recounted that, when inquiring about her Armenian background, Iranian Muslims occasionally with benign curiosity asked whether they as well could become Christian, 'or Armenian' (Radiomarz 2019: m. 6:43). Another respondent, 68-year-old Shākeh, who now resides in the Republic of Armenia, suggested that the confusion regarding the religious and ethnic identities of Iranian Armenians was a matter of the past:

> Whenever people have told us 'Lucky you, when you travel abroad (*khārej*) you can speak English because you are Christian', we reminded them that we are Armenians whose language is Armenian and not English. A Christian is not necessarily English or non-Iranian. This is one example of the unawareness widespread among Iranians who did not distinguish between nationality (*melliyat*), language and religion. That is, they did not know that to be Armenian and to speak the Armenian language is about national identity and that to be Christian denotes our religion. It is possible that an Armenian in fact is not a Christian but an atheist or whatever, a Bahai – everything really, also Muslim, though very rarely of course. But the majority of the Iranian people, those who did not reside in cities like Tabriz, Isfahan or Tehran where there are many Armenians, or in a smaller city like my birthplace Arāk, were not really in contact with the Armenian community. Today of course the situation is different … The awareness has increased markedly and such cute incidents (*ettefāqāt-e bāmazeh*) along the lines of 'Lucky you, you can speak English' no longer happen. (ibid.: m. 4:33–6:24)

Shākeh's account is indicative of a second ethno-religious conflation: that of Christianity with *Western-ness*. In Chapter 1, this topic has been broached in the context of the Western Protestant missions; we have seen how Iranian Protestants themselves have struggled for indigenization and autonomy from the Western churches. Moreover, I have pointed to the ongoing stigmatization of Iranian Christians as supposed 'agents of foreign powers', which ushers in their legal persecution. For non-ethnic Iranian Christians, who consider themselves fully Iranian 'despite' their religion, their association with the West can be a painful experience. The young Hassan Dehqāni-Tafti, when participating in a Shi'ite *ta'ziyeh* passion play in his hometown of Taft, recounts that the locals made him assume the role of a European (*farangi*) who had embraced Islam after witnessing the tragedy of Karbala, thus alluding to his Christian faith. In his English-language autobiography, Dehqāni-Tafti comments on this episode by saying: 'It pained me greatly in my deep pride of being Persian that having a Christian identity made me "foreign" in their eyes' (Dehqani-Tafti 2000: 28).

In conclusion, we can observe that hegemonic notions of Iranian nationhood do not provide space for affiliation with the Christian religion. The dominant logic considers Christianity to be either synonymous with Armenian-ness in the Iranian context or an entirely Western entity. Christianity is ascribed with a double foreignness. As a result, Persian-speaking Christians find themselves in a marginal position. How do they react to their marginalization?

The making of a Christianity in an Iranian idiom

The historical struggle of Iranian Protestants for autonomy from the Western mission churches concerned not only their administrative autonomy, but also their wish for more indigenous forms of worship in their services. Discourses on Iranian nationhood that present Christianity as an essentially foreign entity have further spurred the vision of a truly Iranian Christianity among Iranian Christians. This and the following chapters will provide an overview of the main narratives and practices which nourish the construction of a Christianity in an Iranian idiom. Ultimately aiming at the thorough establishment of an Iranian-Christian national-religious identity – the 'naturalization' of Christianity to the Iranian nation – such narratives and practices, as stated in the previous chapter, are best termed 'narratives and practices of authentication'.

Reacting to the association of Christianity with 'the West', Iranian Christians generally tend to emphasize their patriotism and their faithfulness to Iranian national customs, even after their emigration. 'Isā Dibāj, a main contributor to the magazine *Kalameh* and son of the murdered *Jamā'at-e Rabbāni* pastor Mehdi Dibāj, writes in a 2003 article:

> Indeed, to remain attached to national customs and celebrate ancient rituals like Nowruz, which is in no conflict with the Christian faith and Biblical

teachings whatsoever, more than just being a national duty also contributes to the internalization of the Christian faith in our country and its de-alienation (*bigāneh-zodāyi*), and crosses out the incorrect imagination according to which Christianity is an imposed commodity of the West. (Dibāj 2003a: 36)

Along similar lines, a minister at a Persian-speaking church in Kayseri, Turkey addressed recent converts from Islam who felt insecure about how to, as Christians, position themselves to the national traditions of Iran: it was regretful that some Iranians believed that, with their conversion to Christianity, they as well had to adopt Western culture and values and abandon their own national culture (Kelisā-ye 222 Kāyseri 2019: m. 2:14–4:32). Christianity was not a 'culture of imposition' (*farhang-e tahmili*) of the West, and it did not contradict (*tazādd*) Iranian culture in any way (ibid.). Televangelist Hormoz Shari'at puts it more pithily: 'We have come to believe in Christ – surely doesn't mean we've become Western, right (*Gharbi nashodim hā*)?' (Shari'at 2017: m. 0:57).

Some exiled Iranian pastors, among them the UK-based circle affiliated with Elam Ministries and/or PARS Theological Centre, have even attended to the reconciliation of Iranian national culture and Christianity as a theological task. The publication of both the magazines *Kalameh* and *Shāgerd* must be seen in this context. In a 2004 editorial, Mehrdād Fātehi, another main contributor to *Kalameh* and today the executive director of PARS, elaborated on the magazine's mission (Fātehi 2004). He suggested that God, aware of the human embeddedness in different cultural environments, throughout history had revealed himself in a way attuned to the cultural sensitivities of those receiving his revelation (ibid.: 3). Without this historical-cultural (*tārikhi-farhangi*)[3] framing of the divine message, humans were incapable of correctly discerning it (ibid.). By adopting this view, Fātehi and his colleagues align with the theological paradigm of a culturally sensitive, 'contextual' theology, which was pioneered by Catholic priest Steven B. Bevans.[4] Regarding *Kalameh* magazine, Fātehi points out:

> The mission of the magazine *Kalameh* is to pour Christian message and thought into the mould of Iranian language and culture. It really is spot-on that the magazine on its cover is introduced as a 'Magazine of Faith and Christian-**Iranian** Culture'. For Christian culture in a universal sense does not exist (*beh ma'nā-ye kolli vojud nadārad*). What can exist is Christian-Iranian, Christian-Japanese, Christian-English culture and so forth. In the words of Bishop Dehqāni, who himself on this path has rendered most valuable services to Iranian Christendom, it is 'one well with two sources'. (ibid.: 4, bold in the original)

Other articles in *Kalameh* offer further deliberations on the 'culture question', among them two articles penned by Robert Āseriān, a former *Jamā'at-e Rabbāni* pastor who today as well serves as a staff member of PARS (cf. Āseriān 2004, 2005). Āseriān critically points to the European missions to Africa which, in his view, had tended to impose Western cultural standards (*'anāser-e farhangi*) in realms unnecessary for the delivering of the Gospel (Āseriān 2005: 32). Alongside culinary habits, sartorial preferences and architecture, he mentions music as a primary example (ibid.: 33). For Iran, Āseriān suggests that the country's mixed ethnic, linguistic and religious make-up posed an additional challenge for Christian theologians; likewise, Iranians abroad had to be approached distinctly because of their gradual coalescence into their new countries (ibid.: 37).

Āseriān's and other authors' writings in *Kalameh* thus also recognize the specific circumstances of the Iranian Christian exile community. In 2015, PARS Theological Centre launched the publication of *Shāgerd* magazine. Seemingly catering to a more academic readership, the editors of *Shāgerd*, among them Āseriān and Fātehi, again foreground the question of Iranian culture and explicitly call its preservation in the diaspora a crucial endeavour:

> We are heirs to a unique treasure (*ganjine'i bi-badil*) of Iranian culture and civilization which all of human civilization should feel deeply proud of. As Iranian Christians, the acquaintance with the rich dimensions of Iranian culture and customs is an important part of our culture [as Iranian Christians; *sic*]. We will therefore endeavour to take a small step in the recognition and deeper understanding of another component of our identity as Iranian Christians, through the presentation of articles and research in the areas of poetry, literature, architecture, music, folkloric arts (*honar-e fulklurik*) and everything else that constitutes a part of our cultural and historical heritage, as well as by dealing with the cultural life of contemporary Iran. For those Iranian Christians who for years have lived away from Iran or the new generation of Iranians who have been born outside the country, this topic is of twofold importance. (Āseriān et al. 2015: 3)

Despite this euphoric welcome, the authors do not deem their approach to be uncritically receptive to every single aspect of Iranian culture. Āseriān in his earlier articles explained that national cultures also possessed traditions and customs contradicting the Christian religion (Āseriān 2005: 37). Examples of illicit cultural infringements in the practice of Christians, he suggested, could already be found in the New Testament, where the Apostle Paul reprimanded the Christians of Corinth for allowing their adultery-stricken (*zenā-ālud*) and idolatrous (*bot-parastāneh*) cultural environments to tamper with their Christian orthodoxy (ibid.). Alongside the presentation of the cultural elements positively drawn upon by Iranian Christians, I will therefore in this book also refer to the celebration of *Sizdah Bedar* (in this chapter) and the practice of divination, or *fāl/fālgiri* (in the following chapter), as examples for Iranian traditions frowned upon or even outrightly rejected by Iranian Christians.

The 'treasure of Iranian culture and civilization', as the editors of *Shāgerd* put it, offers Iranian Christians a vast amount of material ready to be utilized for the making of a Christianity in an Iranian idiom. Some Iranian pastors have assumed the roles of 'architects' in this construction process. An early example is Jalil Qazzāq Irvāni (1878/9–1954/5),[5] headmaster of the Isfahan College Branch school who, according to Christian van Gorder, is 'sometimes called the father of Iranian Anglicanism' (Van Gorder 2010: 132). A former pupil of Irvāni, Hassan Dehqāni-Tafti praises his late teacher as a talented artist and an inspiring Iranian theologian who 'taught things Biblical and Christian in a thoroughly Persian idiom' (Dehqani-Tafti 2000: 25). His legacy had a profound impact on Dehqāni-Tafti who, together with his British colleagues at his Isfahan church, endeavoured to merge Anglican liturgical customs and Iranian cultural heritage, for instance, through the composition of hymns (see Figure 1).

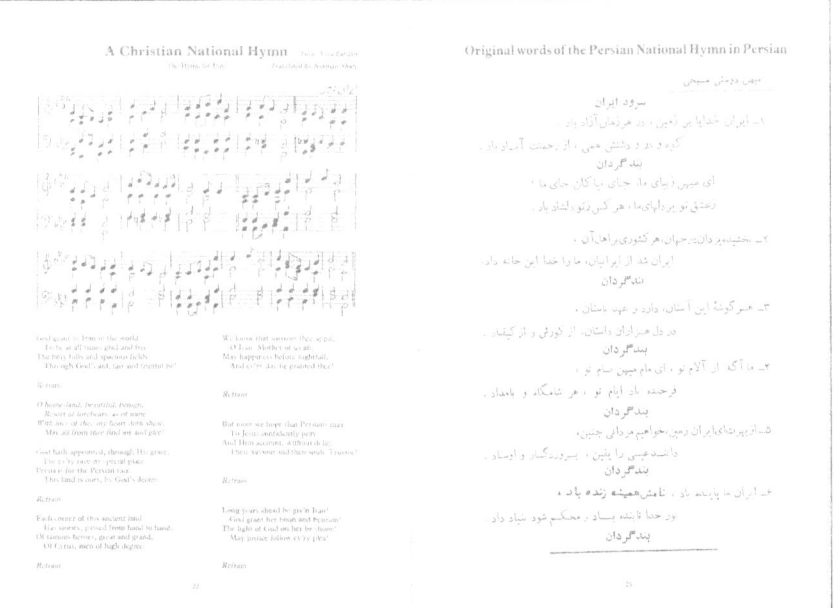

Figure 1 A 'Persian National Hymn', composed by Hassan Dehqāni-Tafti. In Dehqāni-Tafti (1990: 22–3). Used with permission of the Dehqāni family.

A more recent example of a self-described contributor in the making of an Iranian Christianity is the Pentecostal Mohammad Jalil Sepehr who summarizes his biography in a 2009 interview with *Kalameh* (Sepehr and Dibāj 2009). Born into a Muslim family, Sepehr was baptized shortly before the 1979 Revolution at the *Jamā'at-e Rabbāni* Central Church in Teheran to which an Iranian Armenian fellow conscript had invited him (ibid.: 10–11). Later, he served as the assistant to the Mashhad-based pastor Hoseyn Sudmand who was executed in 1990 (ibid.: 12). During prayer meetings that took place in the basement of Sudmand's house, Sepehr regularly recited poetry (ibid.). After the killings of Hāyk Hovsepiān and Mehdi Dibāj in 1994, Sepehr decided to emigrate from Iran (ibid.: 13). Today, he lives in the United States where he often appears on Iranian Christian satellite TV stations.

In the same interview, Sepehr describes the enormous interest in the Christian religion that he observed among Iranians, stating he had never seen an Iranian 'who hears the name of Jesus Christ and remains indifferent to it' (ibid.). This, he continues, made Iranians 'probably the only nation' where this was the case (ibid.). From these circumstances, Sepehr avers, a special responsibility arises: 'As long as Christianity will remain non-native, it will fail to reach people beyond a merely emotional level' (ibid.: 40). His endeavour was therefore 'the promotion of a Christianity that has an air of familiarity (*bu-ye khodemāni*)' (ibid.).

That Iranian Christians have sought to integrate aspects of Iranian culture into their religious practice has been mentioned by some previous works on the subject. Rzepka and Hopkins specifically mention Persian poetry as an example (Hopkins 2020: 165; Rzepka 2017: 81). However, their books are confined to the mere *mentioning* of these tendencies and do not further analyse relevant material. Secondly, one needs to exercise some caution as to whether certain narratives and practices are actually genuine to Iranian *Christians*. Miller mentions the case of an Iranian pastor consciously replacing the Arabic phrase *in shā' Allāh* (God willing) with the Persian *beh omid-e Khodā*, implying that there was a connection between the pastor's Christian faith and his predilection for linguistic purism (Miller 2015: 76). The conscious replacement of Arabic-rooted words and expression with supposedly genuine Persian terms, however, is commonly found among Iranians with a nationalist attitude, irrespective of their religious views. Expertise in Iranian studies can therefore sharpen the view of observers and help them to detect discourses which are peculiar to the Iranian Christian milieu.

Christianizing Nowruz

Nowruz as a subject of ideological contestation

Ringing in the new year in the Iranian calendar, the festival of Nowruz (lit. 'new day') is celebrated at the vernal equinox in Iran, as well as in many other countries and among various ethnic groups in the Middle East, Central Asia, South Asia and beyond. In the Iranian context, where the occasion is followed by two weeks of school holiday, Nowruz is commonly referred to as *'eyd*, a term of Arabic origin meaning festival/feast. In the Islamic tradition, the term is used to denote the two major celebratory dates: the feast at the end of the month of Ramadan (*'Eyd-e Fetr*) and the feast of sacrifice (*'Eyd-e Qorbān*). The Shi'ite tradition, moreover, follows the *'Eyd* of *Ghadir Khomm*, which exuberantly celebrates the appointment of 'Ali Ibn Abi Tālib by the Prophet Muhammad as his successor.

There is a fixed set of customs coupled with the celebration of Nowruz, among them thorough cleaning of the house (*khāneh-tekāni*), buying and wearing new clothes, visiting family members and friends (*did o bāzdid*), distributing gifts (*'eydi*) especially to younger ones, setting the 'Table of the Seven S' (*sofreh-ye haft sin*) and, more generally, socializing in a festive atmosphere. Nowruz is preceded by the celebration of *Chahārshanbeh-Suri* on the last Tuesday night of the year and completed by an occasion called *Sizdah Bedar*, two weeks after Nowruz. I will return to both of these as well as the other Nowruz-related customs further later.

The prevalent designation of the feast as 'Ancient Nowruz' (*Nowruz-e Bāstāni*) enables modern Iranians to, by their participation in the mentioned customs, imagine themselves as continuators of a perennial Iranian national tradition and thus as loyal guardians of their national heritage. Moreover, as Christian Funke has noted, especially after the 1979 Revolution, Nowruz has come to be thought of as *the* manifestation of Iranian-ness in the Iranian calendar and is occasionally pitted against the Shi'ite mourning days of Ashura as its supposed other: the main marker of Iran's *Islamic* identity (Funke 2017: 273–4). This notion is informed by a binary view of Iranian history that represents the pre-Islamic age as a supposed golden age that was abruptly ended with the Arab conquest of Persia (cf. Zia-Ebrahimi 2016). I will return to this influential paradigm when discussing discourses on Islam among Iranian Christians in Chapter 5.

Iranians today, moreover, tend to label Nowruz as a 'Zoroastrian' festival. This idea derives from the nationalist belief that all things pre-Islamic equal Zoroastrian equal authentic Iranian-ness – a notion promoted both by Zoroastrian reformers and by Iranian nationalists since the early twentieth century (cf. Marashi 2020; cf. Ringer 2011). I have consciously decided *not* to introduce Nowruz as a *Zoroastrian* feast to avoid buying into ahistorical narratives. Mary Boyce's detailed observations of Nowruz celebrations in Zoroastrian communities, both historical and contemporary, account for the questionability of a designation of Nowruz as celebrated by modern Iranians as 'Zoroastrian' (cf. Boyce 2016).

The presentation of Nowruz as a vehicle of Iranian-ness throughout the ages, defiant of the supposedly corrosive attacks of Islam, disregards 1,300 years of Islamic Iranian history in which Nowruz was cherished by Islamic rulers under whose patronage Nowruz was celebrated not short of extravaganza (Shapur Shahbazi 2009).[6] It is true, however, that shortly after the 1979 Revolution, during its more 'iconoclastic' stage, there were clerical voices pushing for the removal of Nowruz from the Iranian calendar (Abrahamian 2008: 178; Ansari 2019: 327). Such initiatives were part of a broader impulse to eradicate all ideological remnants previously espoused by the Pahlavi Shahs. As the most famous face of this iconoclasm, the maverick cleric Sādeq Khalkhāli (1926–2003) entered Persepolis with a bulldozer, determined to demolish the highly symbolic remains of the historical Achaemenid city (Amanat 2017: 781). Although his attack was aborted, the memory of such excesses is still very much alive among Iranians who may cite them as supposed evidence for their binary view of Iranian history.

Due to the massive popularity of Nowruz, the Islamic Republic has long come to condone the festival, and both the president and the Supreme Leader deliver an annual Nowruz address. In their legal justification of the permissibility of Nowruz, Shi'ite clerics, among them Supreme Leader 'Ali Khāmene'i (b. 1939) himself, point out that Nowruz, while lacking basis in recognized Islamic sources, was conducive to family gatherings (*seleh-ye rahem*) and thus religiously acceptable (*mostahsan*) (Khāmene'i n.d.). The same reasoning is offered in a legal ruling by the conservative Āyatollāh Makārem-Shirāzi (b. 1927) with regard to the celebration of the Yaldā Night, which I will discuss later in this chapter:

Question: What is the opinion of his excellency with regards to the celebration of the Iranian tradition of the Yaldā Night?
Answer: The Iranian tradition of the Yaldā Night, if celebrated for the sake of a family gathering (*seleh-ye rahem*) and as long as sins are abstained from in its course, is unproblematic (*eshkāli nadārad*). (Makārem-Shirāzi n.d.)

The Iranian state has also tried to provide Nowruz with an Islamic framing (Funke 2017: 275). Despite this overall conciliatory stance, the celebration of

Nowruz is not accepted in all ways and at all costs. A 2011 incidence may serve to illustrate this persisting tension: the president at the time, eccentric populist Mahmud Ahmadinezhād (b. 1956), had intended to hold a pompous Nowruz celebration at the historical site of Persepolis (Takht-e Jamshid) for which he was going to invite royalty and heads of state from around the world. His plan resulted in fierce criticism, with the conservative MP ʿAli Motahhari stating that Ahmadinezhād's plan was reminiscent of Mohammad Rezā Shah's ill-famed celebration of the '2500th Anniversary of the Founding of the Persian Empire' at Persepolis in 1971 (Shojāʿi 2011) – a truly damning comparison. Finally, the event was moved to Tehran's Saʿd-Ābād Palace, adorned by elements of Safavid architecture rather than symbols of pre-Islamic Iran (Sharq 2011). Ahmadinezhād thus remained unable to cross the red line in the amount of acceptance awarded to pre-Islamic national motifs in the state's official self-representation.

Governmental actors in the Islamic Republic are well aware of the expedient symbolic repertoire offered by occasions like Nowruz to voices of dissent. Another potential conduit of resistance, which has been officially outlawed since 2010, is the celebration of Red Wednesday, *Chahārshanbeh-Suri*, marked by the last Tuesday night in the Iranian calendar. A forerunner of Nowruz, the celebration of *Chahārshanbeh-Suri* mainly consists of participants jumping over a bonfire while uttering the phrase 'Let your redness be mine, and my paleness [yellowness] be yours!'. The phrase is believed to possess a purifying power. *Chahārshanbeh-Suri* had already been outlawed during the first two years after the 1979 Revolution and was intermittently rehabilitated (Kasheff and Saʿīdī Sīrjānī 1990). Shahram Khosravi, who calls *Chaharshanbeh-Suri* 'the night the Islamic regime dreads most' (Khosravi 2008: 142), describes the politicization of the event:

> When I was growing up in Iran in the 1970s, Chaharshanbeh souri was an innocent ceremony of youthful entertainment. For us it was merely a neighborhood party. For today's generation it is a political event, pitting national sentiments against the religious identities imposed from above. The ritual has been transformed into a site for defiance toward the social order and 'normative modesty'. Young people have forged (in the sense both of falsifying and of forming) a new version of the ritual. The new, politicized Chaharshanbeh souri has become *a ritual of protest*. (ibid.: 143; italics added)

Its re-conception as a 'ritual of protest' eventually brought about the legal ban of *Chahārshanbeh-Suri* in 2010, the details of which Funke describes in his book (Funke 2017: 278–86). Especially popular among young people who take the opportunity of *Chahārshanbeh-Suri* to meet up for parties and set off fireworks, the occasion had often ushered in clashes between young partakers in the ritual and security forces. After months of demonstrations protesting the rigged 2009 elections, the Iranian state authorities in 2010 were especially alarmed as the last Tuesday evening of the year was drawing near. Moreover, defeated presidential candidate Mir-Hoseyn Musavi, the leading figure of the protest movement, had labelled the event a 'reminder of the festival of light against darkness' (ibid.: 280). Three days before the event, Āyatollāh Khāmene'i stepped in by declaring *Chahārshanbeh-Suri* un-Islamic and thus illegal. The communiqué making his ruling public furthermore cites the Supreme Leader as deriding the occasion as 'fire worship', a long-standing motif of anti-Zoroastrian polemics. Funke rightfully points out that Khāmene'i thus ironically validates the aforementioned equation of authentic Iranian-ness with 'Zoroastrian-ness', at least in the eyes of his nationalist-minded critics (ibid.: 279). Taking the tack of an Islamically justified co-optation in the case of Nowruz, Khāmene'i thus condemned *Chahārshanbeh-Suri* in order to thwart civil unrest. A journalist consequently called Khāmene'i's *fatvā* 'a political argument in the shape of a legal [Islamic] ruling' (Bolhari 2010).

The uneasy stance of the Iranian authorities towards occasions like *Chahārshanbeh-Suri* and their unwillingness to permit the celebration of Nowruz in a fully nationalist dress create a void in the 'battle for Nowruz' which can be filled by differing interpretations. It enables voices of dissent to present themselves as the rightful heirs to Nowruz and the Islamic Republic as a corrupting usurper of Iranian national culture. In the diaspora, these voices can set themselves apart from the Iranian state's cautious and Islamically founded embracing of Nowruz by crossing all the lines that exist in Iran. Whereas they may perceive of the Islamic Republic's celebration of Nowruz as lukewarm and, having in mind the former hostility towards it by leading revolutionary clerics, disingenuous, they can offer self-confident celebrations of Nowruz 'as it is meant to be'.

Research on Nowruz outside the field of philological Iranian Studies has been extremely limited.[7] This comes as a surprise given the ample material it could offer to anthropologists as well as historians and researchers from other fields. Celebrated widely beyond Iran, Nowruz has also elsewhere been subject to vying for its appropriate interpretation and representation. Paula Schrode has analysed the interesting example of modern Turkey where, in the early 1990s, the state appropriated Nowruz (*Nevruz* in Turkish) to stymie Kurdish self-empowerment and resistance through celebrations of the feast (Schrode 2008). Since the late 1980s, Kurdish celebrations of the feast, with strongly political overtones, had evolved into an 'arena of ritualised confrontation' (ibid.: 111). Nevruz was then governmentally reinvented as a perennially pan-*Turkic* occasion, granted extensive attention through official cultural initiatives and even temporarily declared a national holiday in 1994 (ibid.: 113–15). The Turkish case is therefore not at all dissimilar from the Iranian case: in both cases, Nowruz has emerged as a field of ideological contestation with the respective governments being wary of the event's subversive potential. That said, Nowruz of course does not enjoy the same amount of popularity among the ethnically Turkish majority population in Turkey as it enjoys all over Iran.

If Nowruz in fact constitutes the major date identified with Iranian-ness in the Iranian calendar, it can be expected that it is a primary occasion for different actors, including Iranian Christians in the diaspora, to present their own respective readings of what it means to be authentically Iranian. This was the guiding assumption according to which Nowruz services and other forms of engagement with the feast among Iranian Christians were chosen as primary material of pivotal significance for the present book. It appeared plausible that, if Iranian Christians chose to allow Nowruz a place in their religious practice, they would also broach issues of national identity. This assumption has proven to be correct: celebrating Nowruz indeed forms an integral part in the calendars of Iranian churches, much more so than the Yaldā Night in December which featured only in a few of the churches, albeit very prominently. No instances could be observed in which the autumn feast of Mehregān was celebrated or mentioned. Thus, the hierarchy of prominence attributed to the three feasts mirrors the degree of significance that is ascribed to them by Iranians overall, be it in Iran or the diaspora.

Of course, in the diaspora, the celebration of Nowruz additionally sets apart Iranian Christian communities from their general non-Iranian environment as well as other Christian communities who are rarely ever aware of the feast's existence. It is likely that these circumstances further increase the power of Nowruz as constitutive of the celebrating individuals' Iranian identity. This is of course also valid for the non-Christian Iranian diaspora for whom Nowruz usually constitutes the most significant annual community event.

In the following sections, I will illustrate how Nowruz is presented and understood by Iranian Christians. I will first delve into the Christian imagery through which Iranian Christians ascribe new meanings to Nowruz – meanings occasionally postulated to be the *new* and/or *true* meanings of Nowruz only detectable through the lens of the Christian faith. Secondly, I will describe how

Iranian Christians connect the different customs pertaining to the celebration of Nowruz, most prominently the *Haft Sin* table, with Christianity. In line with my broader argument, it shall become apparent how Nowruz is practised to authenticate the practitioners' Iranian Christian identity. Pastors and other individuals make use of Christian motifs and theology to render themselves the legitimate heirs to customs like the *Haft Sin* table, not despite but precisely because of their Christian identity.

The quest for the true meaning of Nowruz

A new day, a new birth, a new creation

'Beloved God, today we have come here to celebrate Nowruz, but without you Nowruz will remain meaningless. You, oh God, are the meaning of our Nowruz. In you, oh God, we have new life' (Habibi 2018: m. 1:22–1:30). With these words, a preacher at a Sydney-based Iranian church calls on God in a prayer commencing the church's service on the occasion of Nowruz 1397 (2018). His prayer is noteworthy in two ways: firstly, the Australia-based pastor claims that only through the Christian God Nowruz could be rendered truly meaningful. Secondly, his prayer introduces the most commonly cited motif of the Nowruz-themed visual and textual sources assessed for this book: the making of a connection between the *newness* Iranian Christians hold to be inherent in Nowruz ('new day') and the experience of newness through the Christian faith, first and foremost the *new birth* and the *new life in Christ*.

Although this book consciously refrains from foregrounding matters of denominationalism, it should yet be mentioned that this motif strongly reverberates with the specifics of Pentecostal Christianity. Individuals who embrace Pentecostalism usually characterize the decisive moment of their conversion or 'spiritual awakening' as a 'rebirth in Christ' – they subsequently deem themselves 'born-again Christians'. Biblical texts, especially when read with a 'Pentecostal bias', certainly offer a rich array of verses and passages ready to be cited in order to underpin notions of newness, rebirth and new beginning. One specific verse from the New Testament, however, stood out in terms of the frequency it was cited in the sources assessed: 2 Cor. 5.17.[8] In the English Standard Version of the Bible, the first half of the verse reads: 'Therefore, if anyone is in Christ, he is a new creation.' Translated to Persian as *khelqat-e tāze'i*, the 'new creation' has served as a guiding motto in many Nowruz sermons, outshining other verses laying emphasis on 'newness' by far.[9]

When cited together with the usual congratulatory phrases for Nowruz, the verse functions as a Christian Nowruz greeting (cf. Hovsepiān-Mehr and Hovsepiān-Mehr 2020: m. 41:14). Pastor Elnātān Bāghestāni of the California-based Ambassadors of Christ Iranian Church went so far as to quote the verse's existence as the main rationale behind a Christian celebration of Nowruz (Bāghestāni 2016: m. 28:21). Nowruz was a feast worthy (*shāyesteh*) of Christians, Bāghestāni suggested, adding that now probably some of the viewers would object and say: 'What are these Christians saying? They have only just appeared and already claim Nowruz as their own! (*nayāmadeh Nowruzo māl-e khodeshun kardan!*)' (ibid.). Bāghestāni then, as a prove to this claim, quoted the first half of the mentioned verse and let the congregation complete it by adding the 'new creation' part (ibid.). It thus appears that 2 Cor. 5.17 is assumed to possess a familiarity big enough among the church attendants that they are able to recognize and recite it from memory.

Because Nowruz is celebrated at the dawn of spring in the Northern Hemisphere, Iranian Christians, when juxtaposing the feast with their 'second birth in Christ', consider themselves to very immediately experience their Christian rebirth in the reawakening of nature after a long and cold winter. Granted that the presence or absence of this long and cold winter may be dependent on where one lives, the end of the cold season at the least can be included into a sermon in the metaphorical sense. Rasul Heydari of the Persian Worshipers of Christ Church in Los Angeles, CA, reminds his congregation and the viewers that God was able to remove this figurative winter (Heydari 2018a: m. 20:07). In times of constant failure (*shekast*) and despair (*nā-omidi*), the message of Nowruz was that of a new beginning (*āghāz-e do bāreh*) (ibid.: m. 13:17). He continues:

> Everyone who has read the Gospel of Christ will understand: the message of Jesus Christ's Gospel is the very same as the message of Nowruz! It is a message giving us a new determination to become active and lead a good life. A life wherein there is joy, a life wherein there is the good news of salvation (*khabar-e khosh-e nejāt*). (ibid.: m. 13:30–14:00)

That the beginning of the new year in the Iranian calendar is dated to the beginning of spring has sometimes even been understood as divine providence. A worship leader playing with her band at the *Shabakeh7* studios (Dallas, TX) for Nowruz 1399 (2020) thanked God for quite appropriately placing the Iranian new year at the beginning of spring (Shari'at 2020: 34:57). Before, she had mentioned that she was aware that different nations in the world had their respective dates for the new year. Iran is so perceived as having received a special blessing by God that is setting her apart from other nations. Pastor Rozitā Zargari (Essen, Germany) confirms this notion, saying that she did not know what other nations felt when they experienced their new birth in Christ, but Iranians, once they were born again, were surely reminded of the moment of their second birth whenever Nowruz recurred (Zargari and Zargari 2017b: m. 8:11). Others, among them the Texas-based pastor Māni 'Erfān, did not ascribe the placing of the Iranian new year to God's will and yet praised this dating for being 'logical' (*manteqi*) compared to the seemingly arbitrary placing of the beginning of the new year at the first of January in the United States and in 'Western culture' ('Erfān 2014: m. 0:09).

'Erfān's 2014 sermon is further instructive to understanding the entangling of Nowruz with Christian notions of newness such as the 'new birth'. His message is built around the biblical passage of Jn 3.1-21 which describes Jesus's encounter with a Pharisee named Nicodemus. Having acknowledged Jesus's authority as a teacher, Nicodemus engages in a theological discussion with Jesus aiming to find out how he could truly please God. The English Standard Version of the Bible translates Jesus's reply to Nicodemus's enquiry in the chapter's third verse as: 'Truly, truly, I say to you, unless one is born again he cannot see the kingdom of God.' 'Erfān suggests that this answer came across like 'a Nowruz' – in fact, Jesus here gave a 'Nowruzian reply' (*javāb-e Nowruzi*) (ibid.: m. 6:03)! Therefore, this episode for 'Erfān had become the message of Nowruz (ibid.). Nowruz and the new birth in Christ are thus virtually rendered synonymous as the interchangeable usage of the two during the remainder of his sermon demonstrates. Further delineating the answer Jesus gave to Nicodemus's question, 'Erfān explains that it was the belief in Jesus Christ that transformed an individual into a loved child of God. He then asks:

> What do I need to do to be included in this [God's] love? What do I need to do to enter *this Nowruz*? Nothing. You do not need to do anything. The only thing you need to do is to say: 'Father, accept me as your own child, in the name of Jesus Christ.' (ibid.: m. 12:35–12:54)

'Erfān's reading of Nowruz through the person of Jesus strongly resembles Heydari's equation of the messages of the Gospel and of Nowruz. In their readings, the defining moment of an individual's turning to Christ becomes 'a Nowruz' as the believer and nature undergo a concomitant rebirth. Following this narrative, it comes almost as a surprise that the experience of *baptism* in the assessed sources was likened to Nowruz in only one instance (Amini 2020: part two; m. 0:36). Because of their refashioning into an Iranian garment, universal categories of (Pentecostal) Christianity can be received by Iranian Christians as authentic and loyal to their native culture. In the Christian faith, they experience the familiar and cherished tradition of Nowruz, albeit, the narrative goes, in a *better* and *more meaningful* way. Moreover, Nowruz 'done the Christian way' is not limited to a few festive days of the year. Rather, Iranian Christians claim to enter a state of *everlasting* Nowruz.

Har ruzetān Nowruz dar ʿIsā-ye Masih!: Everlasting Nowruz in Christ

There are several forms of congratulation on the occasion on Nowruz, the most common one being *Sāl-e Now Mobārak!* – 'A Blessed New Year!'. A more formal and poetic congratulatory phrase is the wish *Nowruzetān Piruz, Har Ruzetān Nowruz Bāshad!* – 'A Victorious Nowruz, may all of your days be Nowruz!'. Some pastors reformulated this phrase to advance the idea that only through Christ would all a believer's days truly become Nowruz. In the words of Pastor Kāmil Navāʾi (Sunnyvale, CA), it was the Holy Spirit who, on Nowruz 1394 (2015), wanted to make all of the audience's and viewers' days Nowruz (Navāʾi 2015: m. 1:31:30). Where in other (Evangelical) services those present are invited to come to the front and 'give their hearts to Jesus', 'accept Jesus as their Lord and saviour' or 'start their new life in Christ', this call here appears as a culturally framed invitation to an everlasting Nowruz.

Numerous other pastors endorsed the notion of an everlasting Nowruz in Christ, among them Rasul Heydari (2019: m. 5:01) and the Netherlands-based Gevik Hāyrāpetiān (2018: m. 32:55). Mehdi Ārshām-Far of the *222 Church* in Stockholm dedicated his entire 1399 (2020) Nowruz sermon to the attainment of 'everlasting Nowruz' through the experience of unconditional love in the Christian community (Ārshām-Far 2020). Māni ʿErfān, to whose 2014 Nowruz sermon I have referred to earlier, asks the viewers of his 2017 Nowruz message:

> Can Nowruz be something permanent? Can newness be there for us every day and forever? Can we live in a Nowruz that not just belongs to the first day of spring and the ensuing one or two weeks but instead accompanies us every day, every hour, every moment and every second because of the life and the hope that we find in Christ? (ʿErfān 2017: m. 5:21–5:55)

He then, not much surprisingly, answers his own questions affirmatively, explaining that Christ could set off an inner revolution for those who believed in him, which was capable of filling the void that was previously spreading (ibid.: 5:57). Earlier in his sermon, ʿErfān had suggested that the life of an Iranian, whether in Iran or in the diaspora, often was a troublesome and depressed one; his Nowruz message should therefore become a beacon of hope (ibid.: m. 10:13). While the customary celebrations for Nowruz maybe for two or three days could seem to make one's sorrows disappear, the spirit of the living God (*ruh-e Khodā-ye zendeh*) could permanently fill the internal void of an Iranian believer (ibid.). Admittedly, a Christian still experienced days of sadness – this was undeniable (ibid.). But when one felt that this despair was coming, when one felt that 'one's Nowruz is fading and winter is returning', it was, as a Christian, possible to seek refuge in faith and say: 'No! I am a new creation … and I refuse to lose this newness and freshness!' (ibid.: m. 17:26).

The motif of an 'everlasting Nowruz' can also be found in Iranian Christian satellite television shows. For the show *Your Church* (*Kelisā-ye Shomā*), streamed on the Toronto-based channel *ICnetTV*, the channel's main face, Pastor Edvin Sāleh, interviewed a fellow Iranian Christian named Nedā on the occasion of Nowruz 1399 (2020) (Sāleh 2020c). Sāleh was curious to know how Nedā dealt with her twofold identity as an Iranian Christian in the context of Nowruz (ibid.: m. 23:30). What special definition had Nowruz gained for Nedā from her Christian perspective? Nedā then pointed out that the view on life of a person who had come to faith could radically change (ibid.). In terms of Nowruz, one consequently could observe from a Christian perspective: '*Zendegi-ye Masihi ya'ni hamisheh Nowruzeh!*' – to live as a Christian meant that it always is Nowruz (ibid.). Her view was enthusiastically confirmed by Sāleh who went on to explain that there was a distinction between the material custom of 'Ancient Nowruz' (*Nowruz-e Bāstāni*) and the setting of a Nowruz table (*sofreh*) in one's *heart* (ibid.: m. 26:17). This distinction, according to which *real* Nowruz was a *spiritual* Nowruz, has also been made by other pastors.[10] As for the notion of an everlasting Nowruz, Edvin Sāleh in his 2020 Nowruz message promised the viewers that according to the Bible, the 'new day' of Nowruz would become *Nowsāl* (new year), '*Nowdaheh*' (new decade) and even '*Nowqarn*' (new century) (Sāleh 2020d: m. 11:20). In other words, believers would enter a day that, different from the fleeting experience of conventional Nowruz, is never ending (ibid.).

Nowruz and Easter

In the Gregorian calendar, Easter follows Nowruz very closely since it is celebrated on the Sunday after the first astronomical full moon in spring, that is, sometime in the period between 22 March and 25 April. It is, however, not solely for practical reasons that some Iranian churches celebrate Easter and Nowruz in one and the same event; the two are also deemed close in terms of their message and meaning. When celebrated in the same service, Iranian Christians can congratulate one other both on Nowruz and on Easter in the same breath (cf. Philadelphia Elam Church 2015: m. 2:00:54). Such a simultaneous mentioning of Nowruz with the universally Christian feast of Easter further increases the plausibility of the celebration of the Iranian new year festival at a church, concomitantly buttressed by its new, Christian meanings. In a way, Nowruz is 'admitted to' the Christian calendar. Kāmil Navā'i of the Iranian Church of Sunnyvale in California names Nowruz one of the three splendid occasions to 'give one's heart to Jesus', the other two being Christmas and Easter (Sālāri, Sālāri and Navā'i 2016: m. 43:51).

The Persian language conventionally renders Easter as *'Eyd-e Pāk*, derived from the French *pâques*. It is noteworthy that this term remained unused in both the textual and visual sources used for this book. In its stead, the terms *'Eyd-e Qiām* and, more rarely so, *'Eyd-e Rastākhiz* which both translate to 'feast of resurrection' were employed. Such a denotation presumably makes it easier for the average Iranian, who is unacquainted with both the French language and the feast of Easter to, by the mere mentioning of the feast, understand what it is about: the resurrection of Christ. The avoidance of the French loan term in a way also contributes to the indigenization of Easter.[11] On a wider note, the word *pāk* already exists in Persian, meaning 'pure, clean'; hence, the usage of *'Eyd-e Qiām/ Rastākhiz* prevents misunderstandings, no matter how unlikely they may be.

How then are Nowruz and Easter tied together beyond their coincidence in the calendar, on a level of meaning? In his editorial to the thirty-third issue of *Kalameh*, Hesām Mortazavi writes that both Nowruz and Easter brought the same gift with them: change (*taghyir*) (Mortazavi 2003a: 2). For Nowruz, this change was very easily observable in the automatic recovery of nature from the coldness of winter (ibid.). But what change could be observed within human beings? Seemingly, humans had an inherent resistance (*moqāvamat*) to change and, more than any other creature (*mowjud*), struggled with their personal transformation (ibid.). Having stated this, Mortazavi declares: 'The triumphant resurrection of Christ from the dead is a definitive and poignant reply to the issue of change and transformation in human beings' (ibid.). With the resurrection of Christ, one became born-again – a sort of change unlike Nowruz not happening automatically but depending on an individual's active decision for it (ibid.). Mortazavi brings his editorial to a close by congratulating the reader on Nowruz and Easter, and by wishing: 'May the arrival of ancient Nowruz and Easter be an impulse for a new outlook on ourselves and on the "change" that has been achieved in us through the act of Christ [his resurrection]' (ibid.).

Related to the notion of change, Mozhdeh Shirvānīān, in her 'Nowruz and Easter Message' as a part of the programme *Women's World* (*Donyā-ye Zan*) at Elam TV, suggested that both Nowruz and Easter were manifestations of God's power of renewal (*qodrat-e nowsāzi*) (Shirvānīān 2018: m. 2:30). This power constituted their mutual message. On Nowruz, God rebuilt nature in a beautiful spring after a cold winter, only to accomplish an even more tremendous renewal on Easter: the renewal of *life*, in the raising of Jesus from the dead (ibid.). She then quotes a poem by the twentieth-century Iranian poet Feridun Moshiri (1926–2000) extolling the miracle of spring. Shirvānīān ends her five-minute address by assuring the viewers that her prayer for the new year was that they would experience the power of Jesus in times of despair – a power that 'is capable of letting arise something new and beautiful even from seed that is seemingly dead and buried in the ground' (ibid.: m. 4:44–4:55).

Finally, a sense of familiarity between Nowruz and Easter can also emerge from very little things. Though unmentioned in the sources, it stands to reason that the painting of eggs for Easter, which is common in some parts of Europe, to an Iranian observer may be reminiscent of Nowruz for which the same tradition exists in Iran. Germany-based Iranian-Kurdish pastor Flor Namdar in her German-language autobiography *Liebe statt Furcht* ('Love instead of Fear') mentions that the Nowruz custom of sowing and sprouting lentils developed into a personal Easter symbol for her (Namdar 2017: 214).

This custom is only one minor component of a whole set of traditions commonly cherished on Nowruz. In the following section, I will describe how these customs are co-opted by Iranian Christians and reinterpreted in a Christian way. While in the present section, the making of connections has mainly remained on a purely symbolical level, Iranian Christian readings especially of the *Haft Sin* table also draw upon supposed historical facts and scientific findings.

Nowruz customs through the eyes of Christianity

I have listed earlier the main components constituting the usual celebration of Nowruz among Iranians. Due to the lamentable lacuna in research, it for now will remain unanswered what general changes celebrations of Nowruz undergo when they take place in the diaspora rather than inside Iran. The *Encyclopaedia Iranica* features brief entries on both the *Haft Sin* table and *Chahārshanbeh-Suri* which I shall refer to. While they to a great deal are occupied with the traditions' origins, they also contain brief descriptions of their contemporary forms. In what follows, I will discuss, most significantly, the *Haft Sin* table, as well as *Khāneh-Tekāni, Did o Bāzdid, 'Eydi* and *Chahārshanbeh-Suri*.

The Haft Sin table

Known in Persian as the *sofreh-ye haft sin*, the table/dining cloth of the Seven S is a beautifully arranged table around which families or other groups of people gather during their celebration of Nowruz. It displays a number of varying items, at the heart of which are seven elements beginning with the letter *s*. These items often include wheat or lentil sprout (*sabzeh*), home sown around two weeks before the festival, apples (*sib*), garlic (*sir*), vinegar (*serkeh*), a few freshly minted coins (*sekkeh*), sumac (*somāq*) and a sweet paste named *samanu*; however, instead or additionally, seeds of wild rue (*sepand*), Russian olives (*senjed*), a sweet named *sowhān* and/or a container with fine herbs (*sabzi*) may be seen as well (cf. Shapur Shahbazi 2002). Further common items of display *not* beginning with the letter *s* are a jar of water with or without a goldfish or a green leaf, a mirror, candles, a bowl of fruits, painted eggs, a flower vase, bread and a bowl with *ājil* (a nuts-and-raisins mix comparable to what is called a trail mix in English). At the table's centre, one moreover often finds a copy of the Quran or, depending on personal preferences, a popular Persian literary work, such as the *Divān* of the poet Hāfez or the *Shāhnāmeh* (Book of Kings) by Ferdowsi. Iranian Christians generally place a copy of the Bible in Persian (see Figure 2).

The *Encyclopaedia Iranica* tells us that the history of the *Haft Sin* custom is 'obscure' (ibid.). Much likely to the chagrin of many of the custom's practitioners, the author nevertheless points out that 'all indications suggest that the haft sin as we know it is not old' (ibid.). Further debunking the popular, albeit ahistorical, propensity to think of traditions like the *Haft Sin* as having persisted linearly since pre-Islamic Iran and thus being automatically Zoroastrian, Shapur Shahbazi explains that Zoroastrians traditionally have *not* set the Table of the Seven S and only very recently adopted the custom from other, non-Zoroastrian Iranians (ibid.). Theories according to which the seven *s* originally were *Haft Shin*, that is, seven *sh*, or that the *Haft Sin* were a corrupted version of initial *Haft Sini* (Seven Trays) are dismissed by the author. These theories will be of relevance in a moment.

Iranian Christians commonly believe the number seven to possess a special significance both in Christianity and in ancient Iranian culture. Several pastors suggested that, in the biblical tradition, seven was a number of perfection (*kāmeliyyat/kamāl*) (Hāyrāpetiān 2018: m. 3:04; Sāleh 2015: m. 7:30; Tabari

Figure 2 A *Haft Sin* table with a Bible. Photo taken by the author at CAS Bayreuth in March 2019. Used with permission of the centre's head of staff.

2018: m. 5:42; Tabdil 2009: 3), or 'the number of God' (*'adad-e Khodāvand*) (Shabānlāri 2019b: m. 34:42). As for the ancient Iranian context, voices range from Edvin Sāleh who simply states that ancient Iranians 'appear to have liked' (*dust dāshtand*) the number seven (Sāleh 2020b: m. 42:07) to Gevik Hāyrāpetiān who claims the number had been 'sacred' (*moqaddas*) among them (Hāyrāpetiān 2018: m. 3:25). A 2007 article in *Tabdil* magazine, a monthly periodical published by US-based former *Jamāʿat-e Rabbāni* pastor Elnātān Bāghestāni, in painstaking detail unravels the multitude of references to the number seven among ancient Iranians (Tabdil 2007c: 10): the reader is told that, in Achaemenid times, seven tribes were known to live in the empire and during the Sassanid Era, seven clans of notables ran the government. The tomb of Cyrus the Great counted seven stairs and Darius the Great teamed up with six fellows (thus forming a squad of seven) to topple King Bardiya (ibid.). Most striking, however, were the traces of the sacred number in literature, be it in the seven mystical cities of love a striving individual had to pass in order to reach true perfection, or the seven labours of Rostam described in the *Book of Kings* (ibid.) – both ironically dating to the Islamic rather than the ancient era in Iranian history. The unnamed author of the article continues: 'The number seven has permeated Iranian stories and legends to such an extent that barely any legend exists in which we do not come across the number seven, or at least hear the phrase "in seven days and nights", pointing to a celebration or another event' (ibid.).

Like the placing of new year at the beginning of spring in the Iranian calendar, the supposedly egregious importance of the number seven in Iranian culture has occasionally been referred to divine will. In a sermon entitled 'Nowruz: A Token of God's Grace' (*Nowruz neshāne'i az feyz-e Khodā'*), Pastor Peymān Shabānlāri (Amsterdam, The Netherlands) points out that the seven items on the *Haft Sin* table were all symbols of life (*namād-e hayāt*) (Shabānlāri 2019b: m. 31:00). Naming the spirit of the Christian God a 'spirit of life' (*ruh-e hayāt*), he argued that the seven symbols of the *Haft Sin* table contained a direct hint (*eshāreh-ye mostaqim*) at the Christian God (ibid.: m. 32:52). In the past, Iranians had failed to understand this, but by becoming Christians, the traces provided by the Christian God in Iranian culture became perceivable (ibid.). Another pastor put it more straightforwardly: the *Haft Sin* table was given to Iranians by the one, good God (Sālāri, Sālāri and Navā'i 2016: m. 2:32:29).

The 'obscure' (Shapur Shahbazi 2002) nature of the *Haft Sin*'s history renders it particularly serviceable to the engineering of historical narratives authenticating it as a component of an Iranian Christianity. That said, the engineers of such narratives themselves quote 'science', first and foremost archaeology and history, as to prove the trajectories they present. Nowhere, however, have concrete works or authors been mentioned. Be that as it may, I am not concerned here either with the historicity of the trajectories presented or with where they have been possibly taken from – which anyway would be difficult to identify. I am interested in the narratives invoked to advance the 'Christianization' of Nowruz and ultimately the naturalization of Christianity to the Iranian nation.

A particularly detailed historical trajectory has been presented by Edvin Sāleh (Toronto, Canada) in *ICnet TV*. Among the sources used for this book, there are two videos in which Sāleh sets forth his theory of the *Haft Sini*, the seven *trays*, the first one dating to 2015 (Sāleh 2015) and the second one to 2020 (Sāleh 2020b). The videos do not markedly differ in terms of their content; still, the later video goes into slightly more details and shall therefore serve as the basis to my account. Sāleh at the onset explains that he always had harboured a curiosity regarding the true origin of the *Haft Sin* custom and because of this interest had looked into what research taught us about it (ibid.: m. 38:45). There was a theory suggesting that, originally, the *Haft Sin* had been *Haft Shin* (seven *sh*), but archaeologists and researchers (*mohaqqeqin*) had proven them wrong; in reality, the custom involved seven *trays* (*sini*) (ibid.: m. 41:07). On all of these trays, one specific item was placed. The trays were divided into two groups of three, with the seventh tray put between the two groups as a connector (*rābet*). While the first group contained items representing the 'material world' (*donyā-ye māddi*), namely a stone (*sang*), herbs (*sabzeh*) and an egg (*tokhm-e-morgh*), the second group represented the 'spiritual world' (*donyā-ye ma'navi*) and featured a candle (*sham'*), a mirror (*āyineh*) and a fish (*māhi*) (ibid.: m. 45:01). These elements, respectively, stood for particular aspects of the material and spiritual worlds.

What then was the seventh, connecting element? Between the two groups of trays stood a jug of wine (*sharāb*) – a symbol for the human being (ibid.: m. 47:37). For centuries, people in Iran (*Irān-Zamin*) used to set this table of seven trays, until the coming of Islam altered their custom (ibid.: m. 49:07). The new rulers, Sāleh tells the viewers, issued a decree (*dastur*) ordering the changing of the table's setting because some of the elements involved were now deemed religiously problematic (ibid.). The stone was prohibited for it could prompt the building of idols (*bot*) (ibid.). Hence, Iranians, 'clever as we were' (*bā hush o zekāvati keh dāshtim*), replaced it with a golden coin (*sekkeh*), an element in essence not much different from stones (ibid.). Needless to say, the new Islamic rulers also took issue with the use of wine which subsequently was replaced by vinegar (*serkeh*) (ibid.: m. 51:17). As a consequence, the spiritual meaning of the seven trays was corrupted – a spiritual meaning that as a matter of fact had been *Christian* in nature (ibid.). For instance, the candle was placed in front of the mirror to disseminate light in a room; Jesus similarly understood himself as a source of light, the 'light of the world' even (ibid.). Paul in his second epistle to the Corinthians called the church the reflector (*mon'akes konandeh*) of this light, making the church what the mirror achieved for the table of the seven trays (ibid.: m. 54:01). A Christian meaning likewise was hidden in the fish swimming in a bowl of water. Most importantly, however, the wine connecting the two groups symbolized the human nature (*ensāniyyat*) of Christ and of course his blood, the shedding of which reconnected humans with God (ibid.). Had ancient Iranians been aware of all this? Sāleh surmises:

> Our ancestors may not have been privy to the meanings in the way that I am understanding them right now. But I think they sensed that the world they were living in was not limited to the very place they were at. Something else must have been behind the curtain. A power must have been behind the curtain, a truth (*haqiqat*) that connected them all. (ibid.: m. 56:30–56:52)

Zoroastrians, Sāleh adds, had to a certain degree understood the meanings behind the seven trays, but only in Christ these meanings became complete (*kāmel*) (ibid.).

The theory of the seven *sh*, quickly dismissed by Sāleh, was not as easily done away with by others. ʿIsā Dibāj mentions that the *Haft Sin* had originally been *Haft Shin* and included wine (Dibāj 2003a: 36). Concurring with Sāleh on this point while advancing a different theory, Dibāj says that with the coming of Islam, wine had been removed from the table and its name been adjusted to seven *s*. This idea is likewise adopted by Siāmak Zargari (Essen, Germany) who plays down the graveness of the alteration: if it is a *Haft Shin*, God wanted to gift us *shālom* (see Chapter 6); if it is a *Haft Sin*, he wanted to gift us *salāmati* (health) (Zargari and Zargari 2017b: m. 2:02:07).

Neither Dibāj nor Zargari cite a source for the *Haft Shin* theory. This also applies to Māziār Tabari, pastor at the *Ruh-e Khodā Church* in Bremen, Germany, who, apart from wine, mentions another of the *former* elements of the table which were supposedly censored after the arrival of the Arab conquerors: a boxtree (*shemshād*), the place of which at the *Haft Sin* was taken by the aforementioned herbs (*sabzeh*) (Tabari 2018: m. 9:33). He joins Zargari in his conciliatory stance towards the corrupted *Haft Shin*, remarking that the joy of spring could equally be experienced in the *Haft Sin* (ibid.). It is unnecessary to go into the details of Tabari's account which, to say the least, is quite multi-layered. Averring that his interpretation complied with the 'original history' (*tārikhcheh-ye asli*) of the table (ibid.: m. 13:38), in summary, Tabari suggests that the items displayed on the table symbolized the Christian trinity (ibid.). His narrative seems to ultimately imply that the *Haft Sin* custom could only with a reference to Christianity be authentically experienced.

Iranian Christian interpretations of the Haft Sin table and its enigmatic items among Iranian Christians do not always make recourse to supposed historical facts. Given that Iranians generally believe the items found on the *Haft Sin* table to symbolize different positive qualities, some Iranian pastors used the opportunity of their Nowruz-themed sermons to casually quiz the present congregants on their knowledge of these qualities. Often, the assumption seems to be that the *Haft Sin*'s components and their figurative meanings were basic cultural knowledge for any Iranian. When testing the present congregation's memory of the Russian olive's (*senjed*) meaning without success, Gevik Hāyrāpetiān jokingly remarked that he as an Armenian was not supposed to know these things by heart, but that the others present were Iranians and therefore ought to know (Hāyrāpetiān 2018: m. 5:21).[12] In several instances, after recalling the seven items' traditional meanings, a second set of seven alternative *s* was presented: the 'Seven S of Christ/God' or the 'Seven S of the Bible'. They enlisted titles or qualities mentioned in the Bible as describing God and/or Jesus, at least in the reading of their respective presenters. Because the sets of *s* differed markedly, I will list all four examples. In three of the four cases, a biblical verse was quoted to locate the respective title or characteristic. In the last case, rather than coming up with alternative *Haft Sin*, the conventional qualities of the seven items were interpreted to also have been qualities of Christ, again corroborated by biblical verses:

Example 1: 'The *Haft Sin* of the Titles of Christ' (*Haft Sin-e Alqāb-e Masih*) (Kalameh 2006: 50; see Figure 3)

1. *Setāreh-ye Derakhshān-e Sobh* – the Bright Morning Star (Rev. 22.16)
2. *Serr-e Khodā* – God's Mystery (Col. 2.2)
3. *Sar-e Kelisā* – the Head of the Church (Col. 1.18)
4. *Sarvar-e Salāmati* – the Prince of Peace (Isa. 9.6)
5. *Soltān-e Jāvedāni* – the Everlasting King (Dan. 4.34)
6. *Sang-e Zendeh* – the Living Stone (1 Pet. 2.6)
7. *Savār-e Amin o bar Haqq* – the Faithful and Righteous Horseman (Rev. 19.11)

Example 2: 'The *Haft Sin* of the Bible' (*Haft Sin-e Ketāb-Moqaddas*), referring to God (Sālāri, Sālāri and Navā'i 2016: m. 24:15–26:32)

1. *Setāreh-ye Derakhshandeh-ye Sobh* – the Bright Morning Star (Rev. 22.16)
2. *Sāyeh-ye Mā* – Our Shadow (Isa. 51)[13]
3. *Separ-e Mā* – Our Shield (Ps. 59.11)
4. *Sar-e Mā* – Our Head (1 Cor. 11.3)
5. *Sardār-e Lashgar-e Āsemāni* – the Commander of the Heavenly Legion (Josh. 5.13-15)
6. *Sarvar-e Salāmati* – the Prince of Peace (Isa. 1)[14]
7. *Sang-e Zāvieh* – the Cornerstone (Isa. 28.16)

Example 3: 'The Seven Characteristics of God' (*Haft Moshakhkhaseh-ye Khodā*) (Kelisā-ye 222 Kāyseri 2019: m. 4:43–27:25)

1. *Sarvar-e Solh* – the Prince of Peace
2. *Sarvar-e Salāmati* – the Lord of Health[15]

Figure 3 The '*Haft Sin* of the Titles of Christ' (*Haft Sin-e Alqāb-e Masih*). In *Kalameh* 45 (2006: 50). Used with permission of Elam Ministries.

3. *Sarvar-e Sarmadi* – the Eternal Lord
4. *Sekhāvatmandi* – Generosity
5. *Saʿādatmandi* – Blissfulness
6. *Sorur* – Joy
7. *Sar-e Kelisā* – the Head of the Church

Example 4: The *Haft Sin* and their meanings in Christ (Hāyrāpetiān 2018: m. 24:05–27:50)

1. *Sir* (garlic): Healing (*shafā*) – Isa. 53.5
2. *Sabzeh* (herbs): Abundance and Blessings (*sarsabzi o barekat*) – Rom. 5.17
3. *Sib* (apples): Health (*salāmati*) – Col. 1.20
4. *Samanu* (sweet wheat paste): Blessings and Strength (*barekat o qovvat*) – 1 Cor. 1.18
5. *Senjed* (Russian olive): Love and Devotion (*ʿeshq o mehrvarzi*) – Jn 3.16
6. *Serkeh* (vinegar): Submission, Obedience and Endurance (*taslim, etāʿat o paziresh*) – Phil. 2.7-9
7. *Somāq* (sumac): Patience and Endurance, the Victory of Light over Darkness (*sabr o bordbāri, gholbe-ye nur bar tāriki*) – Jn 1.4

Other Nowruz customs

Spring Cleaning (*Khāneh-Tekāni*): the term *Khāneh-Tekāni* (or *Khuneh-Tekuni* in colloquial Persian) consists of the noun 'house' (*khāneh*) and the verb 'to shake (out)' (*tekāndan*) and denotes the thorough cleaning of the house before the dawning of the new year. It resembles the tradition of 'spring cleaning' known in different cultural contexts, for example, the Jewish Passover cleaning. *Khāneh-Tekāni* is considered more than just a mundane act of annual house cleaning. As an integral part of the established Nowruz customs, it also has a symbolical aspect: as the old year fades and the new year approaches, one gets rid of old stuff, washes the house's rugs, removes dust and dirt and treats themselves to brand new clothes. ʿIsā Dibāj calls *Khāneh-Tekāni* a tradition that 'for ages has been common among the Iranians' – and, to the best of his knowledge, *only* among the Iranians (Dibaj 2009a: 2). It was not without a reason that the proverb proclaimed: 'Art could only possibly be found among the Iranians (*honar nazd-e Irāniān ast va bas*)' (ibid.).

Even if Dibāj may have cited this nationalist motto tongue-in-cheek, his deliberations illustrate that the performing of *Khāneh-Tekāni* can be tied to an individual's Iranian national consciousness. It therefore seems to suggest itself that pastors have made references to the custom in their Nowruz-themed sermons and addresses, albeit not as prominently as was the case for the *Haft Sin*. A common metaphor has been that God on Nowruz wanted to perform a *Khāneh-Tekāni* on his children's *hearts*. Kāmil Navā'i at the 1395 (2016) Nowruz service proclaimed:

> Just as you have done *Khuneh-Tekuni* in your homes, just as you have cleaned your house, the Lord Jesus today has come and tells you that he wants to free you from sadness, he wants to free you from pain, he says 'Let me free you from all that vindictiveness, from all that hatred!' God today wants to liberate you and me. God today wants to cleanse our hearts … He wants to put new clothes on you. (Sālāri, Sālāri and Navā'i 2016: m. 2:36:34–2:37:09)

What I have translated as 'to free from', 'to liberate' and 'to cleanse' in Navā'i's original Persian is all rendered with the verb *tekāndan* (*az*) to remain within the metaphor of *Khāneh-Tekāni*. A year before, Navā'i had used the same metaphor in the church's 2015 Nowruz event (Navā'i 2015: m. 1:25:55). In a slightly different fashion, the *Khāneh-Tekāni* of the heart was also invoked by Sam Yeqnazar in a 2004 article in *Kalameh*: while it is God who performs the *Khāneh-Tekāni* in Navā'i's metaphor, Yeqnazar invites the readers to *themselves* 'spring clean' their hearts by pondering on their personalities and remove those of their characteristics that are incompatible with the word of God (Yeqnazar 2004).

Writing likewise in *Kalameh* magazine, Khosrow Khezri, who refers to several Nowruz customs and therefore will be of relevance again shortly, points out that in the hassle of physical *Khāneh-Tekāni* one tended to forget the cleansing of one's heart and thoughts (Khezri 2007: 3–4). Specks of dust that have built up there could easily turn into unhealthy seeds (*bazr-e nāsālem*) which in turn could put down deep roots as time went on (ibid.: 4). One had better throw them away together with all the unnecessary stuff found during the literal *Khāneh-Tekāni* (ibid.). We also encounter 2 Cor. 5.17 again in Khezri's article, this time in its complete version not ending with the 'new creature' (*khelqat-e tāzeh*): the English Standard Version of the Bible translates the verse's latter half as 'The old has passed away; behold, the new has come' (ibid.).

The Festive Visit (*Did o Bāzdid*): *Did o Bāzdid* or *'Eyd didani* describe the mutual visiting of friends and family on the occasion of Nowruz. As we have seen, it is this custom that, read as *seleh-ye rahem*, provides the main rationale for the Islamic legal approval of Nowruz and other Iranian celebrations. Iranian Christian pastors likewise have commended Nowruz for bringing together friends and especially families. They have highlighted the mutual visits as an opportunity for reconciliation and forgiveness. Nowruz was a perfect occasion to make peace with each other – real peace, and not just outwardly for the sake of a few festive days. Mehdi Ārshām-Far refers to the constant feud of his uncles who for the days of Nowruz pretended to have put up with each other only to start fighting again soon after (Ārshām-Far 2020: m. 9:24). The message of *Did o Bāzdid* and thus of Nowruz, however, was 'the same, unconditional' forgiveness that believers could find in the New Testament and in Christ, Peymān Shabānlāri avers (Shabānlāri 2019b: m. 35:19).

A second idea advanced in the context of *Did o Bāzdid* is that Iranians should use the occasion to either invite God to their houses for a festive visit or go and visit him themselves. Traditionally, it is especially the younger ones in a family who go and visit the elderly. However, in the words of Rozitā Zargari, God was so humble (*forutan*) that he despite his greatness came to visit us small humans (Zargari and Zargari 2017b: m. 12:29). In making this statement during a prayer, she plays with the words 'big' and 'small' (*bozorg* and *kuchak*) which in Persian are equally used as 'old' and 'young'. Kāmil Navā'i calls upon the present audience and the online viewers that their *'Eyd Didani* should also include a visit to their *heavenly* father (Navā'i 2015: m. 1:21:18). Finally, Khosrow Khezri asks the readers of *Kalameh* to open the doors of their houses for God's Nowruz visit as he truly wished to meet them and gift them an *'Eydi*, a Nowruz present (Khezri 2007: 5). This brings us to the next Nowruz custom integrated into some pastors' Nowruz sermons.

Exchanging Gifts (*'eydi*): Elderly members of a family or a neighbourhood usually gift younger family members and neighbours an *'eydi* for Nowruz, an amount of cash money often in the shape of fresh banknotes. Those families that celebrate the Islamic feasts of *'Eyd-e Fetr*, *'Eyd-e Qorbān* and *'Eyd-e Ghadir Khomm* may also gift an *'eydi* on these occasions. Moreover, the state as well as private companies are legally obliged to pay an end-of-year bonus to their employees which, although having a different official name (*Pādāsh-e Ākhar-e Sāl*), colloquially is referred to as *'eydi* too.

At the end of his sermon at the 1395 (2016) Nowruz programme of *Shabakeh7*, Hormoz Shari'at announced to the viewers that God this year wanted to give them new life (*zendegi-ye now*) as an *'eydi* (Shari'at and Ebrāhimiān 2016: m. 51:58). In the same year, Kāmil Navā'i explicitly addressed those who for the first time had attended the Iranian Church of Sunnyvale and told them that

God had prepared an *'eydi* for them, a 'heavenly *'eydi*' (*'eydi-ye āsemāni*) (Sālāri, Sālāri and Navā'i 2016: m. 2:42:02). Not going into further details, he invited the newcomers to join him at the front of the room after the service and allow him to pray for them (ibid.). Fred Sāleh, the senior pastor at Toronto-based *ICnet TV* and the father of aforementioned Edvin Sāleh, contrasted the gift God has given to humankind by sending his only son and letting him die for the sins of the world (Sāleh 2016: m. 0:57). The gifts people exchanged for Nowruz were transient (*fāni*) in nature whereas God's tremendous gift was eternal (*jāvedāni*) (ibid.). Unlike Nowruz, it was a gift not requiring to be renewed every year (ibid.). Sāleh finishes his short video message by congratulating the viewers on Nowruz – however even greater and better congratulations were appropriate for those who already had accepted Jesus Christ as their saviour (ibid.: m. 2:16).

Red Wednesday (*Chahārshanbeh-Suri*): I have already referred to *Chahārshanbeh-Suri* when analysing the political dimensions of the celebration of Nowruz and its pertaining customs in the contemporary Iranian context. As pointed out, at the centre of the custom stands the jumping over a bonfire with the concomitant utterance of the phrase *sorkhi-ye to az man, zardi-ye man az to!*, 'Let your redness be mine, and my paleness [yellowness] be yours!', which supposedly will shield the partaking individual from harm in the coming year. There are other supplementary rituals which may differ regionally in Iran, among them the smashing of pots, the banging of spoons against plates or bowls, fortune telling (*fāl*) and the burning of rue (Kasheff and Sa'īdī Sīrjānī 1990).

The role *Chahārshanbeh-Suri* played in the sources assessed was marginal. There were no instances of a TV programme or a service specifically dedicated to the occasion which takes place a few days before Nowruz. In two cases, however, pastors made references to the tradition. One of them is, once again, Kāmil Navā'i. It is likely that the frequency in which Navā'i draws upon the various components of the Iranian celebration of Nowruz is owed to the fact that on this particular occasion non-Christian Iranians may be taken along to church by their Christian Iranian friends.[16] By invoking traditions like *Khāneh-Tekāni*, *Did o Bāzdid*, *Chahārshanbeh-Suri* and so on, Navā'i endeavours to create a bond with these individuals who are familiar with and emotionally attached to them while being indifferent to biblical references. Initially sceptical towards the new and – having in mind the double foreignness of Christianity to Iranian nationhood – supposedly foreign environment, the respective individuals may be positively surprised to find that the church they have just entered is tangibly Iranian after all and cherishes national traditions.

How then was *Chahārshanbeh-Suri* integrated into the two sermons? Kāmil Navā'i takes up the invocation of the above-mentioned sentence and reformulates it as a metaphoric quote of Jesus. Today, on the occasion of Nowruz, Jesus from the Cross spoke to the present congregation and the viewers saying: 'Give me your paleness, your pain, your problems, for I in turn will give you my redness, my joy, life and Nowruz!' (Navā'i 2015: m. 1:30:47). Likewise, Andreas Qoli-Zādeh of an Iranian church in Afyon, Turkey refers to this dictum (Qoli-Zādeh 2019: m. 5:57). In his short sermon, he explores the similarities of the Christian faith with ancient Iranian rituals (*āyin-hā-ye bāstāni-ye Irān*) (ibid.). The famous sentence invoked at *Chahārshanbeh-Suri* originally had been a prayer in which an individual called on God to remove their evilness (*badi*), sin (*gonāh*) and maliciousness (*zeshti*), that is, their 'paleness' (*zardi*), and replace it with God's life (*hayāt*) and blessings (*barekat*), that is, God's 'redness' (*sorkhi*) (ibid.). This prayer had been heeded in the coming of the Holy Spirit whose arrival had been announced both by John the Baptist and by Jesus himself (ibid.: m. 6:32). The two pastors thus create an entanglement between *Chaharshanbeh-Suri* and biblical motifs, although in completely different ways.

The limits of an Iranian Christianity (I): Sizdah Bedar

Despite their general emphasis that Christianity and Iranian culture constituted a 'good fit', Iranian Christians reject some components of their national culture and condemn them as irreconcilable with their Christian tenets. The first major example for these limits is the critical engagement of some pastors with *Sizdah Bedar*, the conclusive part of Nowruz which takes place on the thirteenth day of the month of Farvardin (the first month of the Iranian calendar). On this day, Iranians leave their houses to evade bad spirits supposedly haunting the thirteenth of Farvardin and spend the day in nature where they have picnics with friends in merry atmosphere. Another common custom is to take the withered sprout sown for the *Haft Sin* table a month earlier and throw it into a river. This, like the leaving of the house, is believed to have the effect of averting bad luck (*nahsi*). The name of *Sizdah Bedar* consists of the words 'thirteen' (*sizdah*) and 'to drive away, expel' (*bedar kardan*), the latter of which refers to the driving away of inauspicious spirits. Moreover, knots are tied with the withered sprout, especially by young single women and men who believe that, once the knot has loosened, they will have found a partner. Those who kept a little fish in the water bowl of their *Haft Sin* table may also throw this fish into a river.

While these customs in good nationalist fashion are widely believed to directly stem from ancient Iranians, according to the *Encyclopaedia Iranica* there currently is 'no sufficient evidence that would give a solid explanation for the origin of the 13-day period of the Nowruz celebrations with the sizdah bedar at the end of them' (Cristoforetti 2009). Historical records account for the common celebration of *Sizdah Bedar* since the Qajar era (Shapur Shahbazi 2009), which is not to say that they may not have existed earlier. In the Islamic Republic of Iran, *Sizdah Bedar* is officially referred to as 'Nature Day' (*Ruz-e Tabi'at*).

Gevik Hāyrāpetiān and Mohammad Jalil Sepehr have rejected *Sizdah Bedar* with remarkable assertiveness. Interestingly, it is evident from the section of Hāyrāpetiān's sermon in which he raises the issue of *Sizdah Bedar* that the present churchgoers already are aware of the occasion's supposed incompatibility with Christianity. Hāyrāpetiān during his sermon constantly interacts with the congregation which, once the pastor has mentioned the term *Sizdah Bedar*, can be heard pointing out what Hāyrāpetiān then confirms: '*Mā dar Masihiyyat Sizdah Bedar nadārim!*' – 'In Christianity, we do not have *Sizdah Bedar*!' (Hāyrāpetiān 2018: m. 28:21). The reason for this was that Christ on the Cross had already taken all the bad luck (*nahsi*) and curses (*la'nat*) upon him (ibid.). Hāyrāpetiān's verdict on Christians who did not take this seriously and participated in *Sizdah Bedar* is unequivocal: such behaviour amounted to no less than a direct insult (*towhin-e mostaqim*) of Christ's sacrifice (ibid.: m. 29:14). And yet, those who wanted to go out and have fun on the thirteenth of Farvardin could do so as long as it was not in the name of *Sizdah Bedar*. If they went out for a 'Nature Day' (*ruz-e tabi'at*), for instance, this was unproblematic (ibid.). Hayrāpetiān here, interestingly, complies with the official terminology used for *Sizdah Bedar* in the Islamic Republic of Iran.

Mohammad Jalil Sepehr takes a stand on *Sizdah Bedar* in the April 2008 issue of *Tabdil*. In his article, Sepehr levels criticism at the practice of tying knots into withered sprouts and the belief in the practice's miraculous power. He asks: 'Do we really arrive at the nice aims we have got by doing such things? The answer of course is: absolutely not!' (Sepehr 2008: 4). If people wanted to dispel bad spirits (*nahsi*), they had to heed biblical advice:

> As an Iranian Christian appreciative of the beautiful traditions of my country, I am asking you to this year, together with our Nowruz sprout, throw the things Christ orders us to stay away from into the running river of the Holy Spirit (*beh nahr-e ravān-e ruh-ol-qodos*), so they may be as far away from us as sunrise

is from sunset (*mashreq az maghreb*). Let us, instead of tying knots with the Nowruz sprout, uproot the thorns that have grown in our family and social relationships. (ibid.)

Similar to Hāyrāpetiān, Sepehr suggests that Christians, rather than being content with the 'symbolic act' (*kār-e sembolik*) of throwing away withered sprout, trust that their faith in Christ averted bad luck (*nahsi*) in the first place (ibid.).

A third example, Kāmil Navā'i adopts a critical standpoint on *Sizdah Bedar*. It is noteworthy that his California-based church in the past has organized picnic events on thirteenth Farvardin that did not carry an alternative name but were called after *Sizdah Bedar* (cf. Sālāri, Sālāri and Navā'i 2016: m. 2:10:32). These circumstances may be partially explained by a sermon entitled 'Drive Away Bad Spirits!' delivered by Kāmil Navā'i around *Sizdah Bedar* 1398 (2019). *Sizdah Bedar* was a truly historical and ancient ritual (*marāsem-e tārikhi va bāstāni*) in Iran, Navā'i states; however, there was an interesting paradox about it: ancient Iranians actually did *not* consider *Sizdah Bedar* to be a day haunted by bad spirits (*nahs*) (Navā'i 2019: m. 2:17). In reality, they solely went out for the sake of celebrating (ibid.). The notion according to which the day was haunted had entered Iran from Europe in the Middle Ages (ibid.). Navā'i does not explain where he had taken this information from; in any case, his narrative ultimately redefines *Sizdah Bedar* as an unsuspicious picnic, void of any spiritual connotations.

In his sermon, the pastor goes on to explain that the fear of the number 13, called 'Triskaidekaphobia' in Greek, was a superstition (*khorāfāt*) one had to be become liberated from (ibid.). And yet, the danger posed by bad spirits (*arvāh-e palid*) was real. How then were these bad spirits transmitted and, most importantly, how could they be dispelled? Certainly not by throwing withered sprout into a river (ibid.: m. 7:23). Evil spirits sometimes were brought about by the way people spoke, especially when they used curses, but could also be inherent in a particular culture or be transmitted from sinful ancestors (ibid.). For example, the grandchild of an adulterous (*zenākār*) grandfather was likely to become caught up in pornography (ibid.: m. 24:20). Navā'i provides his listeners with three keys (*kelid*) capable of dispelling such spirits: firstly, believers should admit to their sins and repent; secondly, they should always remember that God will forgive them and, thirdly, they should renounce the devil and tell him that Jesus had died for them on the Cross (ibid.). In summary, *Sizdah Bedar* in Navā'i's reading, although historically unproblematic, had been turned by

Iranians under European influence into an occasion offering vain and deceptive solutions to real problems.

Iranizing Christmas: The Yaldā Night

It goes without saying that, if there is a gap in research in terms of the Iranian new year festival of Nowruz, one should not expect a better situation for the far less prominent occasion of the Yaldā Night (*Shab-e Yaldā*). Alternatively referred to as Chelleh Night (*Shab-e Chelleh*), the Yaldā Night is celebrated at the winter solstice, on 21 or 22 December. A short paragraph in the *Encyclopaedia Iranica* describes the main customs commonly engaged in on this night (Omidsalar 1990). At its heart is a family gathering around a dining table (*sofreh*) with an opulent meal; specific foods may be consumed, first and foremost watermelon which is believed to be healthy for the summer months. Secondly, elderly family members entertain those present by telling tales and anecdotes. I shall return to this practice in Chapter 6 during my detailed analysis of diasporic religion among Iranian Christians. Another 'favorite and prevalent pastime of the night of *čella*' (ibid.) is to use poetry by the famous poet Hāfez for the sake of divination (*fāl*). This practice was notably absent in the Yaldā gatherings of Iranian Christians because it, like *Sizdah Bedar*, is deemed incompatible with the Christian religion. I shall address this issue when treating poetry at greater length in the following chapter.

Although it is not politicized in the way described for Nowruz, the Yaldā Night, again once more so in a diasporic environment, can serve to reaffirm an individual's Iranian identity. This assumption is confirmed by Yasrā, a young woman regularly appearing as a member of the *Shabakeh7* team, who on the occasion of the channel's 2016 Yaldā programme is introduced to the viewers as a true Yaldā aficionada (Shariʿat 2016: m. 48:35). Having joined the other team members, including head pastor Hormoz Shariʿat, who have gathered around a Yaldā table, Yasrā avers that the Yaldā Night was truly authentic (*asil*) and traditional (*sonnati*) (ibid.). It, by all means, had to be continued so a young Iranian residing abroad like herself could connect with her origin (*asl*), her validity (*eʿtebār*) and her being authentic (*asil budan*) – Yaldā was 'our Iranian identity' (*hoviyyat-e Irāni-ye mā*) (ibid.: m. 50:26).

Resembling Iranian Christian readings of the *Haft Sin* table, celebrations of the Yaldā Night in Iranian Christian exile churches are framed by historical interpretations of the festival as well as discourses creating a symbolical connection between Christianity and Yaldā. I will address these two aspects in turn. While in the case of Nowruz we have observed how Iranian Christians aim to 'Christianize' the quintessentially Iranian festival of Nowruz, we can interestingly witness an adverse phenomenon for Yaldā: the 'Iranization' of Christmas. Both narratives ultimately serve as narratives for the authentication of an Iranian-Christian national-religious identity.

The Iranian origins of Christmas

Iranian Christians commonly point at the etymological root of the term *yaldā* in the Syriac language, where it means 'birth', corresponding with the Arabic radicals *w-l-d*. Words derived from this root also surface in Persian, among them *tavallod* and *milād* which both as well translate to 'birth'. A short note in the magazine *Tabdil*, as often in the magazine with no author indicated, states that it was not certain when the term *yaldā* entered the ancient Persian (*Pārsi*) language, but that it was likely that it was adopted after mass killings and the forced mass migration of early Syriac Christians from the Roman Empire to the Sassanian Empire (Tabdil 2006b: 1). Moreover, some (*goruhi*) believed that the 21st of December, the date of the Yaldā Night, was the birth date of Christ (ibid.).

While the note in *Tabdil* confines itself to the mentioning of these rather vague assumptions, 'Isā Dibāj in an article for *Kalameh* goes into the depth of the supposed connection between Christmas and Yaldā (Dibāj 2004a). Under the title question 'Christmas: A Western or Iranian phenomenon (*padideh*)?', Dibāj at the beginning of his article recalls how back in Iran, apart from some cursory remarks in the news and a few special TV shows with Iranian Armenian contestants, barely anyone took notice of Christmas (ibid.). He continues:

> In Iran, Christmas is by and large considered a feast of Westerners: a feast specific to Armenians and the Christian minority which starts the new year in the Western calendar and therefore is irrelevant to Iranians who celebrate their own new year with the beginning of nature. This is correct, albeit, as we will see, only one side of the coin. In the present article we will see that Christmas, the feast of the birth of Christ, actually possesses deep roots in the culture and religious beliefs (*bāvar-hā-ye dini*) of Iranians. As a matter of fact, one must state: 'It is *because of* the impact of ancient Iranian customs and traditions that Westerners today celebrate the birth of Christ on 25 December'. (ibid.; italics added)

Dibāj explains that the Yaldā or Chelleh Night dated back to the era before Iranians had embraced Zoroastrianism; in the Yaldā Night, they celebrated the birth of Mithra, the mediator between the creator and creation (*miānji beyn-e āfaridegār va āfaridegān*) (ibid.). When the Achaemenids accepted Zoroastrianism as their new religion (*āyin*), they, rather than eradicating it, maintained this tradition as they saw a connection between Mithra and their 'new' God of light, Ahura Mazda (ibid.). Yaldā was cherished as the night in which light finally triumphs over darkness. Moreover, Dibāj claims that a part of the Yaldā tradition was to place a cypress tree in the Mithra temples on which the younger ones symbolically tied silken cloths and made a wish (ibid.). Under the tree, Iranians presented gifts to Mithra to win his favour (ibid.).

Dibāj then describes how, as a consequence of the Graeco-Persian wars, Mithraism found its way to Europe and experienced a true boom in the second- and third-century Roman Empire (ibid.). Here, by mid-December the feast of Saturnalia in honour of the Roman God Saturn was celebrated. Dibāj does not specify whether there, according to his belief, was a connection between Saturnalia and Mithraism; however, he suggestively mentions that Saturnalia was also the commemoration of the 'birth of the invincible sun' (*milād-e khorshid-e shekast-nā-pazir*)[17] and that those celebrating it 'more or less' (*kamābish*) did what Iranians did on the Yaldā Night: they ate specific food, decorated their houses with green plants, and visited each other and presented gifts (ibid.). When, during the era of Emperor Constantin, Mithraism began to fade in favour of Christianity, the church fathers utilized the popularity of Yaldā and Mithraism for the promotion of Christianity: they, 'by replacing Mithra with Jesus, in one step transferred all of the splendour and grandeur in the celebration for the appearance of Mithra to the event of the birth of Jesus' (ibid.). Why 25 December was finally chosen as the birthday of Christ, Dibāj says, was unclear, averring that, most likely, ancient Romans thought that this was the birthday of Mithra (ibid.). Despite initial resistance, the Eastern Churches also adopted 25 December as the birthday of Christ, with the exception of the Armenians who continue to celebrate it on 6 January (ibid.).[18]

Dibāj then quotes a number of classical Iranian poets who in their work have pointed to the connection between Yaldā and the personage of Christ (ibid.). The article closes with Dibāj's conclusion that Christmas evidently was not a foreign celebration of Armenians or Westerners; therefore, when celebrating Christmas this year, the readers should commemorate its supposed Iranian origins (ibid.).

It is notable that according to Dibāj's narrative, the birth denoted by the Syriac word *yaldā* was *not* the birth of Christ but the birth of Mithra. Others, such as alluded to in the 2006 note in *Tabdil* cited earlier, have contended that the term *yaldā* originally had referred to the birth of Christ and entered Iran because of the presence of Syriac Christians in the Sassanian era (Safāriān 2020: m. 5:18). It was not certain, explains Patrick Safāriān of the Iranian Church of Los Angeles, CA, when this celebration of Yaldā had found its way from the Syriac Christians to 'the Iranian peoples' (*qowm-hā-ye Irāni*) (ibid.). Safāriān's account is remarkable for two reasons. Firstly, it at least partially cites a source for the information presented: the famed Iranologist Ebrahim Pourdavoud (1885–1968). Unfortunately, it is not entirely clear when Safāriān directly quotes from Pourdavoud's work and when he adds his own deliberations. Secondly, Safāriān distinguishes in his historical trajectory between the, as stated, Syriac Yaldā Night based upon the birth of Christ and the *Iranian* Chelleh Night, celebrated by Zoroastrians because of the longest night of the year. Zoroastrians during that night gathered and ate summer fruits to evade evil spirits (*arvāh-e palid*) appearing at the winter solstice (ibid.: m. 6:08). It seems that the Iranian Armenian pastor is of the opinion that the originally distinct celebrations eventually merged into one night, which is interchangeably referred to as Yaldā and/or Chelleh.

Christian meanings of Yaldā

Introducing the ideological contestation surrounding celebrations of Nowruz, I have exemplarily quoted a ruling by Āyatollāh Makārem Shirāzi who frames the Yaldā Night as *seleh-ye rahem*, that is, an opportunity for the coming together of family members, and thus justifies the feast's permissibility in Islam. Christian pastors as well have praised the Yaldā Night's virtue of bringing together even distant relatives. According to Hormoz Shari'at, the importance of familial life even constituted the primary message of Yaldā (Shari'at 2016: m. 6:44).

The dominating motif of Christian celebrations of Yaldā featuring in my set of sources, however, has been that of the triumph of light in the person of Jesus Christ after a long and sorrow-stricken night. On the occasion of Yaldā 1394 (2015), Hormoz Shari'at, whose network *Shabakeh7* seems to broadcast a special Yaldā-themed show on an annual basis, explained that Yaldā was a sign of hope: no matter how long a night lasted, no matter how dark it was, at its end stood light (*rowshanāyi*) (Shari'at and Ebrāhimiān 2015: m. 34:58). This idea was expressed in Ps. 30.5, which the English Standard Version of the Bible renders as 'Weeping may tarry for the night, but joy comes with the morning' (ibid.).

In a similar vein, during the channel's Yaldā programme a year earlier, Shari'at introduced a worship song praising Christ as the 'morning star' (Shari'at and Ebrāhimiān 2014: m. 32:09) – a theme we have already encountered in the different versions of the 'Seven S of Christ'. The Yaldā Night indeed was the longest night of the year, he suggested, but the Bible assured believers that the morning star that is Jesus Christ rose eventually (ibid.). Furthermore, Yaldā and Christianity, in a spiritual (*rowhāni*) sense, had a great deal of congruence (*hamkhāni*), best visible in Jesus's self-designation as the 'Light of the World' (Shari'at 2017: m. 1:10). The corresponding biblical verse (Jn 8.12) has also been invoked in the context of Yaldā by Peymān Shabānlāri (2019a: m. 3:03) as well as by Edvin Sāleh (2020a: m. 49:05) and Patrick Safāriān (2020: m. 10:11). Where 2 Cor. 5.17 serves as an overall motto for Iranian Christians' Nowruz celebrations, Jn 8.12 arguably serves as such for the Yaldā Night:

> Glory to the name of God (*jalāl beh nām-e Khodāvand*)! A blessed Yaldā for you and all Iranians! And we know that our Yaldā in truth is Jesus Christ who came as a light for eternity (*tā abad nureh*), to appear in unbreakable darkness and break it, to appear and thoroughly remove this darkness. (ibid.: m. 18:03–18:24)

Conclusion

In Chapter 2, I have argued that religious affiliation ought to be considered a central component of nationhood. Building upon this theoretical assumption, I have begun this chapter by illustrating how Iranian discourses on authentic national belonging marginalize Iranians affiliated with Christianity. Ascribed with a 'double foreignness', Iranian Christians react to this exclusionary discourse by emphasizing their loyalty to the Iranian nation. They consider the construction of a Christianity in an authentic Iranian idiom a key task to achieve what I have metaphorically termed the 'naturalization of Christianity' to the Iranian nation.

There are several sites in which this process of naturalization is enacted. In this chapter, I have pointed to celebrations of Nowruz and, to a lesser degree, Yaldā as expedient contexts for the promotion of narratives and practices of authentication. Especially since the 1979 Revolution, many Iranians consider Nowruz the main manifestation of an Iranian national identity and contrast it with the Shi'ite occasion of 'Āshurā' as its supposed 'Islamic other'. Iranian Christians offer their very own reading of Nowruz. They reinterpret the newness inherent to Nowruz as akin to the newness experienced in the 'new birth in

Christ', that is, the defining moment of a Pentecostal Christian's turning to the Christian faith. Going beyond merely symbolical aspects, some Iranian pastors moreover refer to the supposed histories of Nowruz customs like the *Haft Sin* table and claim that, in its original version, the table carried a deeply Christian meaning.

References to historical findings equally serve Iranian Christians to frame celebrations of the Yaldā Night. By pointing to the Syriac root of the word *yaldā*, some Iranian Christians claim that there was a connection between the Yaldā Night and celebrations of Christmas, today associated with the 'West'. Celebrations of Christmas thus appear as authentically Iranian, rather than a 'foreign import'. Finally, the symbolism inherent to the Yaldā Night, the longest night of the year, prompts Iranian Christian pastors to invoke the figure of Jesus Christ as 'light' and quote relevant verses from the New Testament.

Occasionally, the Iranian Christian reinterpretations of Iranian national traditions goes so far as to imply an extraordinary affinity between Christianity and Iranian culture. When Peymān Shabānlāri suggests that God, next to the Bible, spoke through occasions like Nowruz (Shabānlāri 2019b: m. 28:42) and Daniel Shayesteh in his autobiographical English-language monograph states that God 'had prepared divine witness in Iranian culture that has been kept alive through tradition for thousands of years' (Shayesteh 2012: x), Iranian culture appears as nothing less than a vehicle for the Christian revelation. Such discourses are prone to segue into a certain Iranian exceptionalism that we will also encounter in the following chapter, when discussing Iranian Christian references to supposedly Iranian figures in the Bible.

Conversely, Iranian pastors occasionally claim that Iranian culture became only complete and meaningful when viewed through the lens of Christianity. Mahyār Ebrāhimiān, assistant of Hormoz Shariʿat at *Shabakeh7*, suggested that Nowruz for Christians gained in conceptual significance (*mafhum*) and became more than just a custom (*rasm*) (Shariʿat and Ebrāhimiān 2018: m. 26:57); the same thought was also advanced by Peymān Shabānlāri (Shabānlāri 2019a: m. 0:50). Hassan Dehqāni-Tafti describes self-doubts resulting from the 'anomaly' of his Iranian-Christian identity and summarizes his conclusive thoughts as follows:

> Nevertheless I am convinced that, far from forfeiting my own identity or being alienated from my personal roots, I have come to know them in a wider and deeper way and to possess them more authentically. My Persian identity is enhanced and fulfilled and this has brought me inward satisfaction and peaceful

contentment: a harmony of soul that, far from being isolated, has been integrated into living community. (Dehqani-Tafti 2000: 2)

Claims of this sort may also address non-Christian Iranians who are among the watchers of Iranian Christian online videos and satellite TV. If Christianity 'fulfilled' Persian identity or supplied Iranian customs with conceptual depth, a Muslim-born Iranian could become more Iranian through his conversion to Christianity – a claim explicitly made by Hormoz Shari'at, as I have referred to at the very onset of this book.

Finally, Iranian Christian claims to the true interpretation of 'Ancient Nowruz' must also be seen in the context of the ideological vying for Nowruz in post-revolutionary Iran and the initial reservations of some leading Shi'ite clerics regarding the occasion. Discourses in Iranian Christian exile churches are embedded in the sociocultural and political discourses of contemporary Iran. This will become even clearer in the following chapter in which I will illustrate further narratives and practices of authentication, namely Iranian Christian usages of Persian poetry, Iranian Christian readings of supposedly Iranian figures in the Bible (among them King Cyrus the Great) and the commemoration of an Iranian Christian canon of post-revolutionary martyrs.

4

Naturalizing Christianity (II): Persian poets and poetry, Iranians in the Bible and the Iranian Christian martyrs

Persian poetry among Iranian Christians

There is a deep and profound pride in the heritage of Persian poetry among Iranians of virtually all sociopolitical hues. Among the most popular Persian poets of the classical age are Ferdowsi, Jalāl-od-Din Rumi 'Mowlānā', Saʿdi and Hāfez – though many more could be named. Their legacy is dear to Iranians who are often able to recite verses or whole poems by heart. From a young age onwards, Iranian children are encouraged to memorize the works of the great masters, and those most talented can even compete against each other on national television. As Hamid Naficy puts it, 'Rich and poor can and do cite Ferdowsi, Sa'adi, Hafez, Rumi, and Khayyam' (Naficy 1993: 148). The fascination with poetry persists in the diaspora, where poetry readings are an inherent part of events organized by Iranian cultural or political organizations.

To define Persian poetry as a core element of an Iranian national self-image has since the early twentieth century been an elitist and later a governmental project. There was a 'broader process of national canonization in which Iranians promoted the likes of Hafiz, Firdawsi, and Sa'di as part of the "national cult of Persian poetry" and embodiments of the "Iranian spirit"' (cf. Ferdowsi 2008; Vejdani 2015: 146). This process culminated in cultural events like the 1934 celebration of the 'millennial of Ferdowsi' with the inauguration of the mausoleum of Ferdowsi in Tus (cf. Marashi 2009), or the pompous visit of Indian Nobel Prize laureate Rabindranath Tagore to Iran two years earlier (cf. Marashi 2020: 97–133).

It is difficult to overstate the prominent place of poetry in virtually all the sources assessed for this book. The magazines *Kalameh*, *Tabdil* and, to some degree, *Smyrna* have dedicated a distinct column to the printing of poetry composed by Iranian Christians. As we have learned in the previous chapter, poetry recitations are also a common feature of the liturgy in Iranian churches. This equally applies to shows broadcasted on Persian-language Christian TV networks. When the necessity of a culturally sensitive rendition of Christianity to Iranian believers and potential converts is brought up, poetry has usually been mentioned as a key vehicle (cf. Hopkins 2020: 165; cf. Rzepka 2017: 81).

Iranian Christians in the diaspora engage with poetry in two main ways, one of which – to remain within the overall analytical frame of this and the previous chapter – is based on narratives while the other one constitutes a practice: they, firstly, point to and emphasize the supposedly exceptional affinities of Persian poets, both of the classical and the modern epochs, with Christianity and the figure of Jesus Christ. In its most assertive form, this narrative portrays the great masters of Persian poetry as pseudo-Christians. Secondly, Iranian Christians assume themselves the role of the poet and compose as well as recite poetry with Christian content. They have done so since the earliest days of a Persian-speaking Christianity in Iran, as we shall see in the example of Jalil Qazzāq Irvāni. Today, Iranian Christian pastors and publishers of magazines actively encourage their fellow Christians to 'versify for the Lord' and send their poems for publication. They believe that God and/or the Holy Spirit gift some individuals with an exceptional talent for poetry, the utilization of which then becomes these individuals' mission and duty. Poems can also function as prayers, as acts of worship and as a means of proselytism.

The following pages will deal with the two mentioned aspects, that is, Persian poetry as a narrative and a practice. It has not been an easy task to decide which material to include here – in terms of the references made by Persian poets to Christianity and Jesus Christ, for instance, a detailed and truly meticulous study by Hassan Dehqāni-Tafti exists. That said, what is of concern for the present book is the *discourses surrounding such references* rather than *the poems' content*. As for the production of poetry by Iranian Christians themselves, the material available is likewise abundant. I have decided to focus on two poets, one from the early twentieth century and one contemporary, at greater detail: Jalil Qazzāq Irvāni and Hanif Avarsaji. I will, moreover, cite examples of poetry published in *Kalameh* and poetry sent to *Shabakeh7* by viewers, to paint a fuller picture.

The section on poetry will close with the illustration of a second example of a component of Iranian culture deemed irreconcilable with Christianity by some Iranian Christians: the practice of *fāl* or *fālgiri*, that is, divination, often practised through the usage of Persian poetry.

Poetry as narrative: Classical Persian poets and Christianity
The works of Hassan Dehqāni-Tafti

> Among the countless Iranian poets, there is not a single reputed poet who has not composed poetry about Christ and Christianity, or who has not spoken about them otherwise. In the endless sea (*daryā-ye bikarān*) that is Persian poetry and literature, passages about Jesus, his religion (*ā'in*) and the lives of his followers are so plentiful that to thoroughly take record of them and mention all the poetic works relevant would ask for the patience of Job and the lifespan of Noah (*'omr-e Nuh*). (Dehqāni-Tafti 1993: 7)

This quote by Bishop Hassan Dehqāni-Tafti is the beginning – and in a way also the conclusion – of his painstaking analysis of Christian motifs among the works of Iranian poets. Dehqāni-Tafti published his study in his own publishing house Sohrab Books in Basingstoke, UK during the first half of the 1990s, as a part of the three-volume series *Christ and Christianity among the Iranians*. Scrutinizing the works of thirty classical and twenty-five modern poets, his choice was, as he admits, to some degree conditioned by the availability of books in his British exile.

Before entering his chronological listing of poets, Dehqāni-Tafti briefly analyses a fundamental question: Where did the awareness about Christianity and the person of Christ among Iranian poets stem from? For the classical age, which in Dehqāni-Tafti's overview reaches all the way from Rudaki (858–940) to Sorush Esfahāni (1813–1868) – a considerable period of almost 1,000 years – the author cites several possible sources: Islamic texts like the Quran and the Hadith, personal encounters with Christians in monasteries and, possibly, direct access to Christian writings (ibid.: 9–10). Most of them, however, must have construed their very own Christianity from hearsay and consequently, in Dehqāni-Tafti's view, were not accurately aware of its rites and contents – sometimes to a degree where poets confused Zoroastrian with Christian clerics (ibid.: 10). As for the modern period, which Dehqāni-Tafti lets include poets from Dāvari (1822–1866) to Nāder Ebrāhimi (1936–2008), Christianity was now approached as a *Western* phenomenon (ibid.: 30). Since poets, 'rather than talking about flowers and nightingales', were now concerned with modernity, freedom and nationalism, Christianity in some instances became a synonym of Western politics (Dehqāni-Tafti 1994: 30).

For the classical age, Dehqāni-Tafti indicates four mutual themes of Christian teachings (*ta'ālim-e 'Isā*) and Persian poetry: the condemning of false piety and hypocrisy (*zamm-e zohd-forushi va riā*), the relationship of body parts with each other (*rābeteh-ye a'zā-ye yek badan bā yekdigar*), love and self-sacrifice (*mohabat va fedākāri*), and prayer and its answering (*do'ā va javāb beh ān*) (Dehqāni-Tafti

1993: 17–24). I will exemplify Dehqāni-Tafti's deliberations by the second theme which is arguably the least self-explanatory of the four. The exiled Anglican theologian here juxtaposes a passage from the New Testament in which the community of Christians is likened to a human body, the parts and well-being of which necessarily depended on each other (1 Cor. 12.26), with the famous[1] poem *Bani Ādam* ('Humankind') by Saʿdi:

> If one member suffers, all suffer together; if one member is honored, all rejoice together. (English Standard Version)

> The members of the human race are limbs one to another, for at
>   creation they were of one essence.
> When one limb is pained by fate, the others cannot rest.
> You who are unsympathetic to the troubles of others, it is not fitting to
>   call you human. (Thackston 2008: 22)

In his short introductory note on the person of Saʿdi, Dehqāni-Tafti states that Saʿdi had been an avid traveller, reaching even Jerusalem (*Beyt-ol-Moqaddas*) (Dehqāni-Tafti 1993: 21). He thus seems to imply that a direct inspiration from Christian sources was not unlikely in his case; whether he actually believed that Saʿdi had borrowed the motif of the interdependent fate of the body parts from Paul's letter to the Corinthians remains unclear.

The content of their engagement with Christ and Christianity transformed among Iranian poets, especially with the dawning of modernity, as Dehqāni-Tafti explains in volume three of his series. He contrasts the approach of classical poets to the person of Jesus Christ, who mainly praised him for performing miracles (e.g. his healing power), with modern poets, who extol Christ as a paragon of steadfastness, brave in the face of persecution and suffering, aiming to achieve the 'salvation of creation' (*nejāt-e khalq*) (Dehqāni-Tafti 1994: 86).

Dehqāni-Tafti's works on the subject at stake can be characterized as comparatively sober in style and guided by scholarly curiosity; nevertheless, he pursues a wider goal – a goal with which we are well familiar by now: all of the three volumes of the series, he explains, serve the 'demonstration of the truth that to be Christian is not inimical to being Iranian and writing and speaking in Persian' (ibid.: 8). Following his conviction, Dehqāni-Tafti has used Persian poetry to better convey Christian ideas, for instance, in a 2007 issue of *Kalameh* (Dehqāni-Tafti 2007). In order to provide the reader with a deeper understanding of Phil. 2.5-7, the then retired bishop lets Saʿdi and Paul – the author of the letter to the Philippians – enter a dialogue. What results 'in fact is a dialectic (*diālektik*) between Saʿdi and Paul' (ibid.: 21).

Discovering divine wisdom in Persian poetry

A common perception among Iranian Christians is that exceptional wisdom dwelled within the words of 'those ever fertile poets' (Dehqani-Tafti 2000: 186). Dehqāni-Tafti, whose English biography teems with quotes from Persian poetry, even quotes Hāfez, Saʿdi and Christ jointly, although adding that 'the ultimate truth is best found in the words of Jesus himself' (ibid.). He is not alone in drawing upon the pronouncements of Persian poets in such a prominent way.

The regular recourse to verses composed by Iranian poets to better advance a particular idea or make sense of the intricacies of life is certainly a penchant of educated Iranians irrespective of their religious affiliation. Iranian Christians are no exception here. One is therefore not necessarily surprised to find Robert Āseriān initiate an article in the magazine *Shāgerd* by quoting a poem by modern poet Sohrāb Sepehri (1928–1980) (Āseriān 2015: 8), nor should it be considered an oddity when Āseriān during a seemingly unrelated review of the Scorsese movie *Silence* in the same magazine suddenly explains that he found himself reminded of a poem by Ahmad Shāmlu (1925–2000) (Āseriān 2017: 29), only to later in the same text also quote the eminent Mowlānā Rumi (ibid.: 31).

But the usage of (mostly) classical Persian poetry by Iranian Christians can go beyond a habitual referencing of this kind. Hormoz Shariʿat during the 1395 (2016) Yaldā Night recites verses from the poet Hāfez in lieu of a Bible reading. He explains:

> In this Yaldā Night, the Bible has a lot of things to tell us about hope and faith as well as hope and love. But Iranian poetry and Iranian poets too possess a lot of content (*mohtavā*). Many of the Persian poets have spoken about faith, hope and love, and even about Jesus Christ. I want to read to you a few couplets from Hāfez. (Shariʿat 2016: m. 1:02–1:26)

He then goes on to recite a part of the 143. Ghazal of Hāfez, ending in the couplet:

> But if the Holy Ghost once more
>   Should lend his aid to us we'd see
> Others perform what Jesus did. (Davis 2012)

Such positive mentions of the Holy Ghost and Jesus conceivably evoke a deep pride among Iranian Christians, like the team of *Shabakeh7* and its viewers, who Hormoz Shariʿat reads the verses to. They enact the established national tradition of reciting poetry at the Yaldā Table and simultaneously experience it in reference to Christianity. In general, the abundance of references to Christianity offers itself to Iranian pastors and ministers as a readily available repertoire which can be put to use especially on 'national occasions' like Nowruz and Yaldā.

Shari'at does not offer any additional exegesis for the couplets he cites – it seems that the text is believed to speak for itself. A different pastor, Daniel Shāyesteh, who published his autobiography *The House I Left Behind: A Journey from Islam to Christ* in English and therefore, as we should keep in mind, primarily speaks to a non-Iranian audience, interprets the prominence of Christian motifs in Persian poetry more daringly. I have so far only very briefly referred to Shāyesteh, namely when pointing to his claim that God consciously prepared divine witness in Iranian culture to draw Iranians closer to him. His take on Persian poetry reflects the same conviction: Shāyesteh first quotes examples of verses by Mowlānā, Hāfez and Sa'di that talk favourably about Christ (Shayesteh 2012: 35-6). Describing how, in his youth, he had failed to question why Persian poets, in his perception, did not talk in the same terms about the Prophet Mohammad, Shāyesteh concludes: 'I believe the writings of these men are a testimony of God's plan for Iranians. He allowed the name of Christ to be magnified in Persian poetry so that Iranians, like me, might see the excellence of Christ without first opening a Bible' (ibid.: 36).

The position and power that is ascribed to Persian poetry in this statement is remarkable. Following this reading, Iranians may discover the 'truth of Christianity' through components of their national culture – or at least experience an initial prompt making them curious to further inform themselves about Jesus Christ and Christianity. The similarities of this idea with the above-mentioned readings especially of the *Haft Sin* table as bearing direct hints to the Christian God are apparent. Different from the rather ponderous interpretation of the *Haft Sin*, however, the references to Christ and Christianity in the poetry of Hāfez and the likes are more straightforward.

It is the prominence of the poet Hāfez as well as the frequency in which he versified about the figure of Christ that have made him subject to speculations among Iranian Christians, suggesting he could have been a secret convert to Christianity. I will briefly expand on this narrative before turning to poetry as a practice.

'Was Hāfez a Christian?'

This question is the title of an undated treatise by Bozorgmehr Vaziri (n.d.), which Rzepka has referred to (cf. Rzepka 2017: 162). Vaziri, himself a regular contributor to the poetry column of *Tabdil*, suggests that, aside from the high amount of references made to Christ by Hāfez, it also appears that Hāfez was fully acquainted with the Bible. At the same time, the name of the prophet of Islam did not feature 'a single time' in Hāfez's poems (Vaziri n.d.: 2). Moreover, Hāfez in some poems seems to suggest that he was wearing the *zonnār*, a compulsory belt for non-Muslims to indicate their status as 'protected people' (*ahl-e zemmeh*) (ibid.: 4). Vaziri closes his treatise by stating that he wanted to leave the final judgement about his initial question to the reader (ibid.).

Similar insinuations were made by Germany-based pastor Siāmak Zargari in his 1393 (2014) Nowruz sermon. Zargari stated that, naturally, all gnostics (*'orafā'*), of which Hāfez was one, were more or less acquainted with the Bible, both the Old Testament and the New Testament (Zargari and Zargari 2014: m. 9:12). One could therefore easily recognize Christian motifs in their teachings and poems (ibid.). However, to truly grasp the immense reverberations of the Bible in Hāfez's works, one had to consult *older prints* of his poems – prints from maybe fifty years ago (ibid.). Why was this necessary? Zargari explains:

> It is interesting: just like you and me actually, he [Hāfez] was Muslim-born (*Mosalmun-zādeh*), but in terms of his understanding – when he died – all of his poems were about Jesus. As an Iranian I want to teach you something about Iran. After the Revolution, they turned this upside down and all prints now suggest that Hāfez *was* a Christian and *became* a Muslim! (ibid.: m. 10:24–10:55)

Zargari does not find the latter hypothesis credible in any way. Instead, he assumes that Hāfez used his rational judgement (*'aql o sho'ur*) to do his research and thus started to praise Christ (ibid.). His late verses, Zargari continues, advanced exactly what today is preached in Christian churches (ibid.). This was a matter of deep pride for Iranian Christians (ibid.).

It should be noted that no other statement suggesting a censorship on behalf of the Islamic Republic's government(s) with the aim of papering over Hafez's supposed turn to Christianity was found in the sources. Where Zargari derives this assumption from remains unclear. That said, it is not off the mark to simply read Vaziri's and Zargari's 'Christianization' of Hāfez as a more assertive form of the narratives surrounding Iranian poets presented previously. Though it has been never put as such, for instance, by Dehqāni-Tafti, the suggested affinities with Christianity among the masters of Iran's poets leave it to the reader/viewer's imagination to think of them as covert Christians. Such assertive readings of course neglect the simple fact that Jesus in Islam likewise features as a prominent prophet; therefore, his mentioning in an Islamic context should not necessarily be considered a surprise.

Poetry as practice: Versifying for the glory of God

A 2004 issue of *Kalameh* features a letter to the editors by a reader named Bahrām (Kalameh 2004). Bahrām describes how, back in high school, he had discovered his 'God-given' (*khodādād*) talent as a poet, but due to personal circumstances had long given up writing verses. By reading the poetry column in *Kalameh*, Bahrām says, a light flashed up in his mind and he suddenly thought: 'Why should I not compose poetry for my faith?' (ibid.). He therefore thanked the editors who he deemed responsible for his rediscovery of poetry, now as a means of worship.

Bahrām's letter is expressive of the two core aspects defining the composition and recitation of poetry as a practice of authentication among Iranian Christians: firstly, the belief that to possess a poetic prowess can be a gift from God and, secondly, that poetry can or should be used for the benefit of Christianity. Iranian Christians have been active in the realm of poetry writing for longer than since they started to publish exile magazines like *Kalameh* and *Tabdil*, roughly thirty years ago. Hassan Dehqāni-Tafti, whose work I have so far used as a *primary* source, has rendered valuable services to the academic observer by chronicling the beginnings of Christian poetry in the Persian language (cf. Dehqāni-Tafti 1994: 453–82). The poets mentioned by him are largely individuals somehow associated with Anglican institutions in Iran, such as their schools (Jalil Qazzāq Irvāni, 'Abbās Āryānpur Kāshāni) or the church itself (Iraj Motahhadeh, successor of Dehqāni-Tafti as bishop). Where available, Dehqāni-Tafti cites excerpts from the introduced poets' works. Especially noteworthy is 'Abbās Āryānpur Kāshāni's work in which Kāshāni poured the entire Gospel of John into the mould of Persian poetry. Furthermore, it would be remiss to not mention that Dehqāni-Tafti also points to the volume of poetry published by Mohammad Jalil Sepehr, a non-Anglican, who I in the previous chapter introduced together with Dehqāni-Tafti as exemplary 'architects of an Iranian Christianity'. Finally, Dehqāni-Tafti mentions his own works, published in two volumes entitled *Divine Suffering* (*Ranj-e Elāhi*) and *Cure* (*'Elāj*).

Four decades before his 1994 overview, Dehqāni-Tafti had published a concise volume wholly dedicated to his former teacher Jalil Qazzāq Irvāni (1878/9–1954/5) (Dehqāni-Tafti 1956). I will use this source to briefly summarize Irvāni's biography and then cite and translate two of his poems. I will then present the example of a contemporary poet Hanif Avarsaji (b. 1981/2).[2]

The poetry of Jalil Qazzāq Irvāni

Born in 1878/9 into a Sunni Muslim family in Tehran, Jalil Qazzāq Irvāni was the son of a Cossack military officer who after the Iranian Qajar Empire's loss of Erevan to the Russian Tsarist Empire in the first half of the nineteenth century resettled in Iran. In his youth, Jalil got seriously ill and was treated at the Christian hospital in Isfahan. Here he discovered his interest in Christianity. In 1922 (Dehqāni-Tafti here indicates the Gregorian year), Jalil received his baptism at St. Luke's Church in Isfahan; his father had long passed away by then. He got married to a woman named Showkat, a fellow convert who had been baptized at the same church, a year before Jalil. Dehqāni-Tafti describes Jalil as a great educator who was an ideal principal to the College Branch School, which Dehqāni-Tafti attended in his youth.

The booklet *Sorrowful, yet Rejoicing* (*Chun Mahzun, vali Shādemān*), the title of which is a quote from 2 Cor. 6.10, contains fifty-three poems of varying length. Some, like the poem *The Wind of Nowruz* (*Bād-e Nowruz*), later became lyrics to popular Persian-language Christian hymns. Others are versifications of biblical passages, among them the *Masnavi of the Prodigal Son* (*Masnavi-ye Pesar-e Gomshodeh*) and *Blessed is the One* (*Ey Khosh ān Kas*) which is based upon the Beatitudes (Mt. 5.3-12). In some cases, the underlying biblical section is indicated at the end of the poem. My selection of the two following poems for translation was partially conditioned by their brevity; however, I have consciously chosen one poem directly inspired by a biblical passage, or more precisely a quote ascribed to Jesus, and another poem written for the occasion of Christmas. One should keep in mind that translating poetry is a tricky business, even more so when translating between two languages neither of which is the translator's native tongue.

بیایید نزد من ای تمامی زحمت‌کشان و گران‌باران⁵

مژده باد آن را که جوید نام تو آن زبان که می‌دهد پیغام تو
زنده جاوید باد آن کو مدام بر صلای فیض تو دارد قیام
مژده باد آن را که هم در تو گریخت رشتهٔ الفت ز غیر تو گسیخت
ای که هستی بر خداوندان امیر ای طبیب اعظم ما دستگیر
در طفیل تو همه دلداری است بی تو سلطانی سراسر خواری است
اینک آن آبی که می‌بخشد نجات اینک آن بخشندهٔ گر خواهی نجات
زد صدای رحمتش بر ما ندا که ای گران‌بار گنه نزد من آ
من ز قید ذلت آزادی دهم در درون جانت آرامی نهم
یوغ من باری خفیف و از وداد تار و پودش بسته است از اتحاد
غیر راه او و مپو که راه نیست غیر او سلطان در این خرگاه نیست
کیست این مولا که عیسی نام اوست مژدهٔ عفو خدا پیغام اوست
از محبت بود او چون بی‌قرار جان‌سپاری کرد نی از اضطرار
جان و تن بخشید در راه شما تا نباشد غیر او تان ملتجا
حق آن سلطان جان نشناختی لاجرم میدان که جان در باختی

> Come to me, all who labor and are heavy laden![4]

Glad tidings to those who seek your name!
    To the tongue that preaches your word
Of everlasting life for those who steadily
    Follow the call of your grace
Glad tidings to those who seek refuge in you!
    Who break their bonds but not with you
Oh, you who are above the this-wordly Lords!
    Oh, our most exalted healer!
In your companionship dwells all relief
    Without you, a king even falls into grief!
Behold, the water that grants salvation
    Behold, the merciful donor of salvation
Whose graceful voice calls out on us
    'Oh, you who are laden with sin, come to me!
I will free you from the fetters of hardship
    And restore your soul to inner peace
My yoke is the light burden of friendship
    Its strings and weft are woven in amity'
Outside of his path, there is no path
    No king but him is under the sky
Who is this master, whose name is Jesus
    Who preaches the tidings of forgiveness?
Out of love it was when he restlessly
    Devoted himself, not out of force
Gave life and body, striving for you
    So he would become your sole sanctuary
Unless your heart will know this king
    Your soul to the square of defeat will cling!

تولد مسیح[5]

یک شبی بود سعد و از این ملکت دور   اختران نور فشان بودی و مه بد پر نور
مژده آمد به شبانان که خداوند ودود   آمد از ساحت قدسی و ز رخ پرده گشود
جمله با شوق دویدند بدان سو بشتاب   پادشه خفته بدیدند در آخور فیاض وجود
با ملائک به ستایش همه خواندند سرود   نزد آن منجی کل شاه جهان منبع خود
به مکانی همه دیوار و زمینش نمناک   به حصاری که شد از پای بهائم پر خاک
آخورش خوابگه و بالش بود زمین   بهر آزادی ما شد به زمین جایگزین
آنکه او بهر گناهان جهان زحمت دید   بر سیه نامه هر یک رقم عفو کشید
هر دم احسان خداوندی او تازه کنیم   رحمتش را به همه ملک پر آوازه کنیم
او پناه است چو ما را نهراسیم دگر   غیر او پادشهی را نشناسیم دگر

The Birth of Christ

In distant lands, on an auspicious night
    Of starshine and of misty light
Good news to the shepherds from the God of grace
    Who descended from heaven and unveiled his face
They longingly ran to him, all together
    To see him, the merciful king in a manger
And there with the angels they all sang him praise
    The newly-born saviour of our human race

That place, its walls and its ground all damp
    All muddied and dirty from cattle, that camp
Where manger turned bed and pillow the ground
    The share of our freedom was only here found
His sufferings lend all the sinners remission
    Delivered their record a stamp of omission
Hence let all our breath his favour anew
    Extol and his mercy, the world shall them view
Our refuge is him, come frighten no more
    But him know no king, henceforth and before!

Hanif Avarsaji: Writing poetry as a spiritual gift

Among the many contemporary Iranian Christians who write poetry and recite it during services, Hanif Avarsaji appears to enjoy a particular popularity. He regularly reads his poetry at California-based Iranian churches, such as the Iranian Church of Sunnyvale. His recitations are uploaded on the church's YouTube channel and the number of views exceeds the usual number of views of similar videos.[6] This together with the fact that Avarsaji has appeared on shows of *SAT7 PARS* and *Shabakeh7* to talk about his life story and about how he came to write Christian poetry have let me choose him as an example of a contemporary Iranian Christian poet.

Hanif Avarsaji grew up in Gorgān, born into a Muslim family that he describes as not very religious and overall 'freethinking' (*āzād-andish*) (Avarsaji, Hovsepiān and Hovsepiān 2019; Avarsaji and Shari'at 2018). His parents were politically active, and in the 1980s, when Avarsaji was a small child, spent years in prison (Avarsaji and Shari'at 2018: m. 7:00). Describing his family as generally fond of the arts, Avarsaji explains that it was his uncle who initially introduced him to poetry (ibid.: m. 3:06). In Iran, he could further develop his talent in poetry associations (ibid.). At the age of twenty, Avarsaji emigrated to the United States in 2002 (Avarsaji, Hovsepiān and Hovsepiān 2019: m. 2:54). He describes the ensuing time as dominated by personal crises and constant restlessness (ibid.). While working in a restaurant in California, his boss, an Iranian Christian, invited him to a church (ibid.: 6:15). After further ups and downs, Avarsaji finally converted to Christianity – or 'entrusted his heart to Christ', to quote his own words (ibid.: m. 14:15). Before his conversion, Avarsaji had further pursued his love of Persian poetry and toured mosques in California to recite his works (Avarsaji and Shariʻat 2018: m. 19:15).

With the embracing of Christianity, a new understanding of what it meant to write poetry ripened in Avarsaji (Avarsaji, Hovsepiān and Hovsepiān 2019: m. 16:12). Now he no longer wanted to versify for a religion (*mazhab*), a person, or one of the Shi'ite Imams, but 'only for God' (ibid.). He names poetry writing an *'atiyyeh*, a gift from God, the same term which in Persian is used to denote the 'gifts of the Holy Spirit' (sometimes referred to the Greek term *charismata* in English), the *'atāyā-ye Ruh-ol-Qods*. Earlier, I have indicated that poetry writing among some Iranian Christians is perceived as a 'God-given' talent. Hormoz Shariʻat as well believes this gift to have been bestowed upon Avarsaji by God. In an interview with Avarsaji, Shariʻat, here functioning as the interviewer, asked his guest: 'People know Hanif because of his poems ... God has given this [ability] to you [Hanif], as an anointment, a talent ... When did you understand that God has given this to you?' (Avarsaji and Shariʻat 2018: m. 1:47–2:24). In his answer, Avarsaji explained that the utilization of this talent for the glory of God for him had become 'the sole reason why I am on this planet' (ibid.: m. 4:21).

The connection of God to the act of poetry writing has at times been described as so close that the poet is thought of as a mouthpiece of God. Hanif Avarsaji has advanced this thought after finishing the recitation of a poem, the first part of which I will cite with translation later. After his recitation, the present churchgoers at the Iranian Church of Sunnyvale applauded him frenetically; on the video recording, one can see the people in the audience giving Avarsaji standing ovations. However, the poet himself was not at all happy with this reaction:

> Please sit, please! I am supplicating (*tamannā*), I am begging you (*eltemās*). I was certain you were going to applaud, so something came to my mind that I would like to tell you. I am not a poet and don't claim to be one (*eddeʻā-ye shāʻeri dāshtan*). Neither am I acting like one of these 'modest' people who are like 'I am a poet but now I am saying that I am not a poet'. When I am writing poetry – and it only ever happens once in a few years – I am only writing down

what God is giving me. All of the credit (*credit*), all the glory and magnificence are God's and God's only. (Avarsaji 2016: m. 9:31–10:00)

In his self-image, Avarsaji thus is a tool of God who uses him as what one might call a 'poet-missionary'. Avarsaji accordingly suggests that he could see the 'fruits' (*miveh-hā*) of God's working through poetry as people could hear Christ through the poems (Avarsaji, Hovsepiān and Hovsepiān 2019: m. 16:30).

To provide a brief impression of Avarsaji's poetry, I have translated the first part of one of his poems which, judging from the number of views on YouTube, seems to be very popular. There is no title indicated, neither in the video title and description nor in the video itself. The whole recitation takes just under ten minutes and thus is by far too long to be quoted fully here. What follows are the first one and a half minutes of the poem, the last verse of which in the video recording is followed by a short interruptive applause by the audience (Avarsaji 2016: m. 0:00–1:32).

من شاعر دلبسته دربار کسی که   سلطان جهان است ولی کاخ ندارد

انگشت ترک خورده زیاد است   ولیکن دستان کسی مثل تو سوراخ ندارد

از دست خداوند اگر جام بگیرم   در دامنه عشق سرانجام بگیرم

تا دلهره در دلم تشویش نباشد   باید که در آغوش تو آرام بگیرم

من در پی یک لحظه تماشا همه جا را   گشتم که تو را در همه ایام بگیرم

ای زیر فلک! اسم تو از عشق فراتر   هر دم مددم را من از این نام بگیرم

ای نام تو بهترین سرآغاز!   در اوج فروتنی سرافراز

ای سر خدا به سینه پنهان   بگذار که فاش گردد این راز

ای مرهم زخم خسته بالی   پرواز هزار دفعه پرواز

ای نام گره گشا که با تو   هر مشکل بسته می‌شود باز

یک بار دگر مدد گرفتم   با نام مسیح کردم آغاز

I am the faithful poet at the court of the one
    who is king of the world but does not have a palace
Chapped fingers there are many
    but the holes in your hands are matchless
If I was to drink from God's cup
    in the kingdom of love I end up
Lest there be fear and oppression
    in your embrace I shall find comfort
In a passing moment I have explored the world
    only to return to you, every day
Oh you whose name under the heavens is higher than love
    As long as I breathe I find help on your way

> In your name, the best name I will start anew
> > You are the most humble, yet glorious are you
> Oh secret of God, still hidden within
> > Reveal yourself, come through!
> Oh almighty healer of broken wings
> > Let us arise and new ways pursue
> All knots will untie in your holy name
> > The utterance of which all stress will undo
> Once more I have sought aid
> > The name of Christ is what I call unto!

Poetry as a means of prayer and worship

Hanif Avarsaji is not unique in his function as a poet-missionary. On another occasion, at the same church where Avarsaji read out the poem I have just cited, an unnamed woman entered the stage under a similar premise. God had spoken to her heart in the form of a poem, she explained; now she wanted to present the poem as a gift to the audience (Navā'i 2015: m. 26:27). Speaking during a Nowruz service, the said woman may likewise have aspired to reach non-Christian Iranians who, as mentioned in the previous chapter, may attend Iranian churches for the first time on the occasion of Nowruz.

Poems in the Iranian Christian context, however, function in manifold ways and may also be addressed the other way around: from humans to God. Especially when intended to eventually become lyrics to a song, poems can serve in worship. More commonly even, at least in the set of sources assessed for this book, are poems as prayers – or rather prayers in the form of poems. Granted that it is up to theologians to determine what defines a prayer, it seems reasonable to assume that a poem addressed to God ending in the utterance 'Amin!' can be heuristically understood as such. Such instances could be observed at least four times in the sources (Bāghestāni 2016: m. 12:36; Heydari 2018b: m. 9:33, 2019: m. 36:59; Shari'at 2017: m. 37:10). On a similar note, in at least two cases a poem ended with an exclamation of 'Hallelujah!' (Navā'i 2015: m. 1:17:27; Shari'at 2017: m. 54:38).

Bearing in mind that most of the video sources used for this book were recorded on the occasion of Nowruz and Yaldā, most poems I have encountered tried to weave Nowruz/Yaldā and Christian motifs into one poem. That said, it is evident from magazines like *Kalameh* that Iranian Christian pastors and ministers encourage fellow Iranian Christians to compose poetry independent of a national occasion like Nowruz. In the poetry columns of *Kalameh* and *Tabdil*, one can find both poems which seem to be sent in by readers, usually only mentioned by their first name,[7] and by recurring contributors. In *Kalameh*, for instance, the regular publication of poems by a person named 'Qarācheh-Dāghi' has been salient; in the example of *Tabdil*, the works of Bozorgmehr Vaziri and 'Ali Yazdiān have appeared frequently (see Figure 4).

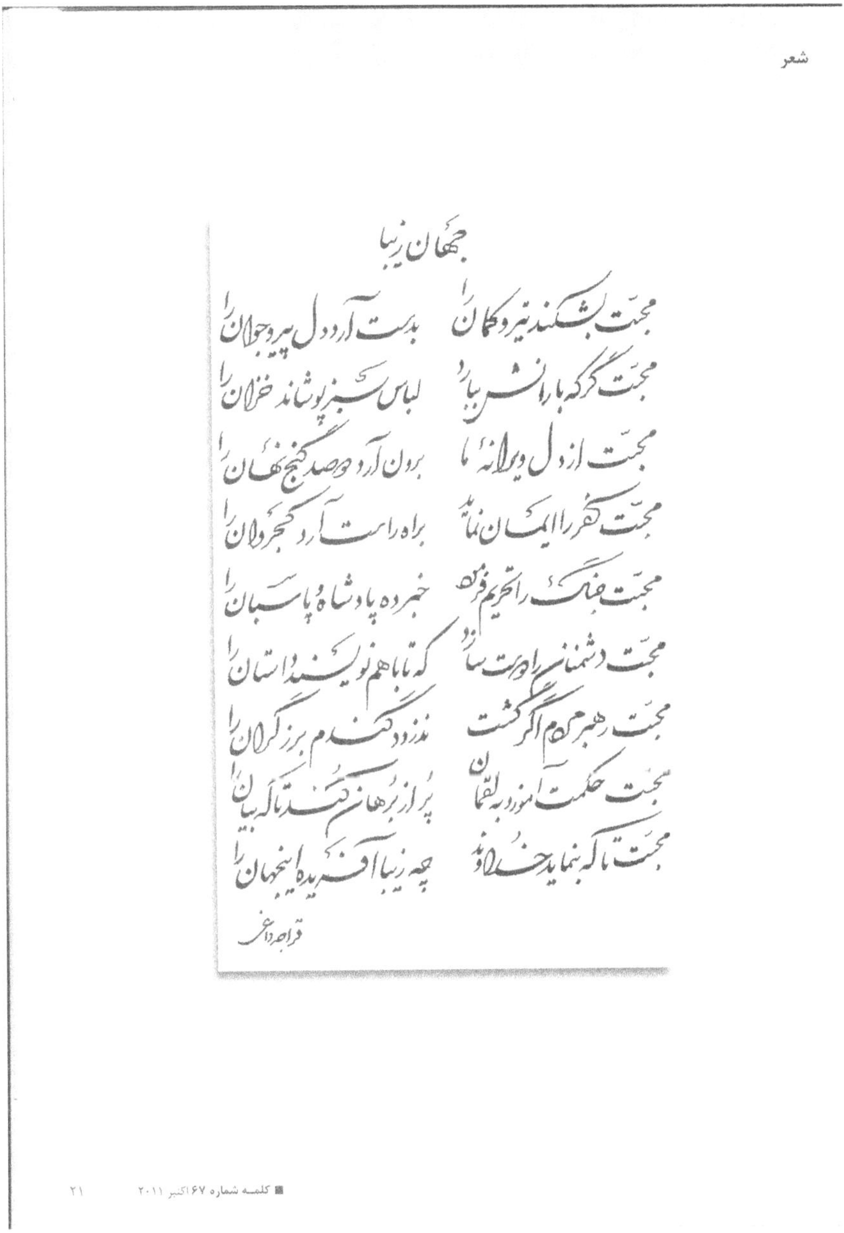
شعر

جهان زیبا

محبت بشکند تیر و کمان را بدست آرد دل پیر و جوان را
محبت گر که بارانش ببارد لباس سبز پوشاند خزان را
محبت از دل ویرانهٔ ما برون آرد دو صد گنج نهان را
محبت کفر را ایمان نماید براه راست آرد کجروان را
محبت جنگ را تحریم فرمود خبر ده پادشاه و پاسبان را
محبت دشمنان را دوست سازد که تا با هم نویسند داستان را
محبت رهبر مردم اگر گشت ندزدد گندم برزگران را
محبت حکمت آموزد به لقمان پر از برهان کند تا که بیان را
محبت تا که بنماید خداوند چه زیبا آفریده اینجهان را

قراچه داغی

■ کلمه شماره ۶۷ اکتبر ۲۰۱۱ ۲۱

Figure 4 A poem entitled *Jahān-e Zibā*, 'Beautiful World', by Qarācheh-Dāghi. In *Kalameh* 67 (2011: 21). Used with permission of Elam Ministries.

Similar to the readers of magazines like *Kalameh*, viewers of Persian-language Christian satellite TV are asked by the channel's presenters to send their poems and songs for broadcast. For Yaldā 1396, 'sister Florā from Iran' sent a pre-recorded *deklameh* (from the French verb *déclamer*) to the team of *Shabakeh7* (Shari'at 2017: m. 46:59). Rezā, one of the show's hosts, explained that Florā was regularly in touch with the satellite TV network and that her poems 'which God and the Holy Spirit give to her' were 'full of wisdom and special meanings' (ibid.). Two weeks before Yaldā, Rezā had texted her and inquired whether she would like to contribute something for the approaching occasion. She then sent her *deklameh*, a poetry reading with accompanying instrumental music, readily edited so that everything left to do for *Shabakeh7* was to click the play button (ibid.).

More frequently, the presenters of the channel themselves recite the poems sent to them and optionally play atmospheric music in the background. In 2014, again on the occasion of the Yaldā Night, Hormoz Shari'at read out a poem sent to *Shabakeh7* by a viewer named Hassan. Shari'at praised the poem for connecting the two occasions of Yaldā and the birth of Christ, which anyway were connected considering the meaning of the word *yaldā* (as illustrated in the previous chapter) (Shari'at and Ebrāhimiān 2014: m. 52:27). He also mentioned that he had met with Hassan in Dallas recently and jokingly declared him the 'poet of *Shabakeh7*'; this, in fact, he continued to explain, applied to many of the viewers who by dint of their contributions could truly be considered members of the network's team (ibid.). I want to close this section by citing Hassan's poem, seemingly untitled, again with my own translation.

به یلدا نشستن، به نام نگار   شب مهرورزی، شب یاد یار
به نام خداوند عشق و کلام   شب دوستی، شب احترام
که باشد خدا در شب شعر ما   به نام خدا شد شب مهر ما
که میلاد عیسی شده بزم من   چه زیبا تقارن در این انجمن
به شامی که باشی در آن مبتلا   چه فرخنده باشد سلام خدا
نخفتن به یلدا به یاد بهشت   چو میلاد عیسی شد اندر سرشت
به یلدا کشیدند تصویر خشت   پرستندگان و سران بهشت
سخن‌پروران و یلان جهان   به زیبایی نام ایرانیان
به یلدای ما نام عیسی رسید   چو نام مسیحا از قلم‌ها چکید
خدایی که به دل آشنا باشدم   که من فخر مهر از خدا باشدم

> Oh night of love, when we remember the dearest
>   when we gather for Yaldā, in the name of the sweetest
> Oh night of companionship, night of veneration
>   in the name of the God of the Word and affection

In his name, the darkness turns into our light
        as God himself becomes our song in the night
How blissful the symmetry of the events
        the birth of Lord Jesus my feast represents
How happily blesses the peace of our God
        the night in which you were intrigued by the thought
Of Jesus's birth which secretly equals
        the waking on Yaldā and heaven's remembrance
The worshippers and the guardians of Eden
        have diamond-like painted Yaldā and proceed in
Their praise for the beautiful name of Iranians
        whose valour and eloquence laud all the nations
When Christ's holy name has sprung from the quill
        the dear name of Jesus let Yaldā fulfil
So we would be honoured to see God's own love
        for he knows our hearts, he who rules from above

The limits of Iranian Christianity (II): *Fāl* and *Fālgiri*

The terms *fāl* and *fālgiri* are best translated to English as 'divination' and broadly describe 'the art or technique of gaining knowledge of future events or distant states by means of observing and interpreting signs' (Omidsalar 1995). Among popular objects serving for the practice of *fāl* are cards (*fāl-e varaq*), coffee grounds (*fāl-e qahweh*) and chick-peas (*fāl-e nokhod*), but first and foremost specific texts. The *Encyclopaedia Iranica* explains in this context:

> Bibliomancy using the *dīvān* of Ḥāfeẓ is the most popular for this kind of divination, but by no means the only kind. The Koran, as well as the *Maṯnawī* of Rūmī may also be used. *Fāl-eḤāfezá* [sic] may be used for one or more persons. In group bibliomancy, the *dīvān* will be opened at random, and beginning with the ode of the page that one chances upon, each ode will be read in the name of one of the individuals in the group. The ode is the individual's *fāl*. (ibid.)

As I have pointed out earlier, the usage of Persian poetry as a means of divination plays a central role on special, national occasions. While the *Iranica* cites *Chahārshanbeh-Suri* as such an occasion, the Yaldā Night could be mentioned as well. The purposeful absence of this practice in celebrations of Iranian Christians is therefore highly significant and would probably come to an Iranian observer's immediate attention.

Iranian Christians have generally situated the practice of *fāl* in the context of 'illicit superstitions' (*khorāfāt*) and ultimately sorcery, witchcraft or black magic (*jādugari*). They have often mentioned *fāl* in the same breath with supposedly related and equally problematic practices like fortune-telling/astrology (*tāle'-bini*), amulet writing (*do'ā-nevisi*), divination through mirrors (*āyineh-khāni/āyineh-bini*), palmistry (*kaf-bini*), the consulting of a Quranic oracle (*estekhāreh*), geomancy (*rammāli*) and so forth. Moreover, the Persian term *fālgiri* verbatim features in different Persian translations of the Bible and therefore enables Iranian Christian pastors and ministers to immediately condemn the practice through the quotation of pertinent verses. In an episode of *Mohabat TV*'s show *The Echo* (*Pezhvāk*), wholly dedicated to the issue of *fālgiri*, one of the three hosts, Jennifer Shamun, read out Deut. 18.10-11 which calls upon its interlocutor to abstain from *fālgiri*, soothsaying (*gheyb-guyi*), geomancy (*rammāli*), witchcraft (*jādugari*) and necromancy (*mashverat bā arvāh-e mordegān*) (Keshish-Ābnus, Shamun and Ansāri 2014: m. 35:33).[8] Shamun then added that rarely ever in the Bible God condemned a practice as bluntly (*rok*) as in the case of *fālgiri*: while her translation used the Persian word *bizār* (disgusted) to describe God's response to such practices, older translations even used the word *makruh*, implying that God harboured a sense of hatred towards them (ibid.). In a different TV channel's show which too exclusively dealt with the topic of *fāl* in one of its episodes, the co-host read out this old translation featuring the term *makruh* to advance the same point as Shamun (Heydari 2014: m. 12:40).

Although some Iranian Christians associate *fālgiri* with the exertion of satanic influence on the individual practicing it (ibid.: m. 5:50), the majority of voices has raised the issue as a supposed remnant of un-Christian cultural practices. The tremendous prevalence of divination and similar practices among Iranians and more broadly among 'Orientals' (*Sharqi-hā*) (Keshish-Ābnus, Shamun and Ansāri 2014: m. 33:02) has generally been acknowledged and bemoaned by Iranian Christians. Regarding the question of where this predilection stemmed from, different suggestions were made in my set of sources. Hormoz Shari'at locates *fālgiri* in the context of Islam when he mentions the practice simultaneously with *estekhāreh*, a sort of oracle inquiry usually involving the Quran, as well as with 'the spirit of the religion of Islam' (*ruh-e mazhab-e Eslām*) (Shari'at 2019: m. 0:39).

Others, such as Fariborz Ansāri, speculate that people out of curiosity began to engage in divination and related practices: what started as a giving in to temptation (*vasvaseh*) could soon become a habit (Keshish-Ābnus, Shamun and Ansāri 2014: m. 42:57). Peymān Shabānlāri, besides slamming professional diviners for economically exploiting their clients, names two different causes supposedly drawing people to *fālgiri*: a lack of identity (*bi-hoviyati*), that is, an unawareness about the fact that they as humans were created in the image of God, and fear (*tars*) (Shabānlāri 2021a, 2021b). The God of Christianity, however, was the God who in his book '366 times' assured humans to 'not fear!' (Shabānlāri 2021b: m. 1:11).

The sources mentioned so far reject *fālgiri* as a generic category. With the exception of the show on *Mohabat TV*, in which Edvin Keshish-Ābnus, Jennifer Shamun and Fariborz Ansāri explicitly reject *fāl-e Hāfez* (and noteworthily also *fāl-e ketāb-moqaddas*, i.e. divination on the basis of the Bible), no explicit mention of the relationship between the beloved Persian poetic tradition and the unwelcome practice of *fālgiri* has been made. Considering that the *Encyclopaedia Iranica* for good reason calls *fāl-e Hāfez* the most popular of all the *fāls*, this has come as somewhat of a surprise. And yet, there is no reason to assume that a generic reference to *fālgiri* should exclude *fāl-e Hāfez*.

Finally, however, in the magazine *Tabdil*, the issue of divination on the basis of Hāfez's poetry is directly targeted. I am referring to two articles here, one of which does not name an author (Tabdil 2006a) and one written by Mohammad Jalil Sepehr (Sepehr 2010). The earlier article, simply entitled 'Hāfez of Shirāz', begins with a praise of Iranian poets and poetry (Tabdil 2006a). Reflecting the Iranian-Islamic binary commonly advanced in Iranian nationalism, it commends the achievements especially of Ferdowsi as a supposed guardian of Iranian language and national identity after 'the attack of the Arabs and the subjugation of Iran to Islam' (*hojum-e Tāziān*[9] *va estilā-ye Eslām bar Irān*) (ibid.). The author then announces that after this 'introduction' (*moqaddameh*), the purpose of which was to highlight the pivotal role of poets among the Iranians, they wanted to get to the 'core issue' (*asl-e mowzu'*) (ibid.). One poet, Hāfez of Shirāz, enjoyed a prophet-like reverence; his main book (the *Divān*) was kept almost invariably in the houses of Iranians who considered it the *lesān-ol-ghayb*, the tongue of the unseen (ibid.). What was truly painful, the author continues, was that many used it for the sake of divination (*az ān fāl migirand*) (ibid.). This was despite the Bible opposing all sorts of divination (ibid.). The article ends with this finding, rather abruptly. The author does not explain what this prohibition was based upon.

In an issue of *Tabdil* published four years later, Mohammad Jalil Sepehr further expounds on the question at stake. His article is entitled with the question 'A Book of Love and Thought, or of Divination and Oracle??? [sic]' and adds a new layer to the discussion in that it argues that Hāfez *himself* would have opposed the (mis)usage of his poetry for divination (Sepehr 2010). To use Hāfez's work for *fālgiri* constituted a 'distortion of his ideas' (*tahrif-e andisheh-ye u*); in reality, Hāfez himself had *combatted* such practices, which in their origins were foreign to Iran (ibid.). Sepehr in his article paints a picture of Hāfez as an 'inviter' to God's revelation and even a preacher of God's good news (*beshārat*) (ibid.).[10] Much resembling the above-mentioned narratives surrounding Iranian poets, especially Hāfez, and their supposed affinities to Christianity, Sepehr implicitly renders Hāfez the archetype of the poet-missionary.

Iranians in the Bible

Thus far, I have treated the Iranian festivals of Nowruz and Yaldā and the usage of Persian poetry as key sites for the construction of an Iranian Christianity. Ultimately, this construction serves the purpose of a thorough inclusion of Iranian Christians in notions of Iranian nationhood. In this section, I am going to deal with Iranian Christians' perceptions of individuals understood to belong to the Iranian nation, which feature in the Bible. Most importantly, these biblical figures include the towering hero of Iranian national self-imagining: King Cyrus the Great, who both seizes an important role in the Old Testament and has been lionized as the iconic embodiment of a virtuous Iranian king by Iranian nationalists (and others). Ali Ansari, who has aptly spoken of the 'cult of Cyrus the Great' (Ansari 2012: 166–78), and other scholars in the field have contributed to a historicization of 'the return of the king' (cf. Marashi 2017). This return has paved the way for the more recent discovery of Cyrus as an icon of resistance against the Islamic Republic of Iran. Discourses on Cyrus the Great thus are a primary example of how Iranian Christian narratives, even in exile, remain attached to sociopolitical developments inside Iran.

The biblical figures identified as Iranians by Iranian Christians surface both in the Old and the New Testaments. Queen Esther and the Prophet Daniel belong to the individuals deemed relevant for the Old Testament; most importantly, however, the Old Testament mentions the Achaemenid kings Cyrus the Great, Cambyses, Darius I, Xerxes I (known in Persian as Khashāyārshā) and Artaxerxes I (Ardashir). A brief anecdote from the limited field research

I was able to carry out in Germany before the Covid-19 pandemic shall serve to demonstrate the immense pride Iranian Christians take in 'their' kings' being featured in the Bible: during a sermon at an Iranian church in Germany, an Iranian Armenian guest preacher asked the present audience whether they knew the names of the Iranian kings mentioned in the Old Testament. After the audience answered successfully, the pastor addressed the interpreter, a bilingual Iranian-born teenager seated at the back of the room with a few Germans, and jokingly advised him to not translate what just was said, lest the Germans get jealous of their Iranian coreligionists.

Cyrus the Great

How Cyrus became an icon

King Cyrus the Great lived around 600–530 BCE and founded the Persian Achaemenid Empire (cf. Dandamayev 1993). His military ventures were vast and successful, making him a ruler over a wide territory from Thrace to Central Asia. After the conquest of Babylonia, Cyrus ended the Jewish captivity and allowed the Jews to rebuild the Jerusalem Temple; this event is celebrated by Jews in the festival of Purim. In 530 BCE, Cyrus was killed during a battle at the Lower Oxus River.

The rise of Cyrus the Great to the position of a primary icon of Iranian-ness is an astonishing one in two ways. Firstly, the discovery of Cyrus as the founder of Iranian monarchy and father of the Iranian nation is fairly recent in occurrence. Ansari, Marashi and Steele in their accounts agree on the fact that it was only in the late nineteenth century that Persianate intellectuals with nationalist propensities first introduced the Achaemenid king to an Iranian audience and stressed his high significance (Ansari 2012: 166–8; Marashi 2017; Steele 2021: 24). In the 1920s, in a history book written by nationalist politician Hasan Pirniā, Cyrus the Great for the first time featured as the 'father of the Iranian nation' (Ansari 2012: 167). Most strikingly, however, the promotion of Cyrus the Great gained pace as a political project of Mohammad Rezā Shah in the 1960s and 1970s. Following Ansari, it was precisely the previous *absence* of Cyrus in Iranian cultural memory – the fact that he offered a 'relatively blank template' – which rendered the figure of the ancient king so valuable to the Shah and his agenda of modernization (ibid.: 175). Mohammad Rezā Pahlavi's government officially recognized the Cyrus Cylinder, a declaration written in the name of Cyrus on a cylinder in the Akkadian language, as the first human rights bill in history (Steele 2021: 1). In 1971, Cyrus the Great was at the centre of the pompous celebrations of 2,500 years of Iranian monarchy, during which Mohammad Rezā Shah addressed his 'earliest predecessor' with a eulogy at Cyrus's tomb at Pasargadae.[11] By associating himself with the figure of Cyrus the Great, Marashi suggests, the Shah endeavoured to achieve the following three political goals: (1) establishing the idea that loyalty to the Iranian nation meant loyalty to the monarchy, as the two became inextricably tied together in the person of Cyrus the Great; (2) representing himself as a true defender of human rights and minorities in times of growing criticism of the Shah's handling of pertaining issues and (3) sending a warning message to neighbouring Iraq, the ancient 'equivalent' of which (Babylonia) Cyrus had triumphantly conquered, while diplomatic tensions were brewing (Marashi 2017: m. 36:15–40:10).

The second astonishing aspect of the Cyrus revival concerns the sources on which it was based. To historians of the ancient period, little is known about the legendary king who notably does not appear in Ferdowsi's *Book of Kings*, the work widely regarded as the Iranian national epos. The textual sources relevant to the reconstruction of Cyrus's biography are 'an amalgam of Greek and Biblical tradition' (Steele 2021: 24). More precisely, it is the ancient Greek historians Herodotus and Xenophon as well as the biblical books of Isaiah, Ezra and the Chronicles that make mention of the Achaemenid king. That in the biblical sources 'Cyrus is regarded with favour' (Dandamayev 1993) is, perhaps unsurprisingly, of central importance to Iranian Christians. In any case, the king's nineteenth century return to the Iranian national stage can be said to have been inspired by his popularity among *European* historians and intellectuals. The European fascination with the figure of Cyrus materialized, for instance, in at least four theatrical plays written about him between the sixteenth and the eighteenth centuries (Steele 2021: 19). No doubt, the discovery of the Cyrus Cylinder by the naturalized British Chaldean archaeologist Hormuzd Rassam in 1879 further sparked this interest. Less than a century later, Cyrus had even entered Iranian pop culture; he was the subject of adventure novels and his tomb and cylinder decorated banknotes and postal stamps.

In the previous chapter, I have described how the revolutionary rejection of Pahlavi nationalism after the 1979 overthrow of the Shah's regime brought with it an uneasy stance towards the Iranian festival of Nowruz. Interestingly, just as a *modus vivendi* was eventually found in the example of Nowruz, the reverence levelled at Cyrus resurfaced on the highest political level in the

Islamic Republic as well. Marashi lists former presidents Rafsanjāni, Khātami and Rowhāni as prominent visitors to the tomb of Cyrus at Persepolis; he also points to 'interesting' remarks about pre-Islamic Iranian history and Persepolis by Supreme Leader Khāmene'i (Marashi 2017: m. 41:21).

No one, however, participated in the 'cult of Cyrus' as extensively as former President Mahmud Ahmadinezhād (in office 2005–13). As illustrated by the case of the aborted 2011 Nowruz party at Persepolis, Ahmadinezhād demonstrated an acute awareness of the popularity of pre-Islamic Iranian motifs among the Iranian population, among them the ubiquitous fascination with Cyrus the Great. In 2010, Ahmadinezhād successfully brokered a loan of the Cyrus Cylinder from the British Museum to Iran – for the first time since the Shah's 1971 celebrations. Cyrus in Ahmadinezhād's reading was 'the epitome of just leadership' and a 'monotheist and just seeking man' (Ansari 2012: 278). Moreover, Ahmadinezhād merged exigencies of daily politics with pre-Islamic cultural resources: Ansari describes a scene from the ceremony introducing the freshly loaned Cyrus Cylinder to the Iranian public in which Ahmadinezhād awards a figure dressed as Kāveh the Blacksmith, a hero from the 'Book of Kings', a Palestinian keffiyeh (ibid.: 279). Thus, the president had the popular figure of Kāveh turn into a pro-Palestinian activist, notably in the presence of the 'first declaration of human rights in history', the Cyrus Cylinder.

Such diverse readings of pre-Islamic Iranian figures, first and foremost Cyrus the Great, demonstrate their adaptability for Iranian narrative-makers of different persuasions. In recent years, Cyrus the Great has evolved into a prominent icon of opposition against the government of the Islamic Republic of Iran. This trend can be observed in the unofficial, annual 'Cyrus the Great Day' during which mostly young[12] Iranians gather at Cyrus's tomb in Persepolis. Such meetings have featured anti-governmental slogans, not rarely with anti-Arab nationalist overtones (see Chapter 5).[13] Slogans directly referring to Cyrus the Great have also been heard at the major uprisings in late 2017 and 2019, during which a considerable number of protestors were killed by governmental security forces. The prevalent chanting of 'Iran is our homeland, Cyrus is our father!' (*Irān vatan-e māst, Kurosh pedar-e māst!*) (Mohammadi 2018) suggests that the invocation of Cyrus has evolved as a universal code of disagreement with the system of the Islamic Republic, the stakeholders of which are deemed to be at odds with the quintessentially Iranian and justly ruling human rights pioneer identified in Cyrus by many. Iranian Christians in exile are by no means disconnected from this discourse.

Cyrus the Great among Iranian Christians: A messiah for the Iranian people

Marcin Rzepka acknowledges the prominence of Cyrus the Great in the perspective of Iranian Christians in his analysis of the Iranian Protestant milieu after the 1979 Revolution. He states:

> They see that without Cyrus they as Iranians would not be who they are: Christians. Kuroš-e Bozorg (Cyrus the Great) linked them with Iranian culture and the Bible, inspiring a personal choice to accept the Christian tradition ... After the revolution and collapse of the monarchy, the Biblical story of the 'anointed Persian king' became an Iranian Christian narrative or rather counter-narrative alternative to the official and Islamic one. (Rzepka 2017: 188)

In what follows, I will further illustrate the (counter-)narrative Rzepka points to. Indeed, the amount of references made to Cyrus the Great in the sources assessed has been very extensive. Even in the English-language monographies by Rezā Safā, Rāmin Pārsā, Daniel Shāyesteh and Hormoz Shari'at, Cyrus the Great has appeared saliently; this suggests that non-Iranian readers who possess a certain familiarity with biblical episodes – and thus potentially with the figure of Cyrus – by the Iranian authors are thought to find it an interesting fact to learn that the much vaunted liberator of the Jews is revered by Iranians as a prominent member (or even the founder) of their nation.

Different churches participate with varying intensity in the 'cult of Cyrus' (Ansari). Two examples in which Cyrus is awarded a noteworthy centrality shall be mentioned here. Firstly, an Iranian church in Apeldoorn, The Netherlands, is named after Cyrus, the *Kores Kerk*, or *Kelisā-ye Kurosh* in Persian. The second example concerns a church to which I have been vastly referring to: Elam Alive Ministries in Essen, Germany, headed by Rozitā and Siāmak Zargari. It seems that at Nowruz 1397 (2018), the church, which in the previous year had celebrated the Nowruz of the year 1396, adopted the Imperial Calendar (*Gāh-Shomāri-ye Shāhanshāhi*) as briefly introduced by the Pahlavi government in 1976. This calendar counts from the accession of Cyrus the Great to the throne in 559 BCE, while the Solar Hejri Calendar, used in Iran before 1976 and again after 1979, starts from the emigration of the Prophet Mohammad from Mecca to Medina (*hejrat*) in 622 CE. Consequently, Iranians in March 1976 found themselves celebrating the Nowruz of 2535 although in March 1975 they had celebrated the Nowruz of 1354.

Similarly, the members of the Germany-based church within a year leaped from 1396 to 2577. Whether its head pastors, the married couple Siāmak and Rozitā Zargari, wished to make a political, pro-royalist statement by the adoption of the Shah's 'Cyrus calendar' remains a matter of speculation. In any event, the calendar change discloses a revering stance on the figure of Cyrus the Great. This attitude has also become clear through Siāmak Zargari's sermons, to which I will turn shortly. Regarding the usage of calendars among Iranian Christians, virtually all of the sources assessed have used either the common Solar *Hejri* calendar or the Gregorian calendar, the latter of course being the common calendar of exiled Iranian Christians' countries of residence. The Imperial 'Cyrus Calendar' of 1976 was only found in one further instance: a short English-language note congratulating on 'Norooz of 2567 (1387)' in a 2008 issue of *Tabdil* (Tabdil 2008b).

Generally, Iranian Christians reproduce the common motifs dominating current popular imaginations of King Cyrus. Among them are Cyrus as pioneer or even inventor of human rights (Parsa 2018: 64; Shabānlāri 2017: m. 5:55), Cyrus as the father of the Iranian nation (Parsa 2018: 48; Zargari and Zargari 2017b: m. 9:39), Cyrus as a just and peaceful ruler (Parsa 2018: 51; Safa 2006: 153; Sharī'at 2018: m. 1:27:19) and Cyrus as the initiator of an uninterrupted 2500-year-long Iranian monarchical tradition (Sharī'at and Ebrāhimiān 2018: m. 6:35; Shayesteh 2012: 30; Zargari and Zargari 2017b: m. 1:38:40). Daniel Shāyesteh also mentions the legacy of Cyrus as a resource to draw upon in opposing the Islamic Republic's government, espousing the nationalist Iranian-Islamic binary:

> It was Islam that guided the heavy hands of Islamic governments to prevent Iranians from relying on the great values of their culture, which cherished individual rights and pushed back Islam's inhumane values. Cyrus the great king left a great legacy for us to resist fascism. This legacy has never been so raised up in the history of Iran since the invasion of Islamists as it was in the time of [*sic*!] Shah. (Shayesteh 2012: 117–8)

How then do Iranian Christian perceptions of Cyrus the Great *differ from* or *add to* the making of Cyrus as it has evolved in Iranian political discourse? As suggested by Rzepka (2017: 188), their particularity lies in the emphasis of biblical representations of Cyrus, first of which is that of him as a messiah, a chosen one or an 'anointed one' (*mash shodeh*).[14] Many Iranian Christians believe that the mission received by Cyrus is ongoing and should concern today's Iranian Christians, who as Cyrus's descendants became the heirs of this mission. This belief segues into the second commonplace perception of Cyrus: that of a spiritual role model. Accordingly, Iranian Christians should become the 'Cyrusses of today'. We will re-encounter this motif several times when engaging with other biblical figures thought of as Iranians. Overall, the stressing of Cyrus's prominence in the biblical tradition should be considered a key strategy in the naturalization of Christianity to the Iranian nation. To demonstrate that the 'father of the Iranian nation' himself was appointed by the Christian God arguably presents a strong narrative making an Iranian-Christian identification plausible.

Introducing the figure of Cyrus the Great, Iranian pastors often assume a sense of familiarity with his personality among the present audience and/or their viewers. Pastor Elnātān Bāghestāni in a 2016 service asked his congregation: 'How many of you know Cyrus the Great?', sarcastically adding 'if you don't know him, you are not Iranian!' (Bāghestāni 2016: m. 1:04:20). The first mentioning of Cyrus the Great is often followed by the introduction of some casual facts, acquainting congregation and viewers with the pivotal role Cyrus supposedly played in the Bible. Most commonly in the assessed set of sources, pastors pointed to the prophecy announcing the coming of Cyrus by name in the book of Isaiah and the claim that the prophecy predated Cyrus's birth by 150 years.[15] Another way to establish an initial association with Cyrus and Christianity is to mention the number of times he was referred to in the Bible – nineteen times, according to Peymān Shabānlāri (2017: m. 15:25).[16]

Most notably, however, the *terms* in which the Bible introduces Cyrus are reiterated with much pride: Siāmak Zargari excitedly tells his audience that Cyrus was the only non-Jewish king in the Bible who was named an 'anointed one', that is, a messiah (*masih*) (Zargari and Zargari 2014: m. 17:17). From here it is only a short leap to direct comparisons of Cyrus with the figure of *the* Messiah, Jesus Christ. Zargari later in the same sermon describes how it was God himself who chose Cyrus's name; this resembled how Mary had had no say in the choosing of Jesus's name (ibid.: m. 22:57). And this was not the only noteworthy aspect of Cyrus's name: the majority of researchers (*bishtar-e mohaqqeqin*) had come to the conclusion, Zargari contends, that *Kurosh* meant 'son of the sun' (*pesar-e khorshid*) (ibid.: m. 23:42). One of the titles (*alqāb*) of Christ was 'sun of justice' (*āftāb-e 'edālat*), he continues; meanwhile, God had called Cyrus to be a beacon of divine justice (ibid.).

The supposed connection between Cyrus and Jesus has also been highlighted by other pastors. In their respective English-language books, Rāmin Pārsā states that 'what Cyrus did for the Jews was a shadow type of what Jesus has done for us' (Parsa 2018: 50), while Hormoz Shari'at avers that 'King Cyrus is a type of Christ'[17] (Shariat 2020: 183). In a Persian-language sermon, Shari'at furthermore contends that, in the Bible, the birth of only two people had been prophesied accurately and by mentioning their name: Cyrus and Jesus (Shariʿat 2018: m. 1:15:15). Finally, one source even claims that Jesus in his last words, the 'Great Commission' of Matthew 28:19-20, alluded to Cyrus (Rāh-e Salib 2016b). Its author points to the edict by Cyrus allowing Jews to return to Israel in order to rebuild their temple, the closing verses of the Hebrew Bible (2 Chron. 36.23) (ibid.). It was not without meaning, the article continues to claim, that Jesus in *his* last words called upon his disciples to spread Christianity all over the world – and, like the returning Jews in the Old Testament, build houses of worship, but this time for all the nations (ibid.).

The mission assigned to Cyrus the Great by God, many Iranian pastors believe, directly translated to a mission for today's Iranians. What began with Cyrus, it is argued, is the starting point of a great divine plan for the Iranian people which will be completed according to the Elam Prophecy (see Chapter 6). Just as Cyrus had been chosen by God, Iranians had been chosen among the nations: the ongoing awakening in Iran, Hormoz Shariʿat suggests, set Iranians apart from other (especially Muslim) nations. As a part of a sermon entitled 'The Anointment of Cyrus for Iran', he says:

> God is working in a peculiar (*ʿajib*) way among Iranians. It is not just me who is saying this, it is the whole world. Do you know what they say? Again and again they are telling me: 'The Iranians are different (*farq mikonand*)! We have travelled to all the countries, especially Islamic countries. In Islamic countries, Muslims don't dare to question their religion, their faith, their [holy] book and their political leaders. But the Iranians are free, they are investigating, they are comparing, they are asking questions!' God has liberated us. All this is from God, let's not think that this is because we Iranians are particularly clever or something! It is the grace of God (*feyz-e Khodā*) ... God has opened the door for Cyrus and now opens it for us. (Shariʿat 2018: m. 1:25:31–1:26:45)

Iranian Christians believe themselves to play a very active role in carrying out God's plan, which had begun with King Cyrus. Pastors have relentlessly called on their brothers and sisters in Christ (and in Cyrus) to embrace the task of transforming Iran and the world. Having identified God's order to Cyrus as equally valid for today's Iranians, Elnātān Bāghestāni asks: 'Are you ready to advance the cause of God? I am' (Bāghestāni 2016: m. 1:15:13). If Iranians, as Rozitā Zargari puts it, are 'the children of Cyrus' (*farzandān-e Korush*), they better be 'good and loyal princes/ses' (*shāhzādegān-e niku o vafādāri*) (Zargari and Zargari 2017b: m. 9:39). Moreover, they ought to become the 'Cyrusses' of the day. Siāmak Zargari addresses his fellow Iranian Christians: 'Cyrusses! Enough sleep, let's awake!'[18] (ibid.: m. 1:53:03). This motif, the idea that Iranian Christians of today were embodiments of their biblical predecessors, likewise comes up in the context of other Iranian-identified figures in the Bible.

Other Iranian kings

Other Iranian-identified kings featuring in the Bible, among them Darius and Xerxes I, can hardly compete in their discursive significance with Cyrus the Great. Simply put, Cyrus overshadows all of them. Whenever other kings were mentioned in the sources, they usually appeared as a joint appendix to Cyrus and rarely were granted a distinct character or narratives of their own. Accordingly, Siāmak Zargari in the same sermon during which he invoked the Cyrusses of the day as well proclaimed that 'God erects the Cyrusses, the Dariusses, the Cambysesses, the Xerxesses and Ardashirs – and not just them, but also the Esthers and Daniels!' (ibid.: m. 2:05:20). Despite their marginal featuring compared to Cyrus, the other four Achaemenid kings have equally been perceived as blessed actors in God's plan. A contributor to *Kalameh* celebrates them as defenders of God's chosen people, the Israelites (Yeqnazar 2003). The parallel mentioning especially of Cyrus and Darius – arguably the second most popular among the mentioned kings – can also be found in a popular Nowruz-themed worship song: 'Cyrus, Darius, and all the kings / Have proclaimed that this day shall be our Nowruz!' (cf. Shariʿat 2020: m. 36:05).

Posing an exception to the overall cursory remarks on the kings succeeding Cyrus the Great, Rāmin Pārsā in his English-language book *From Ashes to Glory: The True Story of a Former Muslim From Iran* dedicates a few more detailed words to King Darius (549–486 BCE; also often referred to as 'the Great') (Parsa 2018: 54–6). His account idealizes Darius as a champion of workers and women's rights, under whose tutelage Persepolis turned into a magnificent city ahead of its time. Pārsā mentions a sophisticated water and drainage system that was 'unparalleled anywhere at the time' and further 'amazing building projects', among them a 1,500-mile-long 'Royal Road' (ibid.: 54–5). More interesting for our present purpose is the religious terms in which Pārsā presents Darius and eventually Xerxes and Artaxerxes (Ardashir): having remarked that Darius's 'rock-cut tomb was carved in the shape of a cross', Pārsā finishes his deliberations on the Achaemenid kings by saying: 'I believe that one day we will see some of these monarchs in heaven since many of them accepted the Lord God of Israel, the only true God' (ibid.: 64). At no point in any of the sources assessed have Cyrus and his successors been honoured with such religiously noble terms. To literally suggest that the ancient Iranian kings had 'accepted' the 'true God of Israel' and thus must have entered heaven amounts to the ultimate 'Christianization' of the mentioned figures. Different from the above-mentioned example of Iranian poets, Pārsā goes beyond a mere insinuation according to which Cyrus and the likes were familiar or maybe sympathized with the 'true God'; instead, they accepted him in the way that Pārsā, the 'former Muslim from Iran' (ibid.: title), had accepted the same God.

The Prophet Daniel and Queen Esther

One could argue that it, as a whole, is an anachronism to use the national epithet Iranian for individuals who were living in ancient times. But even if one was to accept the Achaemenid kings as early members of what was later conceived as an Iranian nation, the labelling of the Old Testament figures of Daniel and Esther as 'Iranian' brings with it yet another set of complexities. Both dwelled in the Achaemenid Empire as Jews in the Babylonian exile. It seems that their geographical connection as well as their ties to the Iranian monarchs, especially in the case of Esther who married Xerxes I, suffices for Iranian Christians to include them into the genre of 'Iranians in the Bible'.

Before I continue to address portrayals of Esther and Daniel in the set of sources used for this book, it should be mentioned that tombs in the names of Esther and Daniel currently exist in the Iranian cities of Susa and Hamadan, respectively. An article in *Tabdil*, after mentioning that Daniel had served at the courts of both Cyrus and Darius, points to his tomb and relates an anecdote according to which the locals after Daniel's death had consciously taken care of his coffin and tomb (Tabdil 2007b). A photo of the mausoleum in Susa has been placed next to the article.

The authenticity of these tombs has been questioned by academic scholarship: Netzer notes in the *Encyclopaedia Iranica* that rabbinical sources maintain that Daniel died *after* returning to Israel (Netzer 1993); likewise, it is only according to *Persian* Jewish tradition that Esther (and her cousin Mordechai) were buried in Hamadan (Netzer 1998). This surely does not affect the pride of Persian Jews for whom the tomb in Hamadan is an important pilgrimage site (ibid.). As for Iranian Christians, the existence of these tombs is yet another argument corroborating an Iranian-Christian identity. The very same is valid for the alleged tomb of the Prophet Habakkuk, although there is 'no evidence that would explain his presence in Iran and his burial in Tuyserkān' (Soroudi 2002).[19]

Two articles in my set of sources speak particularly about Queen Esther, one in the magazine *Rāh-e Salib* (Rāh-e Salib 2016a) and one in the magazine *Smyrna* (Smyrna 2018a). Both texts relate the biblical story according to which Esther saved her people, the Jews, from a planned mass slaughter against them. The unnamed authors praise Esther for her virtuousness, her loyalty to her people and her trust in the God of Israel. While the text in *Rāh-e Salib* suggests that many Persians (*pārsi-hā*) were impressed by Esther's braveness and consequently became 'followers of the one and true God' (*peyrow-e Khodā-ye yegāneh va vāqe'i*), it does not draw a connection between Esther and today's Iranian Christians (Rāh-e Salib 2016a). It thus differs from the (much longer) text in *Smyrna* which, although mainly focussing on Esther's exemplary status as a pious woman, remarks that her connectedness to Iran through her husband King Xerxes 'of Iran' (*Khashāyārshāh-e Irān*) constituted a 'moment of beginning of hope, indicating how valuable we Iranians and Persian-speakers are to God' (Smyrna 2018a: 38).

Representations of Esther among Iranian Christians occasionally emphasize her role model specifically as a *woman*. The cited article from the magazine *Smyrna*, for instance, has appeared as part of a series named 'I am a Woman' (*Man yek zan hastam*).[20] Another notable example of a gendered invocation of Esther as a female believer can be found in the October 2009 issue of *Tabdil*. At the time, two female converts to Christianity, Maryam Rostampur and Marziyeh Amirizādeh, were imprisoned at Tehran's notorious Evin prison.[21] The cover of the issue shows Rostampur and Amirizādeh under the title 'Marziyeh and Maryam, Two Girls from the Stock of Esther (*nasl-e Ester*), the Queen of Iran: Pride of the Persian-Speaking Church'. In the pertaining editorial, Elnātān Bāghestāni condemns the Iranian authorities' treatment of the two women and finishes his statement in the following way:

> It is likewise appropriate that we congratulate these heroic girls who like Esther, the Queen of Ancient Iran, have persevered in their faith and not accepted any compromise just to placate human beings. Dear Maryam and Marziyeh, you make us proud. May the God of the Esthers, Daniels and Cyruses be your refuge and protection and liberate you soon. Amen. (Bāghestāni 2009b: 2)

Iranians in the New Testament

The biblical figures this section has dealt with so far all appear in the Old Testament. With regard to the New Testament, it is two specific passages in which

Iranian Christians retrospectively identify members of the Iranian nation. Both passages serve in the corroboration of the same narrative of authentication: the claim that some of the first Christians in history have in fact been Iranian. The figures in question are firstly the three wise men, also referred to as the Magi, visiting baby Jesus according to the evangelist Matthew (2.1-12); secondly, the mentioned claim is made by pointing to the Parthians, Medes and Elamites present during the event of Pentecost according to the book of Acts 2.9.

The Magi

Mentions of the Magi have been relatively frequent in the sources assessed. The degree of emphasis of their Iranian identity has varied, ranging from an author in *Kalameh* who cautiously and in brackets suggests that the Magi came 'probably from Iran' (*ehtemālan az Irān*) (Rowshan-Zamir 2003), to Peymān Shabānlāri's straightforward assertion that they 'who were the first to witness the birth of that king [Jesus]' were 'our fathers' (Shabānlāri 2019b: m. 13:47). Decades earlier, Hāyk Hovsepiān (d. 1994), in an archived sermon entitled 'The Iranian Magi on the Lookout for Jesus', explained that the Magi most probably originated from Iran, but maybe also Iraq (Hovsepiān 2017: m. 13:05), only to later also call today's Iranian Christians the 'children of the Magi' (*farzandān-e majusiān*) (ibid.: m. 24:39). Thus, a connection is made between the Magi and today's Iranian Christians on the level of biological, or at least symbolical descent.

Going further, Hovsepiān in his sermon draws a parallel between the biblical Magi and today's Iranian Christians in terms of not only their supposed ethnic connection but also their approach to religion. Being Zoroastrian in religion, the Magi were 'truly thirsty' (*teshnegān-e haqiqi*) to find the truth which they finally encountered in Christ (ibid.: m. 24:55). In their spiritual thirstiness, they therefore resembled today's *Muslim-born* Iranian Christians; the Iranian Armenian Hovsepiān contrasted this with the 'nominal [Armenian and Assyrian] Christian minorities' (*aqalliyat-hā-ye esmi-ye Masihi*) who, in his perception, were busy drinking alcohol and gambling and never bothered to even utter the name of Jesus (ibid.: m. 24:17). Much differently, the Magi – and thus implicitly today's Iranian Christians – had been *ahl-e tahqiq*, 'avid researchers' (ibid.: m. 29:15). Through their study of the prophecies in the books of Micah and Daniel, they finally ended up at the stable in Bethlehem (ibid.).

A different pastor, Mozhdeh Shirvāniān, in an article published in *Kalameh* tells that at a conference she recently attended a claim was made that the Magi had been the first Christians in history (Shirvāniān 2006: 2). The (in)validity of the claim aside, what was significant, in her opinion, was the spiritual heritage (*mirās-e rowhāni*) bequeathed upon today's Iranian Christians by the Iranian Magi as well as by many other Iranians in the Bible (ibid.). This spiritual heritage was reason to be proud, even if the world overall did not cherish a legacy of this kind too much (ibid.). But more than just grounds for pride, the heritage should guide Iranian Christians in how they behaved in the *future*: 'On this path, let us follow the example of the Esthers, Daniels, the Iranian Magi and Iranian Christians of the preceding generations and let us carefully examine their points of weakness and strength so that we may benefit as far as possible from our spiritual heritage' (ibid.: 2). In this statement, we re-encounter pluralized Esther and Daniel – certainly, Shirvāniān could have just as well added Cyrus and his fellow Achaemenid monarchs. The last group mentioned by Shirvāniān, that of Iranian Christians from the preceding generations, may refer to the individuals commemorated as Martyrs of the Iranian Church, to whom I will turn at the end of this chapter.

Despite this great pride in the Magi and their legacy among Iranian Christians, a certain controversy seems to surround those 'three wise men'. What kind of 'wise men' were the Magi, who in Modern Persian are either called *majus(ān/iān)* or *moghān*? It is worthwhile to briefly leave the context of Iranian Christianity and unravel the roots of the ambiguities the term 'Magi' produces. The word 'Magi' has entered the English Bible as a Latin plural of the term *magus*. Ultimately, the word can be traced beyond European antiquity and has been 'attested in Old Persian, Elamite, Akkadian, Aramaic, Parthian, and Sasanian documents' (Dandamayev 2000). In Arabic, the term *majūs* has often been used to (derogatively) denote Zoroastrians and their priesthood; the Bible in Arabic uses the same term (or *al-mulūk al-majūs*, the Magi kings) to denote the Magi. However, Dandamayev in his painstaking entry in the *Encyclopaedia Iranica* emphasizes that the relationship with Zoroastrianism of the Magi who 'were the official priests of the Achaemenid kings' is disputed among scholars in the field – just as the question of whether the Achaemenid kings themselves can be justifiably labelled Zoroastrians (ibid.). Later, the term can also be found to describe 'conjurers, sorcerers, and soothsayers' or 'wise men' (ibid.). Thus, in English-language Christian traditions, one nowadays finds the cognate 'Magi' alongside other, more circumscribing translations, most famously 'the three wise men'.

That the three mysterious visitors to newborn Jesus could have been Zoroastrian priests seems to be easily acceptable and even welcome to

Iranian Christians. We have seen earlier that Hāyk Hovsepiān indeed has identified the biblical Magi as Zoroastrians. However, their identification with conjurers, sorcerers and soothsayers may stir a certain unease, given the vociferous rejection of all sorts of magic (and note the etymological roots of the term 'magic'!) that we have encountered in the context of divination. An article by Maryam Dāneshvar in *Kalameh* tries to shed light on these uncertainties, given that the terms *majusi* and *mogh* have 'occupied the minds especially of Christians' due to their affinity to astrology (*tāle'-bini*)[22] (Dāneshvar 2006: 24). After a short etymological assessment, the article concludes that the Magi as 'the wise men of their time' (*mardān-e hakim-e ān dowrān*) pursued all the acknowledged sciences (ibid.: 25). There was no point in denying that this naturally included the practicing of astrology (ibid.). However, this was only one side of the story. Coming from the land in which the Prophet Daniel had been active centuries earlier, the Magi were also familiar with Jewish literature and especially Daniel's prophecies (ibid.). That they ended up travelling to Bethlehem was therefore not just based on their activity as astrologers (ibid.). Dāneshvar then lauds the three wise men as 'seekers of truth' (*juyandegān-e haqiqat*), almost literally complying with Hāyk Hovsepiān's sermon mentioned earlier.[23] Finally, the Magi, according to Dāneshvar, symbolically stood for the many non-Jews who later came to Jesus and 'accepted him as their God' (ibid.).

Iranians at the event of Pentecost

The three Magi seize a central place in Christian tradition. A whole set of customs and stories in diverse cultures have emerged on the basis of their biblical mention. It is, perhaps, for this reason that they are given a fairly prominent position in the genre of Iranians in the Bible. Regarding the Iranians supposedly present at the event of Pentecost, all that is there is a brief biblical mention of 'Parthians and Medes and Elamites' alongside a host of other peoples, such as 'residents of Mesopotamia, Judea and Cappadocia, Pontus and Asia' or 'Cretans and Arabians' (Acts 2.9-11). At least, however, the Iranian-identified Parthians, Medes and Elamites are listed *first* among the other groups. This seems to be the reason for which Hormoz Shari'at in his book *Iran's Great Awakening: How God Is Using a Muslim Convert to Spark Revival* in reference to Acts 2.9 declares that 'the first three people groups who responded to the Gospel … were all Iranians' (Shariat 2020: 182). It was believed that they, having accepted Christ, returned to where they came from and laid the foundation of Christianity in Iran (Shari'at and Ebrāhimiān 2018: m. 13:07).

Dissident martyrs: Commemorating the 'Martyrs of the Iranian Church'

The final narrative of authentication I would like to illustrate in this book is the commemoration of the 'Martyrs of the Iranian Church'. Again, this narrative must be contextualized: notions of martyrdom have been central to discourses on Iranian nationhood in revolutionary Iran. Iranian politicians and clerics have utilized the significance of martyrdom in Shi'ite Islam to postulate a continuity from the martyrs of Kerbela to, for instance, killed demonstrators during the run-up to the 1979 Revolution or Iranian soldiers who perished during the Iran-Iraq war which lasted from 1980 to 1988.

Scholars like Michael J. Fischer and Kamran S. Aghaie have pointed to the reactivation of the Kerbela narrative in the modern political context (Aghaie 2004: x–xii; Fischer 1980: 13–21); thus, the 'Yazids' and 'Hoseyns' of the current moment can be branded and pitted against each other as evil versus virtuous and oppressor versus martyr. A pantheon of prominent martyrs has emerged in the Islamic Republic and entered school curricula as well as popular culture (see Figure 5). The martyrs' faces also can be seen on public squares and busy street corners, exhorting the populace to be mindful of their honourable examples. Even the revolutionary national anthem proclaims: 'Oh martyrs! Your screams echo in the ear of time!'

The supposed moral superiority of the state-promoted martyrs, however, does not remain unchallenged. As anthropologist Shahla Talebi has put it, the position of the 'state martyrs' is questioned by 'dissident martyrs' (Talebi 2012).

Figure 5 Scenes from a children's book narrating the story of a 'martyr' killed during the Iran-Iraq War. In Mirkiāyi (2015).

Naturalizing Christianity (II) 131

Figure 6 Portraits of the 'Martyrs of the Iranian Church'. In *Smyrna* 29 (2018: 30–3).

While Talebi is mainly concerned with leftist dissidents, the 'stark contrast between the hyper-visibility of the "state martyrs" vis-à-vis the discriminatory invisibility and lack of recognition of the "dissident martyrs"'[24] (ibid.: 122) likewise applies to the Iranian Protestant pastors murdered between 1979 and 1996/2005. As victims of the very state that lays claim to the authority over who is admitted as a true martyr and who is not, they offer an alternative canon of martyrs. The collective commemoration of the 'Martyrs of the Iranian Church', irrespective of their affiliation with different Protestant churches, is a regular feature of Iranian Christian exile magazines (see Figure 6).

The catalogue of the 'Martyrs of the Iranian Church' usually consists of Arastu Sayyāh (1928–1979; Anglican), Bahrām Dehqāni-Tafti (1955–1980; Anglican), Hoseyn Sudmand (1951–1990; Pentecostal), Mehdi Dibāj (1935–1994; Pentecostal), Hāyk Hovsepiān (1945–1994; Pentecostal), Tateos Mikā'eliān (1932–1994; Presbyterian) and Mohammad Bāqer 'Ravānbakhsh' Yusefi (1964–1996; Pentecostal). More recent articles, for instance in *Smyrna*, also list the Iranian Turkmen house church leader Qorbān Turāni (1952–2005) (Smyrna 2018b: 30). Occasionally, it is emphasized that, next to the established canon of martyrs, a number of 'lost martyrs' (*shohadā-ye gomnān*) existed; 'Isā Dibāj uses this term, for instance, for Arastu Sayyāh's father who, like his son, converted to Christianity and was murdered, but usually does not appear in Iranian Christian martyrologies (Dibāj 2005b: 8). Similarly, the Christians killed during the Sassanid period can be retrospectively viewed as martyrs of the Iranian church, provided one absorbs the 'Nestorian' Church of the East into one national 'Iranian Church' (cf. Shāgerd 2015).

Iranian Christian martyrs as role models in faith

Another letter to the editors of *Kalameh* shall help us to better understand the significance of the regular promotion of an Iranian Christian martyrology. Under the title 'The Reconciliation of Christianity and Iranian Culture' (*Āshti-ye Masihiyyat va Farhang-e Irāni*), a reader named Farhād addresses the editors of *Kalameh* and refers to the series 'An Overview of the Lives of the Martyrs of the Iranian Church' (*Moruri bar Zendegi-ye Shohadā-ye Kelisā-ye Irān*):

> By reading 'The Lives of the Martyrs of Iran', I have understood that, although these people were normal humans, they even under difficult conditions remained steadfast in their faith and have demonstrated that his [God's] grace is enough. Seeing this kind of people increases the belief and self-confidence of us Christian Iranians, for we comprehend that we have role models (*nemuneh*)

among ourselves and do not need to search for them anywhere else. Role models that, like us, were Iranian and come from a similar cultural background, so we can establish a connection with them. (Kalameh 2005: 14)

The discourses surrounding the collective mentioning of the Iranian Christian martyrs thus strengthen the self-confidence of Iranian Christians. The biographies of the 'Martyrs of the Iranian Church' and their stories are immediately relatable to other Iranian Christians, especially converts from Islam. Photos, recordings of their sermons and worship songs as well as the presence of their children, many of which are prominent faces in the Iranian Christian milieu, create a sense of personal familiarity with the martyred pastors. As Farhād points out in his letter, they become role models in their steadfast belief, even in times of hardship.

As discussed in Chapter 1, the main way of discrimination against leaders of Persian-speaking churches inside Iran since the 2010s has been prison sentences. Extrajudicial killings and trials calling for the death penalty have mainly been a phenomenon of the 1990s. Nevertheless, as can be imagined, leaders especially of the Pentecostal *Jamā'at-e Rabbāni* churches, after the horrifying events of the 1990s, have been very conscious of the potentially severe consequences their continuing activities could have. Robert Āseriān, who served as a reverend at the Tehran *Jamā'at-e Rabbāni* church until its closure in 2013, in an English-language interview explained that, from the beginning of his service, he was aware that 'sooner or later' the fate of his murdered predecessors could befall him as well (Āseriān and Nettleton 2020: m. 21:05). He and his colleagues considered this danger a 'part of our ministry … as Iranian leaders' (ibid.: m. 21:17).

While mentally preparing for times of hardship, Āseriān, who in 2012 spent four weeks in solitary confinement at Evin prison, emphasized the importance of one's 'relationship with the Lord' (ibid.: m. 22:42). Furthermore, however, he also cited the immense importance of 'having that role models [the Martyrs of the Iranian Church]' and of being well aware of 'the legacy and the tradition you are in' (ibid.: m. 22:25). Āseriān and his family now are exiled to the UK where he works at PARS Theological Centre.

Persecution and martyrdom as evidence to Christian awakening

Aside from their functioning as role models, the Iranian Christian martyrs also ascertain other Iranian Christians of what they believe is an ongoing spiritual awakening in Iran. 'Isā Dibāj points out:

> Throughout the history of Christianity, the persecution and discrimination (*jafā va āzār*) of Christians has always resulted in the further growth of the Church. Our dear country Iran is by no means an exception to this principle. In the words of Tertullian, the outstanding thinker of the church: 'The blood of the martyrs is the seed of the Church.' (Dibāj 2004b)

Persecution and martyrdom here become a necessary step on the path to the Christianization of Iran. Suffering for the Christian faith, be it through mere discrimination, imprisonment or martyrdom, is read as evidence to the genuineness of the Christian movement in Iran. The Iranian Christian martyrs become paradigmatic examples of virtue – not much unlike the 'state martyrs'. Their commemoration is also pursued outside of Iranian Christian magazines. In the case of Hāyk Hovsepiān, arguably the most prominent of the martyrs, a memorial service in his honour was celebrated in Glendale, CA, on the twentieth anniversary of his death (cf. Hovsepiān 2014).

Conclusion

This chapter has explored the key sites in which Iranian Christians in exile construct an Iranian-Christian identity. Previous literature has occasionally mentioned Persian poetry as a central element in the religious practice of Iranian Christians. I have added to the existing secondary works by describing the narratives surrounding eminent Persian poets in Iranian exile churches. Having pointed to the conscious promotion of Persian poets as 'embodiments of the national Iranian spirit' (Vejdani 2015: 146) in discourses on Iranian nationhood, I have illustrated how Iranian Christians present poets like Sa'di, Rumi and especially Hāfez as inclined towards Christianity.

Back in Iran already, Iranian Christians composed Persian poetry with Christian motifs and used it in their services. This tradition continues in exile. Poems function in manifold ways, for example, as prayers, means of worship and to attract potential converts. Some Iranian Christian poets believe that God has provided them with an exceptional gift for writing and recitation of poetry. I have used the term 'poet-missionary' to denote the tendency of some Iranian Christian poets to consciously utilize their poetic talent as a culturally sensitive tool for proselytism, targeting non-Christian Iranians residing abroad as well as Iran-based viewers of Iranian Christian online material.

Later, this chapter has discussed Iranian Christian perceptions of Iranian-identified figures featuring in the Bible. Most noteworthy among these figures is King Cyrus the Great; again, the fascination with the Achaemenid king must be seen within the wider political discourse of contemporary Iran where Cyrus has evolved as an icon of resistance against the Islamic Republic's government. The prominence of Cyrus in the biblical tradition and the terms in which he is presented render him a beacon of pride and hope for Iranian Christians in exile. Revered as the 'father of the Iranian nation' by Iranians irrespective of their religious inclinations, Iranian Christian narratives about Cyrus are a central theme in making of an Iranian Christianity.

Other biblical personalities referred to by Iranian Christians include the Prophet Daniel, Queen Esther and the Magi. Through the labelling of the Magi as 'our fathers', Iranian pastors aspire to 'Iranize' the legendary first visitors to newborn Jesus. On a related note, my set of sources suggests that there also is a tendency among Iranian Christians to 'Christianize' prominent *contemporary* Iranians. A relevant example is a *Kalameh* article that speculates whether Nedā Āghā Soltān (1982–2009), the student who developed into an icon of the 2009 protest movement after she was shot dead at a demonstration, could have been 'one of the hundreds of thousands hidden Christians in our country' (Dibāj 2009b).[25] Earlier, a photo showing the young woman with a cross necklace was circulating online.

Finally, the regular commemoration of the 'Martyrs of the Iranian Church' serves as a narrative of authentication. Series on the murdered Iranian Protestant pastors in magazines like *Kalameh* and *Smyrna* constitute an endeavour to establish an alternative catalogue of 'dissident martyrs' (Talebi 2012) who died because of their opposition to the Islamic Republic. In this sense, discourses on the 'Martyrs of the Iranian Church' represent a direct reaction to the Iranian government's promotion of martyrs who passed away in their defence of the Islamic Republic.

In summary, the discourses described in this and the previous chapters are the main themes encountered in Iranian Christian exile churches when the issue of Iranian national identity is raised. They serve the boosting of the national self-confidence of Iranian Christians who can cite them when the authenticity of their Iranian-Christian identity is questioned and Christianity is presented as 'foreign' to Iran. Moreover, casual conversations I had with Iranian Christians during visits to churches in Germany and the UK suggest that especially the narratives surrounding 'Iranians in the Bible' can also function as a means of justification in encounters between Iranian Christians and *non-Iranian*

Christians. Accordingly, a young Iranian man talking to me at an Iranian church in Southern Germany, who once he identified me as a German well-acquainted with Iran and the Persian language, asked me: 'How is it possible that German Christians are completely unaware of the tremendous role Iranians like King Cyrus played in the Bible?'

Another topic featuring prominently in Iranian Christian exile churches and – maybe even more so – in encounters especially of Muslim-born Iranian Christians and non-Iranians is Islam. A portrayal of the Iranian Christian exilic milieu would be incomplete without a discussion of discourses on Islam among Iranian Christians. Furthermore, Islam is *the* contested entity in Iranian nationalism and thus immediately relevant to discussions of the nexus between religion and nationalism in the Iranian context. Therefore, Chapter 5 treats representations of Islam among Iranian Christians.

5

Critical engagement with Islam between expatriation, non-Islamiosity and Islamophobia

Introduction

The vast majority of Iranian Christians today are Muslim-born converts. I consciously speak of 'Muslim-*born* converts' rather than 'Muslim converts' to avoid implying that the individuals in question, before their conversion, necessarily had an affirmative stance on their Muslim identity. Four decades of Islamism have rendered many Iranians tired of Islam, or even of religion altogether, as alluded to in the introduction. While some may cling to their Muslim identity, arguing that the state-promoted version of Islam was a flawed one, others immediately identify the injustices occurring in the Islamic Republic of Iran with the 'actual nature' of the religion of Islam.

This 'image crisis of Islam' certainly is one of the reasons behind the increased interest of Iranians in Christianity. In the opinion of an Iranian Christian refugee speaking on the website IranWire, the restrictions implemented by the Iranian Islamist government towards dissenting ideologies and religions, among them Evangelical Christianity, stirred a certain curiosity among some Iranians precisely *because* of their forbiddenness (IranWire 2022: m. 43:20). Rzepka advances a similar thought when he states that 'in a country that called itself the Islamic Republic … [c]onversion is a means of protest' (Rzepka 2017: 188). To validate or falsify such hypotheses, a thorough study of conversion trajectories would be necessary, the material for which is abundantly available.

In this book, however, I am concerned with the intersection of religion and nationhood in a diasporic setting. The previous two chapters described the 'naturalization' of Christianity to the Iranian nation. One could assume that, if Iranian Christians deem Christianity well suited for Iranians, they may concomitantly deny the suitability of Islam and advance the 'expatriation of Islam'. Indeed, discourses considering Islam a foreign entity to Islam occasionally surface among Iranian Christians who, in making this point, can amply draw on an established intellectual tradition in Iranian nationalism. Nevertheless, discourses on Islam among Iranian Christians are more complex and multifaceted.

Their complexity requires me to, before entering the primary material relevant to this chapter, introduce two further analytical concepts serving to frame critical discourses on Islam: non-Islamiosity and Islamophobia. The former concept was suggested by sociologist Reza Gholami in his study of the Iranian diaspora in London (Gholami 2016); it thus is quite specific to the Iranian context. Islamophobia, much differently, during the past two decades has evolved into an influential analytical tool, both in academia and beyond, to describe anti-Muslim hostilities, usually in settings where Muslims constitute a minority.

After introducing these two concepts, I will separately analyse the Persian-language and the English-language material used for this book. As shall become apparent, critical references to Islam in the Persian-language material are quite specific to the Iranian context. Pastors here speak *as Iranians to fellow Iranians* who were socialized in the Islamic Republic of Iran and are well-acquainted with the specifics of Shi'ite Islam. Much differently, in the English-language sources, Iranian pastors address a non-Iranian audience, presumably comprised in its majority by American Evangelicals. Their main goal here is the 'unmasking' of the true nature of Islam about which they claim to speak authoritatively, given their personal past as (radical) Muslims. In their English-language books, Iranian Christian pastors assume the role of 'crown witnesses' (Shooman 2014) or 'career apostates' (Foster 1984) and promote a discourse resembling that of other outspoken ex-Muslims appearing in the Western media.

Critical discourses on Islam: Two conceptual tools

Non-Islamiosity

Earlier chapters of this book have referred to the binary, Islamic-Iranian view of history characterizing a particular strand in Iranian nationalism. Proponents of this binary hold that Iranian nationhood could most authentically be found in the pre-Islamic era. They view Islam as a foreign, Arab force which was imposed upon 'Aryan' Iranians against their will and ultimately corrupted their national identity. Historian Reza Zia-Ebrahimi has termed this type of nationalism 'dislocative nationalism', explaining:

> Dislocation here refers to an operation that takes places in the realm of the imagination, an operation whereby the Iranian nation is dislodged from its empirical reality as a majority-Muslim society situated – broadly – in the 'East'. Iran is presented as an Aryan nation adrift, by accident, as it were, from the rest of its fellow Aryans (read: Europeans). (Zia-Ebrahimi 2016: 5)

Throughout his book, Zia-Ebrahimi strongly emphasizes the Orientalist legacy in dislocative nationalism – an argument subject to ongoing discussions in scholarly literature on Iranian nationalism.[1] Be that as it may, what is important for the topic of this book is the current popularity the Islamic-Iranian binary wields among Iranians. According to Zia-Ebrahimi, dislocative nationalism 'since the 1980s … has become the most conventional form of secular opposition to the Islamic Republic' (ibid.: 3).

A most instructive study about ongoing uses of dislocative nationalism has been provided by sociologist Reza Gholami who conducted ethnographic field research in the Iranian diaspora of London. Because Gholami's study was published before Zia-Ebrahimi's 2016 book, it does not directly refer to Zia-Ebrahimi's work and his concept of dislocative nationalism. Instead, Gholami proposes the rather clunky[2] concept of 'non-Islamiosity', defining it as 'a mode of the secular by means of which some Iranian Shi'a construct, live and experience diasporic identity, community and consciousness in a way that marginalises, excludes or effaces (only) Islam – it aims to eradicate "the Islamic" from "the Iranian"' (Gholami 2016: 6).

Gholami covers a wide range of examples in which non-Islamiosity surfaces among Iranians in London: its enactment ranges from the abandonment of the 'Arabic/Islamic' greeting *Salām* in favour of the supposedly purely Persian *Dorud*, to decorative writings in Old Persian cuneiform in Persian restaurants, and satirical stage performances portraying the Muslim faith of an Iranian villager as a disease needing to be cured (cf. ibid.). Another relevant area is name giving and name changing practices, where 'Islamic-sounding' names are avoided or discarded in favour of Persian or 'Western' names. Non-Islamiosity, alongside its roots in dislocative nationalism, thus can also be a reaction to experiences of marginalization because of Islamophobia (cf. ibid.: 57–78).

Since the Islamic Republic has failed to live up to its own promises of freedom and social justice, many Iranians see the non-islamious narrative confirmed and consider the Islamic Republic of Iran 'an inevitable outcome of the "misguided" religion of Islam' (ibid.: 8). Identifying the Iranian regime as 'arabophile' due to not only its Islamism but also its foreign policies, protestors draw upon the non-islamious paradigm in their slogans, as I have mentioned when discussing 'Cyrus the Great Day' in the previous chapter. Proponents of non-Islamiosity, noteworthily, equate Islam and 'Arab-ness' and deny the possibility of any positive synergies between Iranian culture and the Islamic religion. This notion should be kept in mind for the discussion of Iranian Christian references to Islam in this chapter.

Islamophobia

The term 'Islamophobia' has been trending during the past two decades in the media, politics and academia. Garner and Selod have recorded the number of scholarly articles featuring the term in their title between 1980 and 2012, finding a long 'first wave' of Islamophobia studies after 9/11 (Garner and Selod 2015: 10). In 2012, the *Islamophobia Studies Journal* was launched under the editorship of Hatem Bazian; furthermore, a detailed and regularly updated international bibliography of Islamophobia under the tutelage of Armin Muftic exists which in 2016 counted more than 1,100 titles (cf. Hafez 2018: 212).

During the past two decades, the concept of Islamophobia has undergone a significant transformation: initially describing a form of prejudice against Islam – defined by a 'closed view', as the pioneering[3] Runnymede Trust Report put it (Runnymede Trust 1997: 4) – the term today is overwhelmingly used to denote a specific anti-Muslim racism (cf. Hafez 2018; cf. Zempi and Awan 2019: 7). Accordingly, Islamophobia targets Muslims as racialized individuals whose behaviour is thoroughly dictated by 'the culture of Islam', understood as a monolithic, unchanging entity. Individual agency and the impact of other factors unrelated to Islam, such as class or gender, are denied. The re-conceptualization of Islamophobia as anti-Muslim racism takes strong cues from post-colonial thinkers like Stuart Hall and Étienne Balibar who proposed the notion of a neo-racism 'without races' (Balibar 1991; Hall 1989). Neo-racism replaces the notion of 'race' with 'culture' while retaining its underlying logic. It has therefore been referred to as 'cultural racism' or 'culturalism'. That said, biological features continue to play a role in cultural racism, as can be observed in practices like racial profiling.

At least in the anglophone world, Islamophobia has become a well-accepted paradigm, attended to by politicians, activists and others. Nevertheless, a number of critical questions persist. Firstly, the term 'Islamophobia' is etymologically misleading, considering that it is used to denote an active hostility rather than a passive, irrational anxiety. Interestingly, the 1997 Runnymede Trust Report already seems to have been conscious of this issue, calling the term 'not ideal' (Runnymede Trust 1997: 1). Following Nathan C. Lean, to maintain the term 'Islamophobia' can be a pragmatic choice since the protracted debate of the term's (in)aptness played into the hands of those denying the phenomenon as a whole (cf. Lean 2019). However, in other languages, among them German, the term 'Islamophobia' has been largely replaced by 'anti-Muslim racism' (*antimuslimischer Rassismus*) in official discourse.

A second major question is how far into the past Islamophobia can serve an analytical tool. Are medieval anti-Islamic polemics and early modern Orientalist discourses forms of Islamophobia? The majority of scholars disagree with such a broad definition of Islamophobia. Yasemin Shooman, though acknowledging the long-standing legacy of some anti-Muslim tropes, concludes:

> It would nevertheless be wrong to assume simple continuities and a linearity in European perceptions of Islam and Muslims since the Middle Ages to the present day. In order to thwart such essentialist notions, it is of vital importance to link an analysis of anti-Muslim discourses to space and time and contextualise them. (Shooman 2014: 17)

Along similar lines, Skenderovic and Späti emphasize that the rise of Islamophobia had to be dated to the 'new geopolitical context of the post-Cold War era' in the 1990s; it was linked to 'questions of global mobility and security issues' and did 'not therefore converge with the history of Orientalism' (Skenderovic and Späti 2019: 136). This qualification appears necessary for Islamophobia to remain a concept of sharp conceptual value. As we shall see, Iranian pastors in their English-language publications connect anti-Muslim discourses with security issues, especially in the context of immigration to the West.

Further contested issues in Islamophobia Studies include the question of whether Islamophobia was akin to or distinct from anti-Semitism,[4] as well as debates regarding the uses of Islamophobia in Muslim-majority contexts (cf. Bayraklı, Hafez and Faytre 2019). The latter discussion can become a linking element with the concept of non-Islamiosity. Although Gholami consciously demarcated non-Islamiosity from Islamophobia (cf. Gholami 2016: 15–18), I would still argue that the two can be mutually constitutive. I will cite examples for this tendency later in this chapter.

Unmasking Islam for non-Iranians: The English-language monographs

The positionality of ex-Muslims: Crown witnesses and career apostates

Different from the Persian-language material assessed for this book, Iranian pastors in English-language books explicitly speak as former Muslims. Through their personal biographies, they seek to claim a position of expertise on Islam and present themselves as predestined to disclose to their readership, presumably in their majority (American) Evangelicals, the 'true nature' of Islam. This emphasis on the positionality as former 'insiders' has been acknowledged in previous research. Shooman specifically points to the role of ex-Muslim women who have presented their dramatic individual stories as a representative view into the supposedly hidden 'world of Islam' (cf. Shooman 2014: 100–23). Some of them have consequently been courted on national television where they were introduced as general experts of Islam and Islamic culture. Following Shooman, it is essential for researchers to critically assess pertaining narratives without automatically accusing the narrators of pandering to their audience (ibid.: 122).

Thirty years earlier, Lawrence Foster in a critical assessment of ex-Mormons Jerald and Sandra Tanner used the term 'career apostates' to describe the Tanners' vociferous activism against their former religious community (Foster 1984). The term, albeit provocative, can certainly be well applied to some ex-Muslim activists. Foster's definition, 'individuals who have devoted their lives to the task of trying to destroy a faith in which they once deeply believed', however, comes across as slightly martial (ibid.: 36–7). Whether or not the Iranian pastors cited in what follows wish to 'destroy' Islam is not of concern as much as their repeated emphasis of their positionality as former *radical* Muslims.

Regarding previous research, there has been relatively little written on outspoken ex-Muslims who in addition to renouncing Islam have embraced Christianity. Larsson has assessed an interview with Swedish Muslim-born convert to Christianity Mona Walter who, as well adopting an expert role on Islam, engages in partially Islamophobic discourse (Larsson 2016). Marti's extensive field research in a US evangelical church headed by a pastor with a Pakistani Muslim background has produced quite a different result: in his example, the pastor went 'out of his way to alleviate the possible fears of his members, new attendees, and visitors, which are rooted in Islamophobia' (Marti

2016: 267). That acknowledged, he too used his status as a former Muslim to speak from a position of authority (ibid.: 262). Most interesting is Christopher Cameron Smith's study of the work of ex-Muslim converts to Christianity Walid Shoebat, Kamal Saleem, Ergun Caner and Emir Caner (Smith 2014). Smith remarks that the four men 'have used their "Muslim-sounding" names and alleged biographies to become … experts claiming an "insider" status aimed at bolstering their credibility' (ibid.: 79). They have actively utilized their backgrounds to present themselves as former Muslim radicals whose task now was to warn the American public of the 'dangers of Islam' (ibid.: 77). Alongside their best-selling books, they have 'appeared on TV news, and have given speeches in front of critical audiences including law enforcement, military, and other government personnel' (ibid.: 91). I shall return to Smith's article when illustrating depictions of Islam in the English-language books of the four Iranian pastors discussed.

Rezā Safā, Daniel Shāyesteh, Rāmin Pārsā and Hormoz Shari'at – the four pastors I am concerned with here – describe their personal biographies in their books. Their conversions happened in different settings: while Safā, Shāyesteh and Shari'at converted after emigrating from Iran (Safa 2006: 53; Shariat 2020: 19; Shayesteh 2012: 193), Pārsā recounts he had converted in Iran already, after watching Iranian Christian satellite TV (Parsa 2018: 24). Pārsā, Safā and Shari'at today reside in the United States, while Shāyesteh settled in Australia. Especially Safā and Shari'at can be considered pioneers of Iranian Christian satellite TV, having started their activities in the early 2000s and today being head pastors of *TBN Nejat TV* and *Shabakeh7*, respectively. All four pastors also beyond their English-language books are active on the English-language Evangelical media, often talking about Islam, as they do in their books.

The mentioning of a supposedly radical Muslim past is given in all of the four Iranian authors' books, albeit to varying degrees. This emphasis is most pronounced in Rezā Safā's books. In 1996, Safā published a book entitled *Inside Islam: Exposing and Reaching the World of Islam* in which he repeatedly described himself as a former 'fanatical Muslim' (Safa 1996: 10, 70). His 2006 book *The Coming Fall of Islam in Iran* introduces Safā as a former 'devout Shi'ite Muslim' on the cover; he himself points out that he used to be a 'hateful Muslim' (Safa 2006: 70). This, he self-consciously contends, was secure proof for his expertise on Islam: 'I know that I know Islam. I was a radical Muslim and well versed in the law and the spirit of this religion' (ibid.: 102). His ostensible insider knowledge was to be preferred over knowledge attainable through the academic study of Islam:

> To really understand the religion of Islam, one must be born into it and spend time practicing the laws and ordinances of the religion. To be honest with you, I am hesitant to read books on Islam written by authors who were not born into a truly radical Muslim family. (ibid.: 25)

Differing voices of 'outsiders' can thus be dismissed *a priori*. What Safā presented was 'more than just book knowledge' (ibid.: 30). Rāmin Pārsā, author of *From Ashes to Glory: The True Story of a Former Muslim from Iran* and likewise born into a 'devoutly Shi'ite Muslim family' (Parsa 2018: 1), concurs with Safā:

> What humbly qualifies me to talk about Islam is the fact that I lived and breathed it for nineteen years, not in democratic America, but in war-torn Iran where I was born, just a few years after the hostile takeover of the Ayatollah Khomeini and halfway into the Iran-Iraq War of the 1980s. (ibid.: xiii)

Pārsā thus establishes his claim to a position of authority at the very beginning of his book. While he does not point to his former Muslimness as redundantly as Safā, he mentions it when necessary to bolster his authority, especially to reject voices of dissent: 'I disagree with people who differentiate between radical Islam and true Islam. As an ex-Muslim, I'm giving you an accurate perspective on Islam and its tenets based on facts' (ibid.: 116).

Daniel Shāyesteh, whose autobiographical book was published under the title *The House I Left Behind: A Journey from Islam to Christ* in 2012, is presented in less sensationalist terms: the cover of his book begins his introduction by stating that he was 'raised a practicing Muslim in Iran' (Shayesteh 2012: cover). It is especially his personal story as an active revolutionary who even ran as a candidate in parliamentary elections, which suggests the image of a 'former radical' to the reader. This presentation is corroborated by photos showing Shāyesteh with his wife (who at the time wore a black chador), during the Islamic ritual prayer and as a member of the revolutionary organization *Jehād-e Sāzandegi* (Jihad of Construction). The photos are each captioned, some with sensationalist remarks, such as 'Daniel while preparing young people for war against Israel and the West in 1981' (ibid.: 92) and 'Daniel praying to Allah in 1981' (ibid.: 94). Eventually, Shāyesteh too resorts to the familiar pattern of claiming authority: 'I was a Muslim leader myself and taught how to permeate the infidel western societies, destroy their cultures from inside and pave the ground for the establishment of Islamic law' (ibid.: 237).

The 'crown witness' paradigm is least outspoken in Hormoz Shari'at's *Iran's Great Awakening: How God Is Using a Muslim Convert to Spark Revival*, even if the title may suggest otherwise. Shari'at's book, as a whole, is comparatively unconcerned with the 'unmasking' of Islam. And still, the author, in the introductory section with the title 'My Journey Out of Islam', does not refrain from mentioning that his grandfather 'had been an Islamic religious leader" (Shariat 2020: 3). The title of chapter one, 'Death to America, Death to the Shah' seems to suggest that Shari'at, who describes that he was active as a hanger-on of his university peers during the anti-Shah demonstrations, had formerly been a devoted enemy of the United States.[5] With respect to his own parents, however, Shari'at acknowledges that they were open-minded Muslims who never forced the religion upon him (ibid.: 4). He thus recognizes the existence of inner-Muslim diversity. In doing this, he differs from Safā, Pārsā and Shāyesteh.

Depictions of Islam and Muslims

Rezā Safā, Rāmin Pārsā and Daniel Shāyesteh all have devoted considerable space to the description of Islam. Safā's earlier English-language publication named *Inside Islam* is entirely concerned with 'the spirit of Islam' (Safa 1996: 10). As for Shari'at's book, references to Islam are scant but existent; however, they are less aggressive than in the other three authors' works. Moreover, Shari'at, unlike Safā, Pārsā and Shāyesteh, refrains from extending his criticism of Islam to a direct attack of Muslims/Muslim immigrants. The following pages will first summarize the authors' depictions of Islam and then describe how, apart from Shari'at, their criticism of Islam directly ushers in the antagonization of Muslims who are presented in culturalist terms.

Depictions of Islam

Hormoz Shari'at's description of his parents as moderate Muslims constitutes a differentiating effort that is conspicuously absent from the work of the other three authors assessed. Pārsā verbatim disagrees with 'people who differentiate between radical Islam and true Islam' for 'Islam is inherently evil and dangerously radical, and it will continue to cause problems in the world if not stopped' (Parsa 2018: 116). Safā operates on the same premise: on the first page of his 2006 book he states that 'an era of warfare with the radical Islam, or the true Islam, has begun' (Safa 2006: 1), thus rendering any effort for differentiation worthless. In a way contradicting his own statement, Safā later in the same book argues that it was the US 'policy of isolation' against countries like Iran or Hamas and Hezbollah which was the cause to 'how Islam became a radical movement' (ibid.: 69).

This historicizing remark poses an exception to Safā's overall depiction of Islam. Similar to Pārsā, who calls Muslims 'constantly jihad-conscious' (Parsa 2018: 94), Safā explains that 'Jihad is the pinnacle of the Muslim faith' (Safa 2006: 39). Ultimately, 'Islam cannot be reformed' (ibid.: 121). Constant essentializations are characteristic of Safā's, Pārsā's and Shāyesteh's deliberations, with the latter stating that 'the heart of Islam was incompatible with freedom and democracy' (Shayesteh 2012: 54). Far from any differentiation, Shāyesteh calls Islam 'a fourteen hundred year old problem' (ibid.: 116).

In his 2014 article on US-based Christian ex-Muslim activists, Smith mentions the linkage of Islam and the Antichrist made by outspoken ex-Muslim Walid Shoebat (Smith 2014: 84). Smith also reports that Shoebat as well as Kamal Saleem have compared Islam to a growing cancer (ibid.: 88–9). The Iranian pastors discussed here have made use of the same and similar vilifying slander, both theological and more broadly polemical in nature, to denigrate Islam. Safā calls Islam an 'antichrist force' with an 'antichrist spirit' as well as an 'antichrist religion' (Safa 1996: 8, 17). Drawing upon descriptions of the Antichrist in the Bible, Pārsā concludes that the Prophet Muhammad fulfilled all the criteria listed (Parsa 2018: 140–2). Even Shariʿat mentions 'a very strong dark spirit called Islam' which has been ruling Iran for the past 1400 years, adding shortly after that some Iranians now dared to say that Islam was 'from Satan' (Shariat 2020: 95–6).

Outside the spectrum of what maybe could be called religion-based slander, Pārsā in very plain terms states: 'Islam is a cancer to the world' (Parsa 2018: 167). Concluding a section on the atrocities committed by ISIS, which in Pārsā's view are based on 'core Islamic teachings', he explains that 'this pandemic is infecting the entire world', to then start a new subsection with the headline 'Mass Migration' (ibid.: 94–5). This structuring follows Pārsā's wider agenda which antagonizes Muslims (and especially Muslim immigrants) in typically right-wing populist terms. In terms of the depiction of Islam, Pārsā moreover avails himself of a Winston Churchill quote, paraphrasing it as 'Islam is as dangerous in a man as rabies in a dog' (ibid.: 66). On the same page, Pārsā notably avers that his book was neither the product of bigotry nor 'so-called "Islamophobia"' (ibid.).

In conclusion, Pārsā's discourse on Islam is remarkably vulgar and uses images of infectious diseases which had to be halted to avoid their further spread. This alone, combined with an omnipresent political discourse warning of the dangers of specifically Muslim immigration, for Pārsā's readership may suffice to identify the 'disease of Islam' in the supposed dangers emanating from Muslim immigrants and generally Muslims. If Islamophobia is understood as culturalist racism directed collectively against Muslims, Safā, Pārsā and Shāyesteh's books are a case in point since their slander is concerned not only with the religion of Islam but also with Muslims themselves.

Depictions of Muslims

In his 1996 book, Safā in alarmist terms warns of the supposed dangers resulting from Muslim immigration. The 'tide of millions of immigrants' was very advanced already: 'The United Kingdom now has more followers of Allah than Methodists and Baptists combined' (Safa 1996: 34). He fuels fears of Muslim takeovers of Western metropoles by claiming that 'Muslims now believe that if they can win London to Islam, it will not be hard to win Western Europe' (ibid.). New York at this point, according to Safā, was already 'a mecca [*sic*] of Muslim believers' (ibid.: 51). Safā's later book offers an paradigmatic example of how Muslims are rendered a collective group in culturalist terms: Safā constantly speaks of 'the Islamic mind-set, which resides in the hearts of millions of Muslims worldwide' (Safa 2006: 1). Muslims here become, very much as described in the conceptual section earlier, helpless victims of 'their culture'. It is not the complex mindset of independent individuals which explains their manifold actions, but simply 'the Islamic mind-set' of passive Muslims.

I have mentioned how the structuring of Pārsā's book leads the reader into making an immediate connection between the 'nature' of the Islamic religion and the supposed behaviour of Muslims. I shall cite a second example. On page 75, Pārsā finishes a section entitled 'Muhammad's Deeds' by calling the prophet of Islam a paedophile and a child abuser, based on his supposed sexual intercourse with nine-year-old Aisha (Parsa 2018: 75). The following page initiates a section entitled 'Inbreeding'. Here, Pārsā laments a commonality of intrafamilial relationships among Muslims, first in Bradford (UK), a city with a high Muslim population of South Asian descent, and then globally, stating that 'another estimate shows that almost half of all Muslims in the world are inbred' (ibid.: 77). The implicit insinuation is clear to every reader: just as the prophet of Islam had lacked control over his sexuality, Muslims today did so as well. Following the logic of culturalism, the underlying message here is: Muslims are what Islam is.

Pārsā in the remainder of his book reels off the whole gamut of right wing slander targeting Muslims: they want to 'take over Europe with mass immigration' (ibid.: 92), create no-go areas and exploit state welfare (ibid.: 96), are prone to rape (ibid.: 97) and are abetted in all this by Western liberals (ibid.: 97–103).

Eventually, Pārsā praises then president Trump's 'Muslim ban' (ibid.: 99) which ironically would have prevented Pārsā himself, who most likely had entered the United States with an Iranian passport, from reaching the safe haven of asylum in America.

Shāyesteh, in a section entitled 'Our Concern for the West', as well warns of what he considers the dangers of Muslim immigration (Shayesteh 2012: 235–42). The fear of infiltration is palpable in Shāyesteh's writing; Islamists as a rule only revealed 'their true colours' after taking power (ibid.: 124). One trope employed most prominently by Shāyesteh, but also featuring in Pārsā's book (Parsa 2018: 128), is that of *taqiyyeh* as a general practice of, in Shāyesteh's words, 'pious deception' (Shayesteh 2012: 70). The concept of *taqiyyeh* by the *Encyclopaedia of Islam* is defined as the practice of 'dispensing with the ordinances of religion in cases of constraint and when there is a possibility of harm' (Strothmann and Djebli 2012). It is strongly rooted in the exigencies of Shi'ite history which witnessed recurring episodes of severe persecution. In contemporary anti-Muslim discourses, as described by Yasemin Shooman for the German example, *taqiyyeh* is reconceived as a general strategy through which Muslims outwardly pretended to be 'moderates' and thus pandered to their naïve non-Muslim surroundings (cf. Shooman 2014: 151). Once the infiltration of society has been completed, the accusation goes, they will reveal their true face of radicalism. This trope is reproduced by Shāyesteh several times throughout his book (Shayesteh 2012: 70, 80, 105, 112).

Non-Islamiosity as a linchpin of Islamophobia

As outlined earlier, I argue that Islamophobia and non-Islamiosity, while being distinct phenomena the separation of which should be maintained, can become mutually constitutive and possess a high mutual permeability. The strikingly casual way in which the Iranian pastors in their English-language publications have switched between episodes attacking Muslims as a collective group and episodes lamenting the supposedly catastrophic reign of 'Arab' Islam over 'Persian' Iran most convincingly suggests this. A constant pitting of Iranian culture against Islamic culture pervades the books of Safā, Pārsā and Shāyesteh (again, not of Shari'at) alongside scathing remarks about Islam and Muslims, as we have already seen.

A sense of Iranian exceptionalism has surfaced occasionally in aspects debated in previous chapters, for instance, in the reading of Iranian feasts like Nowruz as sites of divine revelation. When voiced in the context of Islam, this exceptionalism primarily serves to distinguish Iran positively from other countries with Muslim majority populations. Rezā Safā sets Iran apart from Pakistan, where, as he explains, millions of children eagerly learned the Quran in madrasahs; nor was Iran 'an Arab nation where the Islamic traditions are engraved in the culture' (Safa 2006: 85). The non-islamious (or 'dislocative') reading of Iranian history is easily discerned here: different from other (especially Arab) countries, where a separation between a national culture and Islamic culture can hardly be ascertained, the Iranian nation in its original version was averse to Islam. Following this assumption, Safā states that 'Khomeini brought the reality of seventh-century Arabian culture into the twentieth-century life of Persian people' (ibid.: 165).

The reiteration of the Arab-Persian dichotomy is also omnipresent in Shāyesteh's book. Oddly enough, Shāyesteh throughout his book speaks about '*Saudi*-Arabian' culture – even when talking about the seventh-century conquest of Iran (cf. Shayesteh 2012: 30, italics added). The modern nation state of Saudi Arabia was only founded in the twentieth century. Whether Shāyesteh employs this anachronism out of a misunderstanding or whether he wishes to conjure up an image of the 'most radical' Arabs is a matter of interpretation. What is beyond debate is Shāyesteh's conviction that Islamic culture is wholly alien to Iranian national identity. Veiling, for instance, was against Iranian culture, as was marrying in mosques (ibid.: 88). Talking about 'the mullahs', Shāyesteh contends:

> They were used as the most influential channels for authorizing Shair'a [*sic*] to dominate every area of life, allowing things which were once a disdain to Iranian culture. They loudly and proudly announced the blood-thirsty culture of Muhammad superior over Iranian culture. They wanted to eradicate national identity and dress with hostile Meccan culture. Sometimes, they spoke in favour of Iranian identity but such statements were only for public consumption. (ibid.: 111)

Shāyesteh, moreover, promotes an image of Iranians that chimes with common tropes of non-Islamiosity: he emphasizes that his own ethnic group, the Tāleshis of Iranian Azerbaijan, by historians were believed to be 'the first Aryans, or pre-Aryan nation, to inhabit the northern parts of Ancient Persia' (ibid.: 3). As for religion, Iranians before the rise of Islamism 'were Muslims by name but Zoroastrians (the religion of Persians before Islam) in practice' (ibid.: 31).

Pārsā's view on the Islamic conquest of Persia likewise complies with the general non-islamious narrative: 'A seemingly innocuous ideology caused a supremely formidable and prosperous nation's decent into ashes, and holds it captive to this day' (Parsa 2018: 47). He praises the poet Ferdowsi, in whose *Book of Kings* 'not a single Arabic word was used', as the saviour of the Persian language against the Islamic invaders (ibid.: 78). Concurring with the non-islamious trope of 'book-burning Arabs',[6] Pārsā rejoices in the fact that the *Book of Kings* was 'among the works that remained after Islam destroyed many valuable documents' (ibid.). Finally, Pārsā also pits the figure of Cyrus the Great, whose centrality in discourses on the Iranian nation was discussed in the previous chapter, against his monolithic image of an ahistorical entity called 'Islam': 'Islam turned the initiator of human rights under Cyrus the Great into the second worst violator of human rights. History is the greatest predictor of what's to come. There is no reforming Islam' (ibid.: 98). Here, the non-islamious narrative serves as direct evidence to an Islamophobic attitude: unless the Christian world wanted to become a second Iran, precautions had to be taken now. The boundaries between non-Islamiosity and Islamophobia have virtually vanished.

Disengaging from Shi'ite Islam: The Persian-language sources

The English-language books analysed in the previous section are to a large degree specifically dedicated to the topic of Islam. They, moreover, as was pointed out, speak to a readership accustomed to an established negative discourse about Islam and Muslims, which is usually situated in the context of immigration policy debates. Given their partially harsh content, it is important to not take them as representative of Iranian Christian views on Islam. The separation of English-language and Persian-language sources made in this chapter helps to illustrate the complexity and diversity of discourses on Islam among Iranian Christians. How then are the ways Iranian pastors *more casually* talk about Islam to their Persian-speaking interlocutors different from the Islam-focused English-language monographs?

Admittedly, we are faced with a methodological problem here: the three pastors who have played a central role in the previous section – Rezā Safā, Rāmin Pārsā and Daniel Shāyesteh – do not prominently feature in the Persian-language set of sources built upon video recordings of Nowruz celebrations and Persian Christian magazines. We therefore do not know how Islam would have been portrayed if the pastors mentioned in the following sections were to as well compose English-language books and turn to an audience different from their usual Persian-speaking one. Nevertheless, there are good reasons to assume that discourses about Islam adopt a different shape in the presence of individuals who in their majority have been socialized in post-revolutionary Iran and thus from a young age onwards consumed a similar and very specific presentation of Islam.

Of course, there are also some overlaps between the portrayal of Islam in the English-language and the Persian-language sources. This includes the central trope of the 'expatriation' of Islam: the conviction that Islam was an Arab religion and forced an Arab identity upon Muslims. Most commonly, this assumption, which resonates well with the non-islamious paradigm, has been communicated by pointing to the fact that one had to pray in Arabic in Islam, but was free to pray in Persian, or any other language, in Christianity. The following section will explore this aspect briefly. The remaining sections in this chapter will reveal the distinct character of discourses about Islam in the Persian-language sources and argue that they specifically cater to Iranians disillusioned with a self-proclaiming Shi'ite Muslim state and, by extension, are fed up with everything to do with 'religion'.

Arab Allah versus Christian God of diversity

For the performance of the Islamic ritual prayer (called *namāz* in Persian and *salāt* in Arabic), Muslims of all ethnicities have to memorize a fixed set of phrases and Quranic verses in Arabic. Next to the *ritual* prayer, Muslims can also direct a free prayer of unspecified content to God, which is usually referred to as *do'ā*.[7] The latter can be carried out in the native language of the praying individual. It is, therefore, misleading when Daniel Shāyesteh tells his English-speaking reader that 'one must not pray to Allah in one's mother tongue' (Shayesteh 2012: 32). Pārsā puts it more accurately when he describes the obligatory ritual prayers during his school time as happening 'in a language that we didn't speak' (Parsa 2018: 16). Arabic certainly functions as what could be called the 'liturgical language' of Islam, with the Friday sermon usually being initiated with a brief episode in Arabic and the Quran famously being recited (but not read!) exclusively in Arabic.

Iranians, not just since the 1979 Revolution, study Quranic Arabic as a compulsory subject at school. On an anecdotal level, one will often encounter Iranians whose non-islamious dislike of all things 'Arabic' has been further spurred by the tedium of Arabic verb conjugations during their school time. More recently, the rejection of cultural elements which require the usage of

Arabic-language passages has come to the fore among marrying couples who, out of disdain for the traditional Islamic wedding ceremony (*'aqd*) which is performed by an Islamic cleric and includes set phrases in Arabic, choose to additionally celebrate an unofficial 'Aryan wedding ceremony' (*'aqd-e Āryāyi*). Such ceremonies are held in supposedly 'pure Persian'.

Iranian Christians generally emphasize that the God of Christianity was a God who loved all national and ethnic cultures.[8] What Shāyesteh and Pārsā point to is the negative counterpart to this assertion: Allah, the God of Islam, was *not* a God of cultural diversity. He only spoke and understood Arabic. In the Persian-language sources, this assumption has surfaced as well. During the 2012 (1391) Nowruz celebration of the Ambassadors of Christ Persian Church in Los Angeles, a man called Jamshid entered the stage to recite a self-written poem (Bāghestāni 2016: m. 31:40). Introduced by Pastor Elnātān Bāghestāni as a former member of the Iranian Revolutionary Guard Corps (IRGC) who later converted to Christianity, Jamshid started to talk about his childhood (ibid.). After the early death of his father, Jamshid was raised by his grandfather:

> I was six years old when my grandfather said: 'My boy, you have grown up now, come and learn to pray *namāz*!' So I stood behind him when he said: '*Allāho Akbar, Allāho Akbar*!' I said: 'Granddad, what does this mean?' He said: 'Just say it!' I replied: 'In Turkish please!' I am Turkish and grew up speaking Turkish. He said: 'No, the *namāz* is in Arabic.' – 'For whom do we pray *namāz*?' – 'For God' – 'Doesn't God know Turkish?' [congregation laughs] – 'No, God is an Arab.' [congregation laughs even louder] My grandfather was illiterate (*savād nadāsht*). I said: 'Fine.' Later, in second grade at primary school, they were teaching Arabic. I was longing to learn Arabic, thinking: 'Great, now I am learning God's language and then I will to talk to him!' (ibid.: m. 33:36–34:22)

Jamshid continues to recount that he learned Arabic well, but God did not seem to respond to him (ibid.). Later, during his military service at the time of the Iran-Iraq War, he got acquainted to a Turkish-speaking Christian who gifted him a New Testament (ibid.: 38:02). Eventually, his friend invited him to pray (*do'ā kardan*) together with him and he immediately felt the presence of the Holy Spirit (ibid.: m. 43:25). Jamshid's account thus concurs with the narrative of a Christian God approachable through every language; the Arab God 'Allah' in Jamshid's story did not even respond to his 'own' Arabic language.

Modern Persian, both in the Islamic and in the Christian context, refers to God as *Khodā* or *Khodāvand*. It is therefore easy to distinguish the supposedly Arab God of Islam in Persian by calling him *Allāh*. The distinction between an

Islamic God called 'Allah' and the Christian 'God of Abraham, Isaac and Jacob' has also featured prominently in the English-language sources and has been pointed to in Smith's article for the ex-Muslim Christians studied by him (Smith 2014: 87). In the Persian-language sources, an example of the mentioning of 'Allah' includes a prayer of Siāmak Zargari who asked for the end of the 'age of the power of Allah' (*dowrān-e qodrat-e Allāh*) in Iran (Zargari and Zargari 2018a: m. 1:07:34).

Here and elsewhere, the dissociation from 'Allah' also constitutes a practice. An earlier chapter of this book has referred to an article by Diane Alexander Miller (2015) who observed the tendency of Iranian Christians to use *beh omid-e Khodā* ('God willing') instead of the synonymous Arabic phrase *En shā' Allāh/ Enshālā*. As pointed out, Iranian Christians, in doing this, may not be different from many non-Christian Iranians with a penchant for anti-Arabic linguistic purism. And yet, the firmness with which the usage of the phrase *En Shā' Allāh* is rejected does reach another level when it happens based upon the belief that 'Allah' was not the Christian God.

An episode from the same service in which Siāmak Zargari prayed for the end of 'Allah's' reign over Iran poignantly illustrates this: earlier in the service, his wife, Rozitā Zargari, had asked those willing and not afraid of being filmed to come to the front and pray for Iran in their native languages. Among those taking part was an elderly man praying in Gilaki. Towards the end of his prayer, he congratulated the present congregation on the occasion of the new year and added, seemingly out of habit, '*Enshālā …*' (Zargari and Zargari 2018a: m. 39:22). Having uttered the shunned phrase, he immediately corrected himself, visibly startled and yet amused about his slip of the tongue. The video shows Rozitā Zargari next to him who as well can be seen laughing, but then lifting her hand saying, 'In the name of Christ!' (*beh nām-e Masih*), a phrase then repeated by the elderly man to conclude his prayer. It is unlikely that a non-Christian Iranian mindful of speaking a 'purely non-Arabic' Persian would go so far to apologize and correct themselves when inadvertently using a phrase like *Enshālā*. For the man in the video, however, using the phrase meant not only an unfaithfulness to his true national identity, but the invocation of a wrong God – a God, in fact, who represented the ongoing 'occupation' of Iran by Islam.

Islam as legalist *Mazhab* versus Christianity as a loving relationship

At the heart of Persian-language discourses about Islam has been the emphasis that Islam, *unlike* Christianity, *was a religion* (*mazhab*). Concomitantly,

Iranian pastors have redundantly averred that they were not religious (*mazhabi*) individuals and that churches not religious places. My translation of *mazhab/mazhabi* as 'religion/religious' is admittedly a very literal one;[9] to understand the background of the dissociation of Christianity from *mazhab*, it is necessary to highlight the connotations the term carries for many Iranians who have grown up in the Islamic Republic. At the same time, it should at least be mentioned that there is a broader tendency among Evangelicals to claim that Christianity was not a religion.[10] Yet, I am here more concerned with the roots of this trope in contemporary Iran.

A helpful illustration of the connotations of *mazhab* among many contemporary Iranians can be found in the 1394 (2015) Nowruz service of the Iranian Church of Sunnyvale. In both the event's sermon and the play staged by the church's theatre group, notions of *mazhab* were the main topic. I will first address the play which, notably, did not feature the term *mazhab* literally. It is well possible that the contributors to the service consciously used the theatre play to introduce the topic in a more humorous fashion, while the sermon, delivered after the play, directly addressed the issue. The plot of the play has Āghā Jalil, a middle-aged US-based Iranian Christian, being visited from Iran by his old (non-Christian) friend Khorram (Navā'i 2015: m. 36:16). Having arrived at Āghā Jalil's house, the two friends, who have not seen each other for twenty years, start joking around like in the old days (ibid.: m. 39:48). Eventually, Āghā Jalil mentions that he intended to take Khorram to church on the coming Sunday (ibid.: m. 46:11). Khorram is shocked and leaps from his seat, shouting:

> **Khorram:** What? To church? You want *me* to go to church? Dude, give me a break (*Bābā, vel-e man kon*)! That's exactly the stuff we have escaped from (*az dast-e hamin barnāmeh-hā farār kardim*)! Leave us alone with that. Church ... why would I go to church ...
>
> **Āghā Jalil:** Look, Khorram, my friend (*'azizam*). Every Sunday we go to Sunnyvale, to the Iranian Church. There we worship God with joy. (ibid.: m. 46:11–46:34)

To Khorram, it is incomprehensible why someone who like his friend Āghā Jalil had succeeded in leaving Iran would still bother to be involved in things related to *mazhab* – and a church, in Khorram's perception, surely was such a place. Switching to the plural, Khorram implies that not just he himself, but *all Iranians*, if they left Iran, did this for this very reason: to free themselves from *mazhab* and the challenges coming with it. Āghā Jalil immediately tries to allay his friend's reservations by pointing out that they worshipped God at church 'with joy' (*bā shādi*). Here, Āghā Jalil implicitly draws a boundary to the kind of *mazhab* his friend Khorram is familiar and fed up with: the ritualized sadness and the mourning practices of Shi'ite Islam. I will return to this aspect in a moment. Towards the end of the play, Khorram notices that his old friend had undergone a drastic change of character since the last time they had met. He possessed an astonishing calmness (ibid.: m. 1:00:10). The play ends with Khorram asking whether maybe Āghā Jalil's personal transformation had something to do with his church attendance and that, no matter what its source was, he wanted to experience such a transformation as well (ibid.).

After the theatre play, Pastor Kāmil Navā'i verbatim broached the topic of *mazhab* in his sermon. Addressing the newcomers to the church, Navā'i suggested that they probably had noticed that the Iranian Church of Sunnyvale was different from 'religious places' (*amāken-e mazhabi*) (ibid.: m. 1:18:46). The reason for this was that the church was not a *mazhabi* place, and yet God dwelled (*sāken*) there (ibid.). Neither was it an Iranian club or a charity (ibid.). Instead, it was a family gathering – a loving family with one father (ibid.: m. 1:20:30). Later in his sermon, Navā'i bemoaned that, in his opinion, 79 million Iranians still looked at God through the lens of *mazhab* (*az daricheh-ye mazhab*), ignorant of the God who told them 'I love you' (ibid.: m. 1:29:46). Navā'i's contrasting of Islam, although never mentioned literally, and Christianity identifies the latter as a personal, loving relationship of a believing individual and God. Islam, or *mazhab*, on the other hand, in this reading is characterized by an obsession with legality and the constant question of what is allowed and what is prohibited.

In an earlier sermon archived online, Navā'i expanded on this idea and pointed to a biblical example of *mazhab*. During the time of Jesus, a part of the Jewish 'mullahs' (*mollāyān-e Yahudi*) had turned the laws of God (*shari'at*) into *mazhab* (Navā'i 2009: m. 11:25). The usage of the term *mollā* creates a direct link to the Shi'ite clergy of Iran who, often derogatively, are referred to by the same word. Further, Navā'i defineed what characterized a *mazhabi* individual:

> So, who is a *mazhabi* person? A *mazhabi* person is someone who wants to abide by the law of God. It is very well possible that they are a very genuine individual ... However, they are using the law of God in a way that it turns into a prison, both for themselves and for others. (ibid.: m. 11:32–11:52)

This interpretation complies with the views of a number of other Iranian pastors who, in addition and different from Navā'i, have verbatim made the link to Islam. Edvin Sāleh, for instance, very vociferously rejects the label of *mazhab* for Christianity, explaining that, unlike Islam, it was not based on concrete legal rulings (*ahkām*) by the obedience to which an individual *'en shā' Allāh'* would attain salvation (Sāleh 2018: m. 0:24). In the words of Hoseyn Sālāri, *mazhab* was something 'imposed on us through governments'; Christianity on the contrary was a relationship between people and God (Sālāri, Sālāri and Navā'i 2016: m. 2:50:38). Finally, Hormoz Shari'at explains that, in the past, Christianity too had turned into *mazhab* – it had been the 'Christian mullahs – yes, *Christian* mullahs, not Islamic mullahs!' who until the Reformation were preventing people from thinking freely (Shari'at 2020: m. 48:38). The emergence of a true understanding of Christianity, that is, a non-Catholic one, had 'freed Europe from the captivity of *mazhab*, and today we Iranians need the same thing' (ibid.: m. 50:00).

In conclusion, the term *mazhab* in the sources assessed conjured up notions of rigid legality preventing Iranians from truly being free. Following this notion, Iranians, by turning to the loving and approachable God of Christianity had to liberate themselves from all remnants of *mazhab*. Moreover, although the notion of *mazhab* has not appeared as genuine to Islam, virtually all of the pastors have made implicit or explicit connections to contemporary Iran. This connection is further bolstered by the occasional linking of *mazhab* with 'mullahs' (*mollā-hā*), a term unmistakably interwoven with contemporary conceptions of Shi'ite clergy in the Islamic Republic.

Another term directly linked to *mazhab* by Iranian pastors is the title *hazrat*. Used in Persian as well as other languages (e.g. Turkish), the term may be translated as 'his/her holiness' and is usually put before the names of Islamic prophets as an expression of reverence.[11] This includes the Prophet Jesus ('Isā) who is often referred to as *Hazrat-e Masih* by Muslims. It appears that some Iranian Christians, whether out of habit or purposefully, continue to use the title; Peymān Shabānlāri during the 1398 (2017) Nowruz service at his *Kelisā-ye Navid-e Rahāyi* in Amsterdam mentioned that he was talking to someone who kept saying that *Hazrat-e Masih* 'indeed was a great man' (Shabānlāri 2017: m. 32:55). Shabānlāri then had told him that throughout history, no one had found salvation in someone that was defined as a *hazrat* (ibid.). The empty tomb of Christ accounted for the fact that he was not a *hazrat*, for all the *hazrats* now were below the soil (ibid.: m. 35:15). What he was talking about in his sermon, Shabānlāri continued, was not *mazhab* and had nothing to do with it – it was 'liberation' (*rahāyi*) (ibid.: m. 33:50). Again, the concept of *mazhab* is pitted against the freedom of liberation by the salvation through Christ; parallel to that, the (Islamic) *hazrat*s are juxtaposed with the Jesus of Christianity who, different from the Islamic narration, rose from the dead.

Mournful Shi'ite Islam versus joyful Christianity

In her ethnographic study of a London-based Iranian Church, Kathryn Spellman observed how Iranian Christians espoused a dichotomous view of Christianity and Shi'ite Islam that contrasted 'the joyous disposition' of Christians with 'the mourning and crying' prevalent in Shi'ism (Spellman 2004: 184). Mourning rituals constitute a central – though not the sole – element of Shi'ite religiosity, culminating in the month of Muharram during the initial days of which the martyrdom of the Prophet Muhammad's grandson Husayn is commemorated. In acts of self-flagellation, Shi'ite Muslims display their regret and repentance that, historically, they did not come to the support of Husayn in the Battle of Karbala, in which he and other members of the Prophet's family (the *Ahl ul-Bayt*) were killed.

Two excerpts from Nowruz sermons in Iranian Christian exile churches shall illustrate how Shi'ite mourning practices are referred to by Iranian pastors as supposedly representative of Islam as a whole. Speaking at an Iranian church in Almere (the Netherlands), Iranian Armenian Pastor Verzh Bābākhāni explained:

> God wants us to have a joyful life, in high spirits, full of freshness, did you know this? This is the desire and wish of God! His wish is not for us to be depressed, in grief and sadness or that we cry and constantly beat our chests (*hey sineh bezanim*) – none of these things. (Bābākhāni 2019: m. 0:32–0:49)

The mentioning of chest-beating makes clear to his Iranian audience that Bābākhāni here is referring to Shi'ite mourning practices. In the remainder of his sermon, Bābākhāni introduces numerous biblical hints aiming to characterize Christianity as a cheerful religion. Using the epithet *ahl-e shādi*, 'people fond of joyfulness', for Christians, Bābākhāni explained that Christ himself, even on the way to Golgotha, had continued to sing joyful songs of praise (*sorud*) with his disciples (ibid.: m. 20:28). This joyfulness, Bābākhāni continued, chimed well with the spirit of the Iranian people; the Christian God's cheerful disposition even extended to an Iranian culinary favourite: as a last biblical hint, Bābākhāni argued that the Bible introduced God as a God in love with celebrations and a God who loved Kebab (*ahl-e kabāb*) (ibid.). It was not for no reason that God in the Bible repeatedly asked people to bring a sacrifice, it was for them to *consume* it – 'and boy did they eat!' (*hesābi ham mikhordand māshāllā!*) (ibid.: m. 22:54)

Siāmak Zargari implicitly contrasts Christianity with Islam by quoting a video clip he had seen on the internet (Zargari and Zargari 2019: m. 1:06:26). Somewhere in Iran, a neighbourhood had gathered to celebrate Nowruz when a cleric (*akhund*)[12] came along and broke up the get-together. Zargari concludes:

> These people [Shi'ite clerics] as a principle have a problem with happiness. They have a problem with laughter, they have a problem with getting together. They have a problem with dancing. These are people who only like *rowzeh*,[13] mourning, suffering, misery, crying, blood, killing, and war. (ibid.: m. 1:06:40–1:07:05)

Descriptions like this one, albeit in a less harsh tone, have also surfaced at other points in the sources assessed for this book, including a sketch performed by Hormoz Shari'at and the team of *Shabakeh7* (cf. Shari'at and Ebrāhimiān 2016: m. 25:30–28:35). Usually, however, the word 'Islam' remained unuttered. In the Persian-language sources, Iranian pastors have generally refrained from directly attacking Islam. Unlike in the English-language sources, such attacks would have simply been unnecessary as the described implicit references are completely sufficient for the Iranian audience to understand the conveyed message.

Conclusion

Given the fact that Muslim-born converts today constitute the vast majority among attendants of Iranian Christian exile churches, a portrayal of Iranian Christian exilic milieu would be incomplete if it refrained from discussing references to Islam in services, written publications and beyond. Moreover, negotiations of what defines Iranian nationhood have often featured the question of whether Islam should be considered a disruptive, Arab element – and consequently, 'the Islamic' be eradicated from 'the Iranian' (cf. Gholami 2016: 6) – or whether (Shi'ite) Islam should be integrated into the Iranian national self-image, as has been the case in post-revolutionary Iranian state discourse. This chapter has illustrated the complexity and diversity discourses about Islam take on among Iranian Christians, highlighting the differences between portrayals of Islam in English-language monographs written by Iranian Christian pastors in exile and in the Persian-language set of sources used for this book.

The English-language works especially of Rāmin Pārsā, Rezā Safā and Daniel Shāyesteh refer to Islam *and* Muslims in deeply vilifying terms, including the portrayal of Islam as a cancer and an infectious disease. By highlighting their supposed past as 'radical Muslims', Pārsā, Safā and Shāyesteh aim to speak from a position of authority which they derive from their 'insider knowledge'. In typically culturalist terms, Muslims appear as passive executors of the 'spirit' or the 'mindset of Islam'. Lest the West wanted to turn into a second Iran, the mentioned pastors argue, Muslim immigration had to be drastically regulated. The culturalist portrayal of Islam combined with the recurring warning of Muslim immigration arguably justifies the labelling of the English-language monographs as Islamophobic.

Occasional overlaps aside, the Persian-language sources assessed for this book display a different discourse on Islam. While direct attacks on Islam and Muslims are avoided, including even a hesitancy to literally mention Islam,[14] references are more specific to the lived experienced of individuals who were socialized in post-revolutionary Iran. A vociferous disengagement from *mazhab*, or '(legalist) religion', accounts for the disillusionment for the sort of religion promoted by the Iranian state. Strongly reflecting the Protestant and Evangelical tenets of the pastors speaking, Christianity, in contrast with Islam, is portrayed as a loving relationship between a directly accessible God and his children.

In the previous two chapters, we have observed how Iranian Christians strive for the 'naturalization' of Christianity to the Iranian nation. Does this endeavour go hand in hand with its counterpart – the 'expatriation' of Islam? Some narratives presented in this chapter go into this direction. The portrayal of the Islamic God as a distinct Arabic God, Allah, surfaced occasionally in the sources. Furthermore, the portrayal of Christianity as a cheerful religion, as opposed to a 'mournful' Shi'ite Islam, can be supplemented by a reference to the joyful elements in Iranian culture. As we have seen, this portrayal, in its most pithy form, pictures the God of Islam as a God of self-flagellation and the Christian God as a God holding barbecue parties.

Albeit with different nuances, references to Islam in the sources assessed were invariably negative. This may not necessarily come as a surprise considering that this book deals with individuals who (in their majority) have converted away from Islam and have been exiled at the hand of an Islamist government. There is, however, one exception to this seemingly unequivocal attitude: Hassan Dehqāni-Tafti. It is speculative whether Dehqāni-Tafti, whose father was a Muslim and mother an early Muslim-born convert to Anglicanism, possessed an additional degree of emotional involvement with Islam because he until his youth actively practised Christianity (at an Anglican boarding school) and Islam (when visiting his village during summer holidays) (Dehqani-Tafti 2000: 27). In any case, Dehqāni-Tafti in a 1981 book reflecting on the hardships suffered by him and his family after the 1979 Revolution chose to entitle the closing chapter with a quote ascribed to the Shi'ite Imam Hussain: 'Truly Life is but Belief and Struggle' (Dehqani-Tafti 1981: 98). He explains:

> The title of this chapter is one of the sayings of Imam Hussain, revered in the Shi'ite tradition as Lord of the Martyrs–a man who believed in what he said, and who died for his belief ... They much impressed me when I went back to Iran after the Lambeth Conference, with the idea of martyrdom gnawing at my mind. (ibid.)

Earlier in the same book, Dehqāni-Tafti stresses that the brutal and often arbitrary death sentences occurring after the 1979 Revolution were 'in no way in accordance with Islamic justice or with Shar'ia law' and 'totally unislamic' (ibid.: 58). Considering the tragic personal fate Dehqāni-Tafti and his family suffered as a consequence of the 1979 Revolution, his vocal defence of Islam appears astonishing.

Such episodes in Dehqāni-Tafti's writing are reflective of his wider endeavour to differentiate when discussing the 'Islam question'. In the English-language version of his autobiography,[15] published in the year 2000, Dehqāni-Tafti ponders on whether the 'Khomeini Revolution' was 'the doing of Islam' (Dehqani-Tafti 2000: 257) – a question self-evidently answered affirmatively by pastors like Rezā Safā (cf. Safa 1996: 43). The conclusion Dehqāni-Tafti draws from his discussion is that 'certainly *an* Islam was guilty' (Dehqāni-Tafti 2000: 260, italics in the original). He thus, again different from the English-language books discussed earlier, recognizes the existence of plurality among Muslims. Finally, there is another remarkable aspect about Dehqāni-Tafti's discourse on Islam: he uses the terms 'God' and 'Allah' synonymously in English (ibid.: 262). In doing this, Dehqāni-Tafti was unique in the source material used for this book.

6

Diasporic religion among Iranian Christians: Meanings of exile, visions of return and the Elam Prophecy

Introduction

Of the manifold media productions of Iranian Christians in the diaspora, one category has remained completely unmentioned so far: films. The sons of Hāyk Hovsepiān, who are now residing in the United States, have produced several Persian-language films of different genres. Most notable among them is the 2007 documentary *A Cry from Iran* which tells the life story of their father and other 'Martyrs of the Iranian Church' (Hovsepiān and Hovsepiān 2007).

In 2003, Joseph Hovsepiān produced the movie *The Tune of Nostalgia* (see Figure 7) which features his brother Gilbert in the main role (Hovsepiān 2003). Gilbert plays Vahid Akbari, a young Iranian man who is disillusioned about his personal future in Iran and, entertaining a utopian imagination of what life in 'the West' could be like, decides to immigrate to Austria. Having arrived, he soon realizes that life as a refugee brings with it severe hardships. Eventually, he even falls into dodgy dealings under the influence of his criminal roommate. Then, at the peak of Vahid's despair, his other roommate, an Iranian Armenian Christian, invites him to join a Sunday service at a Persian-speaking church. Vahid reluctantly agrees. The next scene shows him at the church, struck by the sermon which seems to speak directly to him. In the final episode of the movie, Vahid, now a baptized member of the church, can be seen playing the piano during the service while his criminal roommate enters the room and approaches the altar in repentance.

The Persian title of the movie *The Tune of Nostalgia* is *Āhang-e Ghorbat*. While the Hovsepiān brothers decided to translate the term *ghorbat* as 'nostalgia', there are other possible translations. *Ghorbat* is one of the possible Persian equivalents

Figure 7 Film poster of *The Tune of Nostalgia*. Reprinted in *Kalameh* 41 (2005: 36). Used with permission of Elam Ministries.

for 'diaspora': a Persian-English dictionary suggests 'the state of being away from one's home' and 'life in exile' as possible translations (Emami 2006: 620). Young Vahid's nostalgia therefore is not any kind of nostalgia; it is the bitter nostalgia of exile. It appears that the Hovsepiān brothers, through their movie, intended to send a warning sign to young Iranians who may envision life in emigration in all too bright colours. Furthermore, however, the movie sends a religious message. Although Vahid, who thinks of himself as a talented musician, did not find the shining career he had dreamt of, he found something else: the faith in Jesus Christ. Ultimately, his departure from Iran was not in vain. Hence, his exilic suffering was alleviated and his painful dwelling far from home rendered meaningful.

This vignette seemed suitable to introduce the last chapter of this book which deals with notions of exile and visions of return among Iranian Christians. While exile in the previous chapters has only come up implicitly, I would like to draw upon the theoretical framework developed in Chapter 2 of this book to analyse diasporic religion in Iranian Christian exile churches in the present chapter. After illustrating how Iranian Christians attribute meaning to their forced displacement in reference to their religion – or, in the words of Thomas Tweed, how 'people and the clergy compose stories about the suffering and disorientation of displacement' (Tweed 1997: 95) – I will address how religious visions of the future of Iranian Christians and Iran are tailored according to a soteriological scheme. I will use Baumann's conceptualization of the Jewish diaspora as a fourfold soteriological course of 'sin or disobedience, scattering and exile as punishment, repentance, and finally return and gathering' (Baumann 2000: 317) to frame the most prominent of Iranian Christian visions of return: the Elam Prophecy.

Finally, this chapter will briefly glimpse into the future and describe the expectations first-generation Iranian Christians in exile have for the second and future generations, for which Tweed and others expect the emergence a 'supralocal', and thus de-territorialized, approach to religion (Tweed 1997: 97).

Meanings of exile and the alleviation of its pain

First-generation Iranian emigrants expectedly feel a strong sense of *ghorbat*, the painful estrangement caused by exile. It is not an overstatement to say that the event of leaving their home country constituted the most significant turning point in their personal biographies. Edward Said, an exile himself, poignantly stated:

> Exile is strangely compelling to think about but terrible to experience. It is the unhealable rift forced between a human being and a native place, between the self and its true home: its essential sadness can never be surmounted. And while it is true that literature and history contain heroic, romantic, glorious, even triumphant episodes in an exile's life, these are no more than efforts meant to overcome the crippling sorrow of estrangement. The achievements of exile are permanently undermined by the loss of something left behind for ever. (Said 2001: 173)

While the sentiment described by Said surely can only be fully related to by fellow exiles, the unsurmountable sadness mentioned by him was occasionally palpable to me during personal interactions with individuals who (in some cases very recently) saw themselves forced to leave Iran. Martin and his wife, for example, by the time of our interview had only arrived in Europe little over a year earlier, after both had endured imprisonment under inhumane circumstances. And yet the couple would strongly disagree with Said's thoroughly negative characterization of exile. Instead, they would emphasize their obedience to what they perceive as God's personal plan for their lives which, for whatever reason, included their emigration from Iran. Iranian Christian exiles often cite their religion as an alleviating force to the pain of *ghorbat*. The following pages will describe different religious readings of exile prevalent among them.

Ghorbat from the heavenly homeland

One way to adopt a mitigating perspective towards the pain of exile is to universalize it for all Christians. Some Iranian Christians do so by claiming that a sense of painful estrangement was mutual to Christians, who, as long as they sojourned in this world (*donyā*), experienced a *ghorbat* from their 'heavenly homeland' (*vatan-e āsemāni*).

In a 2005 article appearing in *Kalameh*, 'Isā Dibāj elaborates on the 'pain of *Ghorbat*' (Dibāj 2005a). Reflecting on exile as a punishment (*tab'id*)[1] and the emotions evoked by it – emotions well familiar to many of the readers, as Dibāj suggests – he quotes the first lines of Rumi's *Masnavi* which, in his view, offered an apt portrayal of exilic sentiment (ibid.: 13).[2] Entering the context of the Bible, Dibāj explains that all humans through their sinfulness had been estranged from God (ibid.). Even Christians, who through their faith in Jesus Christ could establish a relationship with God, remained in this earthly *ghorbat* as long as they had not died and ascended into heaven (ibid.). In this world, Christians were strange (*gharib*) and scattered (*parākandeh*), as their true homeland (*vatan*) was heaven (ibid.: 45).

To understand this, Dibāj admits, did not mean that the longing for Iran vanished; Iranian Christians continued to see Iran in their dreams, to miss their family back home and to pine for a return to their country of origin (ibid.). Nevertheless, it did offer some consolation to know that 'as followers of Christ ... we actually are strangers everywhere in this world, even at our own birthplace' (ibid.).

The notion of a 'heavenly homeland' also featured in one of the video sources. At the 1398 (2019) Nowruz service at the California-based Worshippers of Christ Church, a puppet artist performed a short piece, presumably to entertain the children present in the congregation (Heydari 2019: m. 28:10). Entering a dialogue with his puppet, the performer started to ask her questions about what it meant to be a Christian. After the question 'who is our king?' ('Jesus Christ!'), he tested his puppet by asking 'where is our homeland (*vatan*)?' – a question promptly answered by the puppet saying 'heaven!' (ibid.: m. 30:26). The audience, that cannot be seen in the video recording, confirmed the answers given by the puppet with a loud 'Yes!' (*Baleh!*); this was also the case for the artist's question about the 'earthly homeland' (*vatan-e zamini*), which the puppet correctly identified as Iran (ibid.).

It is thus noteworthy that the notion of the 'heavenly homeland' does not jettison the concomitant acknowledgement of Iran as the homeland of Iranian Christians. Rather than doing away with notions of national origin, the emphasis of the estrangement of *all* Christians shifts the focus to the transitory nature of earthly life. In other words, while Iranian Christians may have lost their homeland in *this world*, they can rest assured that they, by having come to faith in Christ, have won a superior and eternal homeland in the afterlife.

Ending up in *Ghorbat* by divine will

As we have seen earlier in this book, some Iranian Christians have only converted to Christianity after leaving Iran. The reasons for their emigrations are diverse; some may have arrived to their new country of residence on student visas while others may have emigrated as professionals. Others, like the movie character Vahid from *The Tune of Nostalgia*, may have tried their luck in claiming asylum in Europe and ended up attending Persian-speaking or other churches.

One of my interlocutors, a woman named Mahlā, openly admitted that she and her husband initially had started to attend a church solely with the goal of being admitted as refugees and receive a residence permit (interview with Mahlā, 2021). Later, however, they genuinely embraced the Christian faith and now serve as ministers at a Germany-based Iranian church (ibid.). Such trajectories enable Iranian Christians to read their emigration as divine providence. Ultimately, they would argue, the path leading them outside of their home country also led them to salvation.

Despite the possibility of a genuine later conversion, as in the case of Mahlā, Iranian Christian leaders in Europe generally discourage Muslim-born Iranians from faking their conversion to Christianity in order to receive asylum in Europe or North America and refuse to baptize individuals who come 'for the wrong reasons' (Spellman 2004: 193). 'Isā Dibāj directly addresses this issue in a 2003 article in *Kalameh* (Dibāj 2003b). As a young man back in Iran already, Dibāj felt uneasy about individuals who acquired a residency permit outside Iran by untruthfully claiming their lives had been in danger at home (ibid.: 37). Apart from being a lie, Dibāj considered this an insult to the 'Martyrs of the Church' – one of them being his father Mehdi (ibid.).

Dibāj continues his deliberations by telling the story of an Iranian man who attended an Iranian church in Birmingham, UK. When this man had arrived in the UK, he had applied for asylum on untruthful grounds (ibid.). Later, however, Dibāj recounts, the man genuinely came to faith in Christ (ibid.). At the decisive court hearing, he admitted to the judge that his initial claims had been bogus and that he, having become a Christian, wished to no longer lie, even if this meant his deportation (ibid.). Much to his surprise, he was admitted as a refugee and received a permanent residency (ibid.).

What theological lessons did Dibāj derive from this story? In his view, the story was indicative of the fact that a full surrender to God's will should be at the heart of an individual's decision to emigrate or stay in Iran:

> In my view, this sort of attitude should be an example to each and every true Christian. Maybe, for some people, emigration (sometimes even without them knowing this) has actually been God's will, and God himself miraculously opened all the doors in their way and removed all the obstacles, so they could become markedly more useful for him than they would have been inside their country. Likewise, there may be people who (again sometimes without them knowing themselves) against God's will have settled abroad and amidst a world full of wealth and comfort have experienced only misery, frustration, betrayal and separation, and their lives have ultimately fallen apart. Outside the will of

God, even the best, safest and greenest countries are nothing but hell (*jahannami bish nist*). But if we step forward within the will of God, if the receiver of our heart is tuned to the frequency of God's voice, even the corner of a prison cell will become a centre of joy and happiness for us – just as it has been for the heroes of faith (*qahramānān-e imān*). This is because it is their true place of refuge. (ibid.: 37)

In this reading, even an emigration in the face of real persecution becomes a wrong decision if God intended an individual to serve him inside Iran rather than in the diaspora. Indeed, some Iranian church leaders, led by what they perceived as the will of God, have consciously decided to remain in Iran, even at the height of violent oppression in the mid-1990s. A case in point is Tākush Hovsepiān, the widow of Hāyk Hovsepiān. In a 2007 interview, she explained that, originally, she and her children had intended to leave Iran for the United States a year after the murder of her husband (Hovsepiān and Dibāj 2007: 43). Then, however, she felt that the Holy Spirit was telling her that the time to leave Iran had not come yet (ibid.); they subsequently remained in Iran for five more years.

Conversely, there are other pastors who believe they have specifically been called to *leave* Iran. Church planting abroad has become a core activity for Iranian Christians who consider the growing Iranian expat community an opportunity for unimpeded missionary activities. Accordingly, Dāvud Thomas, an Iranian Assyrian pastor who was among the early leaders of the Pentecostal *Jamā'at-e Rabbāni Central Church* in Tehran, describes how his decision to stay in the United States in the mid-1980s was founded upon his gradual realization that 'God had called us to serve him among the Iranians here [the US]' (Thomas and Dibāj 2010: 12).

Nowruz and Yaldā in *ghorbat* and the creation of a translocal space

Iranian national occasions like Nowruz and Yaldā immediately confront an exile with the foreignness of their new environment – an environment that does not celebrate these occasions. The festive atmosphere of Nowruz which in Iran permeates the public sphere of the whole country in exile is confined to the private sphere of family and, in the case of Iranian Christians, church gatherings. Many of the voices speaking through the sources used for this book have bemoaned that Nowruz in a 'strange country' (*keshvar-e gharib*) remained almost unnoticed (Kelisā-ye Jāme'e Fārsi-Zabānān 2020: m. 11:16). This realization immediately evoked the longing for a celebration of Nowruz back in

Iran one day; a short article in a 2009 issue of *Tabdil* entitled 'A Blessed Nowruz in *Ghorbat!*', for instance, connects its congratulations directly with the poetic wish for 'the days when we again will celebrate our festival (*'eyd*) in the embrace of the proud Damavand and Alborz mountains' (Sepehr 2009).

Mahyār Ebrāhimiān of the *Shabakeh7* team as well acknowledged that the atmosphere of Nowruz as experienced by people in Iran was absent abroad (Shariʻat and Ebrāhimiān 2020: m. 29:30). However, the TV channel's team endeavoured to create this unique atmosphere as much as possible (ibid.: m. 29:37). Broadcasting live to Iran, the US-based team of *Shabakeh7* is directly connected to their homeland through its viewers; the channel, in a way, is therefore inherently translocal. Alongside the decoration of the studio, the performance of traditional Iranian music and the joint counting down to the moment of the new year (*tahvil-e sāl*), a central means through which *Shabakeh7* tries to re-enter the authentic atmosphere of Nowruz and Yaldā at home is the staff members' telling of memories from the time before their emigration.

The contrasting of the *before* and *after* of emigration lets exiles count the number of years they have been away from home. Iranians abroad may similarly count the numbers of Nowruzs and Yaldās they have spent outside Iran. At *Shabakeh7*'s 1399 (2020) Nowruz programme, Mahyār Ebrāhimiān interviewed a young staff member of the channel, asking her: 'How many Nowruzs has it been since you have left Iran?' (ibid.: m. 26:52). Similarly, during the channel's Yaldā programmes, the team members, who gather around a set Yaldā table, regularly mention the number of years since their emigration from Iran.

An established habit, they then go on to one by one tell their personal memories of Yaldā celebrations in Iran. Often, the atmosphere is joyful and humorous as the team members joke about the generational differences becoming apparent in their stories. During the 1394 (2015) Yaldā programme, for instance, the older team members present were reminiscing about gatherings around the *korsi* with their families in the Yaldā night. A *korsi* is a low table which, traditionally, during winter was used by placing a heater underneath it and covering it with a large blanket; the family members would then sit or sleep under the blanket to stay warm. A younger team member, Musā, when being asked to share his memories smirkingly remarked that 'actually, I can't really remember those times where there was *korsi* and all these things' (Shariʻat and Ebrāhimiān 2015: m. 27:54). Mahyār Ebrāhimiān, who had just finished recounting his detailed memories of gatherings at the *korsi*, immediately retorted: 'Needless to say, I as well mostly have heard about these things in stories!' (ibid.).

Aside from the more joking episodes, however, the telling of memories creates a sense of nostalgia among the *Shabakeh7* team. Anecdotes about the *korsi* also bring back memories of their early childhood days for some of the team members:

Mahyār: So they [his family members] brought these very beautiful old, thick quilts (*un lahāf-hā-ye koloft-e qadimi-ye kheyli khoshgelo dar miāvardand*), some of them with flowery ornaments. They brought colourful velvet cloths, threw them over the *korsi* and went underneath it. The top of the *korsi* was turned into a table with nuts, pomegranates, watermelons, sunflower seeds, and so on

Farzāneh: Mahyār, you have made this picture really alive for me! (*Mahyār jān, tasvir rā kheyli zendesh kardi hā!*)

Hormoz: Absolutely …

Farzāneh: Believe me, I can smell the coal of the *korsi*! (ibid.: m. 22:06–22:37)

Mahyār's narration creates a momentary translocal and transtemporal space which conjures up a past experience for him and some of his interlocuters. This experience inextricably belongs to another time and another space: the Iran of his childhood. Just as the days of his childhood have passed (together with the tradition of the *korsi*), the original environment of his Yaldā memory has become irretrievably lost with his forced displacement to the United States. The presence of the '*Shabakeh7* family' (*khānevādeh-ye Haft*), as the team members of the TV channel like to address each other, helps him to at least fragmentally relive an authentic Iranian Yaldā, together with other Christian exiles.

The telling of Nowruz and Yaldā memories is not exclusive to the programmes of *Shabakeh7*. Edvin Sāleh of *ICnet TV* on the occasion of Nowruz 1399 (2020) as well exchanged his memories about Nowruz in Iran with his guest, a woman called Nedā (Sāleh 2020c: m. 18:41). Among other anecdotes, they were jointly reminiscing about the long Nowruz holidays and how they as pupils always had left their homework to the last day (ibid.). The effect created resembles what I have just described for *Shabakeh7*. Furthermore, the telling of episodes from daily life in Iran also helps channels like *ICnet TV* and *Shabakeh7* to create an atmosphere of familiarity with their live viewers back in Iran. The implicit message behind seemingly mundane anecdotes from Edvin's and Nedā's school time is that they, although they have lived outside the country for decades, still are able to relate to the daily lives of their non-emigrant audience. Potential converts thus are also reminded that becoming a Christian does not mean to automatically assimilate into, in this case, Canadian or American society.

Iranian Christians and the Biblical Israelites

Notions of exile among first-generation Iranian Christians can hardly be separated from visions of a future return to Iran. These visions may be more or less concrete. Generally, Iranian Christians, like many other Iranian exiles, deem a return to Iran impossible and undesirable as long as the Islamic Republic persists. Prayers for a downfall of the Islamist government are therefore commonplace. Many believe that only with the help of God, Iran will experience true changes and the ongoing hardships would come to an end.

Occasionally, Iranian Christians compare their own fate to that of the paradigmatic diaspora: the scattering of the Jews. Passages from the Old Testament recounting the journey of the Israelites into captivity in Egypt and their subsequent exodus seem relatable to some Iranian Christians. They as well experience their scattering as a 'thoroughly religious crisis' (Johnson 2012: 100) and trust in God to provide them soon with a 'gathering of the scattered' by God's grace (Baumann 2000: 317) back in their homeland. In what follows, I will illustrate how Iranian Christians interpret their own and their country's fate along the lines and imagery of the biblical Israelites. Among some, comparisons of this kind are complemented by the appropriation of Jewish symbols and Hebrew terms as well as a pro-Israeli political stance. After a brief assessment of this tendency, I will move on to the most pronounced and prominent Iranian Christian vision of a return to Iran, the Elam Prophecy.

Forty years in the desert

In 2019, the Islamic Republic of Iran completed the fortieth year of its existence. The longevity of the revolutionary state has surprised many observers and frustrated the Iranian exile community. In the early years of the Islamic Republic, many exiles firmly believed in imminent political change that would allow them to return soon. By the early 1990s, however, many saw their hopes dashed; there was, consequently, an 'increasing awareness among Iranian exiles that their conditions of exile were perhaps not, in fact, temporary' (Malek 2015: 25).

Some Iranian Christians although they did not leave Iran in 1979, with the approaching of the fortieth anniversary of the Iranian Revolution, have compared their dwelling outside the country with the forty-year wandering of the biblical Israelites through the desert (Safā 2019; Zargari and Zargari 2018a: m. 8:30). Thus, the term *biābāngardi* (desert roaming) has evolved as a shorthand for the plight of Iranian Christians in exile (cf. Shabānlāri 2017: m. 1:18; Shari'at and Ebrāhimiān 2020: m. 38:07).

One should not forget, however, that this characterization also engenders a certain optimism – after all, the Israelite sojourn in the desert *ended* after forty years. The comparison thus also offers a beacon of hope. Accordingly, Rezā Safā in a short video published in January 2019, a month before the revolution's fortieth anniversary, speculates about the collapse of the Islamic Republic during its fortieth year (Safā 2019). Alongside the wandering of the Israelites in the desert, Safā mentions other biblical episodes in which the number 40 plays a central role, such as the forty-day fasting of Elijah in I Kings and the temptation of Christ in the Gospels of Matthew, Mark and Luke (ibid.). Safā suggests that, in a biblical perspective, the number 40 was 'a number for trial, effort and temptation' (*mohākemeh, kushesh va āzmāyesh*) (ibid.: m. 1:48). Likewise, the people of Iran for forty years had been tried. The video ends with the question 'The 22nd of Bahman 1397 [the fortieth anniversary of the Iranian Revolution], the year of Judgement for the Islamic government?', placed under photographs alluding to the brutality of the Iranian Islamist government.

The tyranny of Pharaoh

When Rezā Safā describes the hardships suffered by many under the Iranian Islamist government, he does not speak only about Iranian Christians, but about the whole of the Iranian people. The dissatisfaction with the revolutionary Iranian state connects Iranians of many backgrounds, especially those in exile who blame their personal fate on the 1979 Revolution and its ramifications. Similar to Safā, Hormoz Shari'at in his 2020 English-language book, while acknowledging the distinct discrimination experienced by Iranian *Christians*, laments the oppression that, in his view, is mutual to all Iranians:

> The way the Iranian government treats its people is similar to how Pharaoh treated the captive Israelites in Egypt. Iranians are crying out to God for salvation, just as the Israelites did. And what God is doing now is similar to what he did then. He sent Moses to save the Israelites long ago. Today, He is sending His own Son to save the Iranians. (Shariat 2020: 140)

Both in Safā's and in Shari'at's portrayals, visions of a liberation of Iran from its current government are tied to the 'salvation' of the Iranian people, that is, their Christianization. The collapse of the Islamic Republic is thus situated at the end of a soteriological pattern. I will turn to this aspect later.

What is notable for now is that Shari'at too uses the image of the biblical Israelites, this time their captivity in Egypt and their liberation through Moses. The deployment of the 'Mosaic myth' to describe the political situation in Iran has got prominent antecedents: interestingly, not to say paradoxically, Islamist revolutionaries, among them Khomeini himself, had used the image of Pharaoh to vilify the *Shah*'s government and characterize their own struggle against it (cf. Chehabi 2010).[3] Identifying the Shah as an embodiment of Pharaoh because of his supposed 'injustice', 'polytheism', 'disbelief' and 'arrogance' (cf. ibid.: 18), the revolutionary Islamist discourse is striking in its similarity with Iranian Christian characterizations of the Islamic Republic:

> 'But Pharaoh said: Who is the Lord, that I should obey his voice' – he didn't know him! – 'and let Israel go? I do not know the Lord, and moreover, I will not let Israel go'. [Exod. 5.2, English Standard Version] Exactly like the government of the Islamic Republic! They don't know the true God, they don't know Jehovah. And they don't stop the injustice and oppression against our people. (Heydari 2018a: m. 24:42–25:08)

The perceived commonalities between Iranian Christians and the biblical Israelites/the Jewish people among some Iranian pastors constitute a recurring element in their sermons and other addresses. One narrative likely to be cited in this context is the supposedly perennial connection of Jews and Iranians spawned by the Babylonian Exile and the freeing of the Jews through King Cyrus the Great. Occasionally, such discourses usher in vocal support for the state of Israel. At times, moreover, Iranian Christians appropriate Jewish cultural elements and Hebrew terms.

Christian Zionism and the appropriation of Jewish symbols

Writing about the global dimensions of Christian Zionism, specifically in the Brazilian context, Manoela Carpenedo argues that scholars ought to not treat such tendencies as mere imitations of Anglo-American Christian Zionism (Carpenedo 2021: 205). Indeed, for Iranian Christians, as for Iranian dissidents of other backgrounds, outspoken support for Israel may also constitute a component of their active dissociation from the Islamic Republic. Provocatively put, precisely *because of* the Iranian government's fierce hostility towards Israel and Zionism, the two may appear worth supporting to some. According to historian Abbas Amanat, many Iranians look up to Israel as an industrialized and developed role model for the region; rather than the United States or Israel, their 'number one "other"', in any case, was the Arab world (Amanat 2018: m. 3:50).

While these may be contributing factors to Iranian Christian perceptions of Israel, matters of course are more complex. In a way contradicting Carpenedo's argument, my set of sources suggests that it is primarily Iranian pastors based in the United States who are vocal in their support for Israel. There are entanglements between pro-Israeli organizations and some US-based Iranian pastors. Rāmin Pārsā's English-language book in which he, albeit in a passing remark, praises the former Israeli occupation of Gaza (Parsa 2018: 100) includes a two-page endorsement by Nonie Darwish, founder of the organization Arabs for Israel. Another case in point is the invitation of a representative of Christians United for Israel to the Los Angeles–based Iranian church headed by Rasul Heydari. Asked why he and his church supported Israel, Heydari points to Gen. 12.3 which promised those who blessed Israel to receive blessings in return (cf. Heydari and Melāmed 2018). Functioning as the 'commonly cited … rationale for the restoration of the Jewish state by early and contemporary Christian Zionists' (Carpenedo 2021: 207), the verse is also cited by Hormoz Shari'at who calls it a 'promise' that 'has no expiration date' (Shariat 2020: 185).

It is important to not use such examples to make generalizing statements about Iranian Christians and their views on Israel and Zionism. Articles in *Kalameh* suggest that Israel and Zionism constitute a tricky subject in the Iranian Christian exile community, with a potential to create divisions. The question of whether the establishment of the state of Israel in 1948 was or was not the fulfilment of a biblical prophecy, for instance, is viewed upon differently by different Iranian Christians. In the last article of a series entitled 'What Does the Bible say about the Land of Israel?', the editors of *Kalameh* point out:

> The editorial board of *Kalameh* is aware that this is a sensitive topic and that Christians from all over the world have different views in this regard … Until the second coming of Christ, Christians will disagree about many issues and the topic of the land of Israel is certainly one of them. (Kalameh 2003: 34–5)

Beyond the question of attitudes towards the state of Israel, some Iranian churches during their services appropriate Jewish symbols and Hebrew terms. Again, Manoela Carpenedo has observed similar tendencies in the Brazilian context, where, rather than being part of a thought-out theological dogma, they are 'mobilized only at a superficial level' and appear 'arbitrary' in use (Carpenedo 2021: 211). My observations from the Iranian case suggest a similar arbitrariness (see Figure 8), although more research would be needed.

Examples of Jewish symbols displayed include the Star of David (Habibi 2018: m. 1:10) and the menorah (Philadelphia Elam Church 2015: m. 14:15; Zargari and Zargari 2020: m. 1:30). Among the two churches prominently featuring a menorah on their stage, the Gothenburg-based *Philadelphia Elam Church* runs a dancing group which during its 2015 Nowruz/Easter service performed two Hebrew-language songs by Israeli-Kurdish singer Itzik Kala (Philadelphia Elam Church 2015: m. 9:50; m. 47:50).[4] Music appears to be a primary realm of the adaptation of Jewish and Hebrew elements. Among the Persian-language worship songs circulating online, one can find a Hebrew-Persian rendition of the song '*Kadosh*' ('Holy'), originally performed by Messianic Jewish Israeli singer Elisheva Shomron.[5] It bears mentioning that the song's Hebrew-*English* version is equally popular;[6] the song may therefore have entered the Persian-language worship repertoire through its English rendition. A more curious case is a Persian-language adaptation of the song '*Abba*' ('Father') by Haredi Jewish popstar Avraham Fried.[7]

Such adaptations, again, are likely to be random rather than systematic; the latter song, for instance, may simply be the product of a devoted individual who covered it and made it available online. Much differently, a phenomenon constantly recurring in the sources used is the appropriation of the Hebrew word *shalom* – a term not usually part of the Persian lexicon. Usually, the word is used as the *shalom* of God (*shālum-e Khodāvand*) to express a wish for peace or to invoke a blessing.[8] The background for this adaptation is speculative. Potentially, its usage offers an alternative peace greeting to expressions including the word *salām* (the Arabic cognate of the Hebrew *shalom*) which by some may be perceived as an explicitly Islamic greeting.

Academic literature on Christian Zionism (particularly in the United States) has occasionally emphasized the relevance of dispensationalist theology, or 'premillennial dispensationalism' (cf. Clark 2007; cf. Spector 2009). Comprising a complex hermeneutical scheme of biblical texts, one of the notable tenets of dispensationalism is that the return of the Jews to the land of Israel was a prerequisite for the return of Christ. Thus, dispensationalist ideas in the United States immediately evoke sympathies with Israel in the Israeli-Palestinian conflict

Figure 8 A 2015 issue of the magazine *Rāh-e Salib* seemingly arbitrarily features the Hebrew name of the Feast of the Ascension of Christ (*Khag ha-Aliyah*). In *Rāh-e Salib* 13 (2015: cover).

(Reed 2012: 479). The arguable embeddedness of US-based Iranian pastors in the wider Evangelical milieu has already been alluded to during my discussion of discourses on Islam in Chapter 5; relatedly, recent scholarship has pointed to the increasing adoption of Islamophobic views among dispensationalist theologians (cf. Smith 2014). Another central characteristic of dispensationalism is prophecy belief (cf. Boyer 1992). Iran and Israel, like the whole of the Middle East, feature centrally in the speculations of dispensationalist theologians and authors regarding what the Bible supposedly foretold about the future of human history (cf. Reed 2012). This should be kept in mind as I discuss the Elam Prophecy in the following section, the most pronounced vision of return among Iranian Christians in exile.

The Elam Prophecy

35   Thus says the Lord of hosts: Behold, I will break the bow of Elam, the mainstay of their might.

36   And I will bring upon Elam the four winds from the four quarters of heaven. And I will scatter them to all those winds, and there shall be no nation to which those driven out of Elam shall not come.

37   I will terrify Elam before their enemies and before those who seek their life. I will bring disaster upon them, my fierce anger, declares the Lord. I will send the sword after them, until I have consumed them,

38   and I will set my throne in Elam and destroy their king and officials, declares the Lord.

39   But in the latter days I will restore the fortunes of Elam, declares the Lord.

(Jer. 49.35-39; English Standard Version)

Introduced by the biblical text as the 'Prophecy *against* Elam' and referred to by Iranian Christians as 'The Elam Prophecy' or 'The Prophecy about Elam' (*nabovvat-e 'Īlām/pishguyi dar bāreh-ye 'Īlām*), the cited biblical episode has constantly recurred in the sources assessed for this book (see Figure 9). Many Iranian Christians identify 'Elam' as it is mentioned in the book of Prophet Jeremiah with modern-day Iran. Some, for example, Elam Alive Ministries in Essen, also include today's Afghanistan and Tajikistan in their interpretation of 'Elam' – the two other modern nation states with considerable Persian-speaking populations. Historically speaking, Elam and the Elamites comprised an ancient civilization which was at home in large parts of the modern Iranian

Figure 9 A video screened during a worship session at Elam Alive Ministries in Essen, Germany. The Persian text reads 'Come and establish your throne in Elam!' In Zargari and Zargari (2017b: m. 1:15:31).

territories. The history of this civilization, 'despite recent progress … remains largely fragmentary' (Vallat 2011). As for the present, a province in Northwest Iran is named *Ilām*, derived from the ancient Elamite kingdom. Most Iranian Christians, when referring to the biblical Elam mentioned in Jer. 49, spell it with an initial *'eyn* (*'Ilām*). It can thus be distinguished from the modern Iranian province and in its spelling complies with the toponym's Hebrew spelling which as well begins with the letter *'eyn*.

Despite the salience of the Elam Prophecy among Iranian Christians in exile, the degree to which it is relevant to their religious practice and the self-understanding strongly differs on a very individual level. I asked Mahlā, who works for Elam Ministries in Germany, what role the prophecy played for her and her colleagues. She emphasized that its relevance went beyond a merely slogan-like character; the vision (*ro'yā*) of Elam Ministries was based on Jer. 49 (interview with Mahlā, 2021). At the same time, Mahlā mentioned that the Elam Prophecy did not manifest in her work on a daily basis (ibid.). Throughout her service for Elam Ministries, the topic was only debated once in her presence (ibid.).

Another of my respondents, the Iranian Armenian Henrik, explained that a diverse range of readings of the Elam Prophecy existed among Iranian Christian pastors and ministers – in fact, some believed that the prophecy had already been fulfilled (interview with Henrik, 2021). For himself, the Elam Prophecy did not seem to play a central role, but he stressed that he generally believed in the ongoing occurrence of prophecies (ibid.). Henrik claimed that while he was serving as a pastor within Iran, he had seen prophecies come true in front of his own eyes (ibid.). Generally, Henrik was much more enthusiastic to talk about what he sees as the current awakening (*bidāri*) inside Iran than about Iranian Christians in the diaspora.

Other pastors possess a very concrete idea of how the Elam Prophecy is supposed to speak to Iranian Christians in the diaspora. For pastors like Rozitā and Siāmak Zargari, Kāmil Navā'i, Hormoz Shari'at, Peymān Shabānlāri, Māni 'Erfān and Rasul Heydari, among others, visions of a future return to a transformed Iran originate from the Elam Prophecy. Moreover, the prophecy succours them in their quest for answers to the *why* of the, in their view, catastrophic event of the 1979 Revolution and their subsequent emigration from Iran. At the beginning of *Shabakeh7*'s 1397 (2018) Nowruz programme, Hormoz Shari'at, sitting in front of a small replica of the ruins of ancient Persepolis, explained to his viewers:

> You have seen our set: it is ancient Persepolis, a set that reminds us of what our past was and what our future will be. Sometimes, we Iranians look at the past and say: 'We used to be this and that!' (*khob, mā in budim, mā in budim!*) But we who know the Bible well are not just concerned with 'We used to be that!', but also with 'We *will* be that!' Because the Bible also talks about our future. (Shari'at and Ebrāhimiān 2018: m. 1:06–1:37)

What Iranians 'used to be' and 'will be' in the reading of Shari'at and others directly correlates with the Iranian people's chequered journey on the path to salvation. The final gathering back in Persepolis stands at the end of this path – but what has happened so far and what must be done to accelerate the return of Iranian Christians to their homeland? How will the 'religious crisis' of diaspora (Johnson 2012: 100) be eventually resolved?

To illustrate possible answers to these questions, three of the diverse readings of the Elam Prophecy will be presented in the following pages. All of the three readings can be structured according to the fourfold soteriological pattern of sin and disobedience, scattering and exile as punishment, repentance, and return and gathering described by Baumann (2000: 317). Reflecting the diversity of the sources used for this book, the sources in which the different readings of the prophecy can be found are videos comprised of several sermons by Rozitā and Siāmak Zargari, a series in the magazine *Tabdil*, and a section from Hormoz Shari'at's English-language monograph.

Sin and disobedience

According to Jer. 49.35-39, God will harshly punish the people of Elam. His 'fierce anger' will be upon them. The question immediately arising from the initial verses of the prophecy is: Why? What is it that caused God to rage so heavily that he decided to punish the Elamites by 'sending the sword after them' and 'scatter[ing] them'?

Rozitā and Siāmak Zargari in their services regularly point to what they consider the historical disobedience of Iranians to the true God. Ultimately, in their reading, the main rupture distancing Iran from God was her people's submission to Islam; earlier, Siāmak Zargari explains, Christianity even had been one of the official religions of the Iranian empires (Zargari and Zargari 2014: m. 41:10). But then Islam appeared and Iran entered its ongoing decay (ibid.: m. 42:00). The Zargaris frequently refer to Islam as 'the Prince of Persia' (*Mālek-e Fārs*), an allusion to the book of Dan. 10.13.[9] Its dark power, according to the two Germany-based pastors, culminated in contemporary Iran, which 'has thoroughly been consumed by evil' (*sharir kāmelan chatresho pahn kardeh*) (Zargari and Zargari 2017b: m. 19:55). The description of these evils, such as poverty, drug addiction and chronic lying, constitutes a recurring element in the Zargaris' addresses.

The anonymous author of the series 'The Prophecy about Elam' (*Pishguyi dar bāreh-ye 'Ilām*), which was published in thirteen parts between August 2007 and July 2008 in *Tabdil*, situates the moment of rupture much later. They aver that it was only with the 1979 Revolution that God 'broke the bow of Elam', as described in Jer. 49.35 (Tabdil 2008f). Only with the fall of the Pahlavi government, Iranians lost their power in the region, the author argues (ibid.). Regarding the present, the author much like Rozitā and Siāmak Zargari excoriates the supposed sin-stricken state of Iranian society as well as naivety of Iranians who assumed they could appease God with 'sentences in Arabic and a few ritual prayers' (*jomelāt-e 'Arabi va namāz-hā*) (Tabdil 2008h). Judgement and punishment awaited Iranians, as announced by the prophecy (Tabdil 2008e).

Following both the Zargaris and *Tabdil*, the prophecy has started to transpire but not yet reached its critical stage. The third example I am concerned with here, Hormoz Shari'at's reading of the prophecy, locates the prophecy's unfolding entirely in the future. In Shari'at's interpretation, 'the bow of Elam' has not been broken yet. Going into remarkable details, he suggests that Iran soon will experience a harsh military attack during which its nuclear arsenal, its oil reserves and the office of the Supreme Leader will be attacked (cf. Shariat 2020: 79–100).

That Iranians will suffer to such an extent seemed harsh, however: 'As we will see later ... Iranians will be involved in a major offense that *will* warrant this level of divine punishment' (ibid.: 86, italics in the original). This offense, Shari'at later reveals, would be a future attack of Iran and its allies (among them Russia) against Israel (ibid.: 115).

Scattering and exile as punishment

Jer. 49.36 entails the sinister promise that God will 'bring upon Elam the four winds from the four quarters of heaven' and 'scatter them [the people of Elam] to all those winds, and there shall be no nation to which those driven out of Elam shall not come'. The verse appears easily relatable to recent Iranian history as, undoubtedly, Iranians have experienced a tremendous scattering after the 1979 Revolution. In what ways do the three interpretations of the prophecy relate this scattering to Jer. 49:36?

In a 2017 address, Rozitā Zargari explained that God punished people disobedient to his commandments by taking their land from them and displacing (*āvāreh*) them (Zargari and Zargari 2017a: m. 9:35). The fate foretold by the Prophet Jeremiah for the Elamites – that is, for Iranians, Afghans and Tajiks – in this regard completely complied with that of the Israelites (ibid.: m. 39:11). More than that, Rozitā Zargari in a different sermon pointed out that what Jer. 49.36 announced, namely that 'there shall be no nation to which those driven out of Elam shall not come' had evidently become true: even in poor African countries, she suggests, one could find Iranians who had come there as refugees (Zargari and Zargari 2018a: m. 14:11).

The account in *Tabdil* again refers Jer. 49.36 to the emergence of the Islamic Republic of Iran in 1979. After a description of the manifold hardships caused by the revolution, the author turns to the ensuing mass emigration:

> Consequently, those who saw this massive flood and were faced with their own death, screamingly fled their own country in all four directions. The borders of Iran became a centre of terror-stricken masses (*markaz-e farār-e vahshat-zadegān*) in search of rescue. Human traffickers were thronging at every Iranian border to transport Iranians against exorbitant charges across the sea, deserts and mountains or streets and airports – in the four directions of its borders. (Tabdil 2008d)

If one did not know that this citation directly refers to Jer. 49.36, the emphasis put on the '*four* directions' would come across awkwardly to the reader. Bearing this in mind, however, it becomes obvious that the author wants to underpin the connection of the recent exodus from Iran to the biblical verse's announcement that God 'will bring upon Elam the *four* winds from the *four* quarters of heaven'. Different from Rozitā Zargari, the anonymous author in *Tabdil* does not put their emphasis on the immense range of countries Iranians have fled to, but on the diverse routes they have taken to leave Iran.

Again, Hormoz Shariʿat's reading differs quite markedly from that of the other two interpretations. The 'four winds', he avers, should not be taken literally but rather denoted the fact that all 'heavenly spirits' would be involved in the dispersion (Shariat 2020: 102). This dispersion indeed had already begun. However, the *main* dispersion foretold in Jer. 49.36 would only unfold with the horrible attack awaiting Iran and with the ensuing war (ibid.). Despite this, Shariʿat, much reminiscent of Rozitā Zargari's remark about Iranian asylum seekers on the African continent, attempts to baffle his readers by mentioning that recently he had encountered an Iranian man who previously was residing on the remote Southern Pacific archipelago of Tonga (ibid.: 105).

Repentance (conversion)

Approached through a soteriological pattern, it is up to the dispersed to take the initiative and accelerate their return to the homeland. They are the ones who need to make up for the sin committed by themselves or by their ancestors. The first step on this path is to acknowledge that they indeed have gone astray and therefore express repentance. In the Pentecostal Christian context, repentance also paves the way for the thorough embracing of Christianity or the second birth in Christ. Moreover, if the great sin committed by the Iranian people was their turning to Islam, as some of the pastors discussed here would argue, the reasonable reaction of those repenting would be to leave Islam again. For this reason, step three in the soteriological pattern envisioned by the Elam Prophecy may also be described as 'conversion'.

Siāmak Zargari, in a 2018 sermon, fervently called upon his fellow Iranians (not just Christians) to do repentance (*towbeh*) (Zargari and Zargari 2018b: m. 7:38). Again, Zargari compared the Iranian situation with that of the captive Israelites in Egypt (ibid.). Interestingly, Iranians of different backgrounds now gradually discerned the necessity of repentance, Zargari suggested, as one in recent demonstrations could hear the chant '*Mā eshtebāh kardim!*' – 'We committed a mistake!'[10] Later in the same service, Zargari called his congregation and online viewers to actively disseminate the message of the Gospel among friends and family (ibid.: m. 22:22). As proposed, repentance and conversion here are closely connected; accordingly, the active prayer for awakening inside Iran constitutes a constantly recurring element in Zargari's church and other communities.

Similarly, in the *Tabdil* series 'The Prophecy about Elam', the focus is not so much on repentance as it is on awakening and conversion. Still, the author implies that Iranians will experience a sense of regret about their turning to Islam; right now, more than ever, Iranians 'have become acquainted with the true face of their inherited religion (*din-e pedari*)' (Tabdil 2008g). For the first time, they consciously were comparing Islam and Christianity (ibid.). Despite all the discrimination and repressions, the article continues, house churches grew steadily (ibid.). This was because it was not humans who were at work but God himself (ibid.).

Hormoz Shari'at as well enthusiastically describes the awakening supposedly happening in Iran. The country, as the title of his book's twelfth chapter claims, had 'the fastest growing Christian population' (Shariat 2020: 133). Meanwhile, Islam lost its grip on Iranian society 'as if a veil was lifted from the minds of Iranian Muslims' (ibid.: 134). Yet, until God will finally 'set [his] throne' and 'restore the fortunes of Elam' (Jer. 49.38-39), a great transformation was necessary in Iranian society. Like his descriptions of the coming military skirmishes between Iran and other countries, Shari'at again goes into astonishing detail and enlists 'seven areas of transformation', namely family transformation, church transformation, marketplace transformation, media transformation, arts and sports transformation, education transformation and government transformation (ibid.: 151-68).

Return and gathering

The final verse of the Elam Prophecy nourishes the hope of many Iranian Christians that God will lead them back to their homeland, like he had led the exiled Israelites to the Promised Land. But the Iran they are hoping to return to is not envisioned as any kind of Iran. It is, to say the least, a post-Islamist Iran. For some, the promise that 'in the latter days [the Lord] will restore the fortunes of Elam' (Jer. 49.39) entails the vision of an Iran where Christians will enjoy full freedom and Persian-speaking churches will be as visible and accessible as mosques. For others, it means a thorough Christianization of Iran. Where on this spectrum do the three sources assessed here lie? To what extent do they possess a vision of what an Iran post Jer. 49.39 could look like?

For Siāmak Zargari, the answer to the question of how a future Iran will look like was hidden in verse 38 of the prophecy, where, in the Persian translation, God promises to establish the 'throne of his reign' (*takht-e saltanat*) in Elam (Zargari and Zargari 2014: m. 36:06). The concept of *saltanat* (reign), he explains, implied that at least 50 per cent of a country's population voted for the same head of state (ibid.). Translated to the context of the Elam Prophecy, this meant that more than 50 per cent of Iranians will accept the *saltanat* of Christ in their hearts (ibid.: m. 37:08). As Iranians were converting to Christianity in a staggering amount, this great transformation, in the view of Zargari, was palpably in process (ibid.).

The unnamed author writing in *Tabdil* does not go into details as much as Zargari. They state that Iranians always had been on the lookout for a king; now, however, religious bigots (*mazhabiun*) and 'people of the Sharia' (*ahl-e shari'at*) had usurped the position of the king (Tabdil 2008c). The author scathingly criticizes the Islamist government of Iran which, they argue, preached much about God but did not act accordingly (ibid.). Soon, in accordance with Jer. 49.38-39, a new government would emerge in which 'the people at last will worship the true God, rather than a human being' (ibid.).

It is again Hormoz Shari'at who possesses the clearest idea of what Iran after the Elam Prophecy's fulfilment will look like. His deliberations even include a discussion of what it meant to be 'a Christian nation' (Shariat 2020: 142–7), since, in his expectation, Iran would become one:

> After Iran's political leaders are judged and removed, millions of persecuted (but strong) Iranian Christians will have the freedom to function in the society. As a result, they will transform Iran. This will turn Iran into an openly Christian nation, via a natural transforming influence of Christians over Iran's government, media, finance, education, and artistic community. (ibid.: 120)

Shari'at provides his readers with further details. Alongside mentioning Iran's future constitution, which will be 'very brief' and 'might contain only two items' (ibid.: 146), Shari'at pictures 'large crowds gathering in numerous megachurches' and 'stadiums hosting great services' (ibid.: 149). Once God has established his throne in Elam, not just Iranian Christians will return to Iran, but the entire Iranian diaspora, 'because they will be proud of what Iran has become. (Today, conversely, they are embarrassed to call themselves Iranians)' (ibid.: 126).

No matter the individual reading of Jer. 49.35-39, no matter whether an Iranian Christian considers it already fulfilled, in the process of its unfolding or belonging entirely in the future – as of the year 2023, the Islamic Republic of Iran, albeit crisis-stricken, persists and the oppression of Persian-speaking churches continues. Those Iranian pastors who left Iran in the mid-1990s meanwhile have lived abroad for almost thirty years, a considerable amount of time. Their children and – depending on the emigrants' age – their grandchildren have spent their formative years outside Iran or have never even been to the homeland of their parents and grandparents. As the second generation of Iranian Christians in exile is growing, questions regarding their willingness to maintain an Iranian identity arise. What is the first generation's perspective on this issue? How important is it for them that their children keep an explicitly Iranian or Persian-speaking Christian identity?

Maintaining Iranian-ness in exile: What about the second generation?

In a 2007 paper, Cameron McAuliffe poses the question of whether the religious affiliation of second-generation Iranians in the diaspora contributes to the persistence or fading of their felt attachment to Iran (McAuliffe 2007). Engaging with Shi'i Muslims and Bahais in London, Sydney and Vancouver, McAuliffe finds that a sense of belonging to Iran was much more developed among his Muslim respondents than among Bahais (cf. ibid.). This divergence, he argues, can on the one hand be explained by the simple fact that most of the Iranian Muslims interviewed were free to travel back to Iran whereas the Bahais usually were exiled due to their religion (cf. ibid.). On the other hand, however, Bahais tended to de-emphasize the significance of their national identity by alluding to the post-nationalist attitude inherent to the Bahai faith (cf. ibid.).

How does McAuliffe's study compare with the case of Iranian Christians? Iranian Christians are distinct from the bulk of their Shi'ite compatriots and similar to Bahais in that they are unable to return to Iran. However, unlike what McAuliffe's Bahai interviewees have advanced for Bahai tenets, Iranian Christian churches do not by any means promote a post-national sense of belonging. Chapters 3 and 4 have offered rich evidence for the constant emphasis of an Iranian national identity. Besides, it bears mentioning that, contrary to McAuliffe's findings, Mehdi Bozorgmehr and Eric Ketchman in their study of second-generation Iranians in the United States have found that the will to maintain fluency in Persian is 'more pronounced among Iranian *exiles*' (Bozorgmehr and Ketchman 2018: 37; italics added) who, they claim, have a higher drive to preserve a connection with Iran. Accordingly, being exiled, rather than weakening a diasporic consciousness, can strengthen an individual's determination to maintain ties with their family's country of origin.

During the interviews I conducted with exiled Iranian Christian leaders, I sought to find preliminary answers to the question of what level of importance first-generation Iranian Christians ascribe to the transgenerational maintenance of an Iranian identity. All of my respondents acknowledged the active integration of the second generation into their churches as a pressing challenge. However, the degree to which the maintenance of an Iranian identity was deemed worthwhile varied. The matter is especially complex among members of the ethnic Christian minorities who need to navigate between three languages and cultures in the education of their children.

Henrik, who together with his family has lived in the UK for eight years, told me that his teenage son's level of Persian was not sufficient to understand sermons at their church (interview with Henrik, 2021). Speaking Armenian at home and English at school and with his friends, Henrik's son picked up his Persian mainly in the environment of the Persian-speaking church (ibid.). In a way, the church was thus credited with providing the Iranian-Armenian-British teenager with at least a basic knowledge of Persian. Another respondent, Ānāis, who left Iran with her Armenian parents aged nine and spent her formative years in Germany, similarly described the different Iranian churches she attended in the diaspora as the main site where she could maintain her Persian skills (interview with Ānāis, 2021). That said, Ānāis, with whom I conducted the interview in German, stressed that she was not happy with her own level of Persian (ibid.).

The attendance of Persian-speaking churches in the diaspora may have a similar effect on non-ethnic Iranian Christians as described by Henrik and Ānāis for Iranian Armenians. According to Zahrā Sālārī of the Iranian Church of Sunnyvale, Iranian churches abroad bolstered the Iranian identity of the second generation. Addressing viewers of the church's 1395 (2016) Nowruz programme tuning in from inside Iran, Sālārī averred that to maintain an Iranian identity in the United States was a big challenge, especially for children who were born in the United States (Sālārī, Sālārī and Navā'i 2016: m. 2:47:05). While many of the second-generation Iranians who grew up outside of the Sunnyvale church even shied away from calling themselves 'Iranian', young second-generation Iranians attending the church 'with pride' (*bā eftekhār*) called themselves Iranian and actively participated in Iranian cultural events (ibid.: m. 2:47:11). Churches, next to strengthening the second generation's language skills, thus can function as guardians to exiled Iranians' cultural heritage.

Beyond the question of language, Henrik told me that for him it was not important whether his children ended up attending a Persian-language or an English-language church (interview with Henrik, 2021). What counted for him was that they remained steadfast in their Christian faith (ibid.). Henrik thus differed from some of my other respondents. Daryā, who converted from Islam in the 1980s and left Iran for Germany in 1994, said that she consciously raised the youth group of her church to become the future of a *Persian-speaking* church (interview with Daryā, 2021). Her attitude was strongly informed by the vision of a potential return to Iran, in the event of which the second generation could become a pillar of the church inside Iran (ibid.).

Amir, who has a similar biography to Daryā but emigrated to the UK, pointed out that he did not want Iranian churches abroad to adopt a 'national dimension' (*janbeh-ye melli*) but still wished for the second generation to maintain a connection with an Iranian church (interview with Amir, 2021). He emphasized the importance of transnational Iranian Christian unity as a main concern to Iranian Christian leaders (ibid.). Like Daryā, he also raised the potentiality of a future return and the important role subsequent generations of Iranian Christians could play then (ibid.).

The active maintenance of an Iranian identity can also mean to draw boundaries to one's new cultural surroundings in exile. A potential negative influence originating from 'Western culture' that has been raised several times in the sources is its supposed individualism or isolationism (*enzevā-talabi*). In the editorial of a 2003 issue of *Kalameh*, Hesām Mortazavi mentions the latter as an increasing global phenomenon which was particularly palpable in the West (Mortazavi 2003b: 2). Since Iranian culture lent itself to get-togethers and community, Iranians abroad were easily affected by this; consequently, Iranian churches ought to maintain a communal spirit, also to attract non-Christian Iranian emigrants (ibid.). In a similar fashion, a member of the *Shabakeh7* team contrasted the importance of community in Iranian families with the, in his view, inherent individualism inside American families (Shari'at 2016: m. 13:32). A challenge for Iranian parents abroad arose here, as they should be careful 'to pass on the good things that exist in our culture to the next generation' (ibid.: m. 13:44).

Conclusion

In Chapter 2 of this book, I have argued that conceptualizations of diaspora in the study of first-generation emigrants must put notions of the homeland front and centre. By drawing upon Thomas A. Tweed's pioneering study of religious exiles, I have foregrounded the salience of religious narratives in visions for the homeland and its future among individuals who were exiled as a direct consequence of their religious affiliation. This chapter has illustrated such visions among Iranian Christians. Visions of a future return to Iran invariably are *religious* visions; they go hand in hand with the belief in a divine plan foreseeing the transformation of Iran which, as some insist, will become a Christian country.

In the view of some Iranian Christians, exile and return are necessary steps on the path to the salvation of the Iranian people. In this regard, the religious narratives of Iranian Christians resembles Jewish conceptualizations of diaspora, as described by Martin Baumann. I have used Baumann's enquiry on diaspora as a soteriological concept entailing a fourfold course of sin and disobedience, scattering and exile as punishment, repentance, and return and gathering to frame the most vibrant vision of return among Iranian Christians, the Elam Prophecy.

I have emphasized the multiplicity of readings of the Elam Prophecy and pointed out that the degree to which it is deemed relevant to the religious practice of Iranian Christians varies on a very individual level. Nevertheless, the Elam Prophecy can be justifiably called the major mobilizing narrative in the Iranian Christian milieu. It lends its name to many churches and the main publisher of Persian-language Christian literature, UK-based Elam Ministries.

Jer. 49.35-39 underline the perception of many Iranian Christians that Iran was the venue of an ongoing awakening. Moreover, in times where Iranians living abroad suffer from their association with a country which in the eyes of many is ill-famed as a supposed hub of Islamist extremism, they can take pride in the biblical significance of Iran. Discourses on the Elam Prophecy here resemble the narratives surrounding Iranian-identified biblical figures, as presented in Chapter 4. Notions of chosenness reverberate in the ample presence of the Elam Prophecy, strengthened by occasional comparisons drawn between Iranians and the Jewish people. However, especially in dispensionalist circles, references to biblical prophecies are by no means unusual or genuine to the Iranian case; rather, they are a central component of biblical exegeses.

Tweed hypothesizes that the second and subsequent generations of religious exile communities will no longer be attached to their parents' homeland to the same degree and display a 'supralocal' approach to religion. Given that the voices speaking through this book are almost exclusively first-generation emigrants, it will be left for future studies to inquire potential new, de-territorialized understandings of Christianity among their children and grandchildren. My sources suggest, however, that first-generation Iranian Christians wish for their children to not lose touch with their Iranian roots; some have even emphasized church as a sphere where these roots should be consciously maintained to prepare for a potential return to Iran.

Conclusion

Iranian Christian exile churches are becoming an ever more significant part of the religious landscape of the Iranian diaspora. Scholars from different fields may choose to study these churches from different angles. In this book, I have combined expertise in the study of religions and Iranian studies to describe Iranian Christian exile communities as a movement rooted in a wider religious transformation occurring in contemporary Iran. Analysing the publications and media productions of Iranian Christians active in countries like the UK, Germany, the Netherlands, Turkey, the United States and Canada, I have foregrounded notions of Iranian nationhood and the construction of a distinct Iranian-Christian national identity in Iranian Christian exile communities.

Historically speaking, a Persian-speaking Christianity in Iran first emerged as a result of Western Protestant missionary endeavours, particularly of British Anglicans and American Presbyterians. Over the course of the twentieth century, Pentecostalism gained increasing influence, leading to a 'pentecostalisation' (Rzepka 2017: 174) of Iranian Protestantism after the 1979 Revolution. Violent repercussions against Persian-speaking churches inside Iran, especially during the 1990s, have accelerated the emergence of a growing transnational community of Iranian Christian exiles. Rather than identifying through their affiliation with a particular denomination or church, Iranian Christian exile churches usually prefer to emphasize their *national* origins, using labels like 'Iranian' or 'Persian-speaking'.

Several factors lie behind this 'nationalization'. During the twentieth century, Iranian Protestants have striven for their independence from the various Western mission churches and sought to emphasize Iranian unity over denominational difference. This quest for indigenization made a major step in the early 1960s, when Hassan Dehqāni-Tafti became the first native Iranian Bishop of the Anglican Diocese of Iran. Ever since the 1979 Revolution, use of the Persian language for Christian purposes has been a particular target for Iran's Islamist government. Whether they are Muslim-born converts or Iranian Armenians and Assyrians, individuals active in Persian-speaking churches find themselves accused of engaging in subversive activities and of being agents of foreign, Western powers. These circumstances have further galvanized the national consciousness of Persian-speaking Iranian Christians.

Most importantly, however, I have pointed to the marginalization of Iranian Christians in discourses on what supposedly defined true Iranian-ness. Hegemonic notions of the nexus of religion and nationhood in the Iranian context have tended to represent Christianity as a thoroughly foreign entity, either conflated with Armenian-ness or belonging to 'the West'. I have termed this phenomenon the 'double foreignness' of Christianity in conceptions of Iranian nationhood and on a theoretical level argued that religious affiliation ought to be considered a central component of nationhood, that is, the traits considered to define authentic belonging to a particular nation. Notions of nationhood are subject to change; accordingly, religious groups and individuals marginalized by dominant understandings of nationhood can react by promoting differing notions and struggle for their thorough inclusion in the nation in question.

Iranian Christians use the freedom available to them in exile to present narratives and practices aiming for the 'naturalization' of Christianity to the Iranian nation. At the heart of these narratives and practices lies the conviction that one indeed can be both authentically Iranian and Christian at the same time. In Chapters 3 and 4 of this book, I have described in detail the sites at which this conviction materializes, using Iranian Christian celebrations of the Iranian new year festival of Nowruz as a starting point. While some pastors emphasized the symbolical overlap between Nowruz and the Pentecostal Christian notion of a 'new birth in Christ', others go so far as to cite 'scientific research', though vague regarding the exact source, to claim that the 'original' version of the *Haft Sin* table set on Nowruz bore a Christian meaning. Ultimately, proponents of this narrative would argue that Nowruz can only be truly understood through the lens of the Christian faith.

Further narratives and practices of authentication can be found in the context of Iranian Christian uses of Persian poetry. On the one hand, Iranian Christians claim that the famed classical poets of Iran – especially Hāfez – had an exceptional predilection for the figure of Jesus Christ or may even have been covert converts to Christianity. On the other hand, Iranian Christians themselves compose poetry with Christian content. Some, believing that the Holy Spirit has provided them with an exceptional gift, write Persian poetry as a means of worship and proselytism. They assume the role of what one might term 'poet-missionaries'. Persian poetry is a recurring component of Iranian Christian exile magazines; moreover, its recitation features in some Iranian Christian exile churches as a part of the liturgy.

Likewise prominent in the publications and media productions of Iranian Christians are references to Iranian-identified figures in the Bible, both the Old and New Testaments. Most significant among these figures is King Cyrus the Great. Over the past two centuries, Iranian intellectuals and politicians have discovered Cyrus the Great as the supposed 'father of the Iranian nation' and the epitome of a just and tolerant ruler. More recently, Cyrus has also become a primary icon of resistance against the Islamic Republic of Iran, the injustices of which protestors contrast with the ideal of Cyrus's government. Iranian Christians in exile proudly draw upon positive biblical mentions of Cyrus and call themselves the 'Cyrusses of today'. As in the case of Iranian Christian readings of the *Haft Sin* table, such portrayals are not lacking in a certain Iranian exceptionalism. This also applies to the Iranian Christian claim that the first Christians in history were Iranians, based upon the identification of the Magi with Zoroastrian priests.

Throughout the book, I have aimed to demonstrate how discourses prevalent in Iranian Christian exile churches are embedded in the sociocultural and sociopolitical exigencies of post-revolutionary Iran. In the examples of the Iranian national festivals of Nowruz and Yaldā, Iranian Christians represent themselves as the true heirs to these celebrations, which are understood by many Iranians to be perennial embodiments of Iranian culture. The Islamic Republic of Iran's hesitant and, at least historically speaking, hostile approach to occasions like Nowruz creates a void for differing interpretations which can freely be promoted in exile. Similarly, Iranian Christian commemorations of the 'Martyrs of the Iranian Church' offer an alternative canon of 'dissident martyrs' (Talebi 2012) challenging the moral superiority of the state-promoted martyrs who died in defence of the Islamic Republic.

Although Iranian Christians generally reiterate that Christianity was a religion most suitable for Iranians and Iranian culture a culture most harmonious with Christianity, there are nonetheless cultural elements deemed irreconcilable with the Christian faith by Iranian pastors. Most noteworthily, they read the festival of *Sizdah Bedar* and the practice of divination (*fāl/fālgiri*) as conducive to sinful practices, which a 'true Christian' should do away with. But even these practices are not unsalvageable. In an attempt to recuperate *Sizdah Bedar*, one pastor argued that it had only become a vehicle of illegitimate superstition as a result of Western distortion; along similar lines, a different pastor claimed that the poet Hāfez himself would have opposed the practice of divination based on his poetry – arguably the most popular variant of *fāl* today.

The forced displacement of Iranian Christians is directly connected to their religious affiliation. Even if many Iranian Christians emigrated for reasons unrelated to their religious identity, their open affiliation with Christianity justifies their assumption that it would not be safe for them to return to Iran. As a result, Iranian Christians make sense of their exile in religious terms: they ascribe religious meanings to their painful dwelling abroad and entertain religious visions for the future of Iran and the Iranian people. Drawing on Tweed's conceptualization of diasporic religion and Baumann's inquiry into the early Jewish understanding of diaspora, I have described how Iranian Christians perceive of their forced displacement as a necessary step in a soteriological scheme, at the end of which stands their return and the 'salvation' of Iran. Yearning for 'Next Year in Persepolis!', prayers for the unfolding of this scheme are commonplace.

Iranian Christians' hopes for a transformation of Iran that will allow them to return are concretely inspired by the Elam Prophecy, a biblical passage from the book of Jeremiah which provides rich material for worship songs and has inspired the names of various exile churches and other institutions. Different sources provide differing interpretations of this prophecy, but what generally unites them is a reading of the Islamization of Iran as a lamentable rift that must be surmounted through prayer and missionary work. Believing in an ongoing 'spiritual awakening' among Iranians, many Iranian Christians consider the 're-conversion' of their country to be in the making.

Despite the historically significant role played by Iranian Armenians and Assyrians in the development of a Persian-speaking Christianity, Iranian Christian exile churches today in their vast majority are attended by Muslim-born converts. Iranian Christians are thus eager to dissociate themselves from Islam. Depending on the audience, this dissociation can adopt a thoroughly different tone. In English-language books, some Iranian Christian pastors wage a vulgar attack on Islam and Muslims, aligning with Islamophobic tropes prevalent especially in right-wing circles in the West. In doing this, the pastors use their Muslim background to speak from a supposed position of authority – as 'crown witnesses' (Shooman 2014) or 'career apostates' (Foster 1984).

In the Persian-language sources assessed for this book, however, discourses on Islam appeared much more specific to the Iranian context and were mainly preoccupied with the contrasting of Christianity with the negatively perceived specifics of Shi'ite Islam. A key trope here is the representation of Christianity as a religion affirmative of joyfulness. Christianity is pitted against Shi'ite mourning practices, seemingly identified as the defining essence of Islam by Iranian Christians. Moreover, Iranian Christians emphasize that Christianity, in contrast with Islam, was not a (legalist) religion (*mazhab*). They foreground an Evangelical Christian understanding of Christianity as a 'loving relationship' and present it as a suitable alternative for Iranians who are fed up with the – as they would see it – paternalistic and suffocating variant of Islam imposed by Iran's Islamist government.

In the introductory chapter of this book, I set the stage for the ensuing chapters by pointing to a large-scale disillusionment with Islam among Iranians. Taken together with a strong and amendable national identity that does not depend on Islam – and, as we have seen in the case of non-Islamiosity, occasionally harbours an explicit loathing for it – the ongoing religious transformation of Iran appears sociologically explicable. Iranians who turn to Evangelical Christianity benefit from a readily available religious infrastructure (in the Persian language) which is well-accustomed to accommodating new followers and thus differs from other religions, among them Zoroastrianism[1] – a religion many Iranians otherwise possess a strong emotional attachment to.

Disillusionment with Islam is not necessarily a phenomenon restricted to the Iranian context. Neighbouring Turkey, for example, increasingly witnesses a young generation 'tired of religion'.[2] Wherever a government vocally espouses religious identity politics, its failures may be perceived of as a failure of religion too. If slogans like 'Islam is the Solution!',[3] systems like an 'Islamic Republic' and Islamically tinged promises of 'justice and development' fail to deliver, dissent emerges and a transformative potential arises. The case studied in this book is but one product of this potential. Given the ever-changing nature of seemingly static categories like religion and the nation, scholars should approach the 'Islamic World' and its large diaspora communities as spheres of diversity in which any (non-)religious alternative to Islam may evolve at any time.

Notes

Introduction

1 It bears mentioning that Philip O. Hopkins repeatedly and specifically maintains that 'both Persian and English sources from Iranian and Western authors are used' in his book (Hopkins 2020: 14). Overall, however, Persian-language sources play only a minor role in his book which focusses on the perspectives of mid-twentieth-century American missionaries. Rzepka mentions a Persian-language article by Ārmān Roshdi from *Kalameh* magazine but does not further engage with Persian-language Christian magazines (Rzepka 2017: 56). Regarding the works concerned with Iranian Christians in the diaspora, Krannich mentions that he started to learn Persian but nevertheless carried out his interviews with Germany-based Iranian converts in German (Krannich 2020: 26). Similarly, Kathryn Spellman notes that she 'was frustrated that I could not speak fluently and understand the Persian language' (Spellman 2004: 40).

2 This is most palpably the case for the books by Mark Bradley (2008, 2014). His 2008 book, for instance, begins with the following statement: 'Early on I noticed that Iranians were willing not to just give Christians a hearing, but some were ready to actually become Christians. As someone who wants people to respond to the Christian Gospel this was of course encouraging' (Bradley 2008: ix). He is therefore accused by Hopkins of not being 'an unbiased observer accounting the facts of a movement; he [Bradley] is a Christian who desires Iranians to convert to Christianity' (Hopkins 2020: 22). A similar point could be made for Van Gorder's book *Christianity in Persia* in which he states that 'it is hoped by this author, and many other believers worldwide, that Christianity will always be able to flourish in Persia's rich and ancient soil' (Van Gorder 2010: 212). Even Hopkins at times struggles to leave the normative perspective of an Evangelical theologian and uses terms like 'the message of the gospel' (2020: 12) or 'theologically orthodox' (ibid.: 177) without further elaborations.

3 The Netherlands-based Iranian scholars Ammar Maleki and Pooyan Tamimi Arab in an online survey asked over 50,000 adult Iranians (90 per cent based inside Iran, 10 per cent abroad) the question: 'Which of the following is closer to your beliefs and faiths?' They received the following responses: 32 per cent Shi'ite Muslim, 22.2 per cent none, 8.8 per cent Atheist, 7.7 per cent Zoroastrian, 7.1 per cent Spiritual, 5.8 per cent Agnostic, 5.0 per cent Sunni Muslim, 3.2 per cent Mystical (Sufi), 2.7

per cent Humanist, 1.5 per cent Christian, 0.5 per cent Bahai, 0.1 per cent Jewish and 3.3 per cent others (Maleki and Tamimi Arab 2020: 6). This, only in theory, would amount to roughly one million self-identifying Iranian Christians among a total population of eighty million.

4 Already before the recent study by Maleki and Tamimi Arab, scholars have pointed to the shrinking religiosity of Iranian Muslims. Axworthy poignantly stated that Iran 'is an Islamic republic, but one in which only 1.4 percent of the population attends Friday prayers' (Axworthy 2008: xiii). Khosravi referred to a governmental report from the year 2000 according to which '75 percent of the total population and 86 percent of the students do not practice Islam' (Khosravi 2008: 126). He added that *din-gorizi* (the 'escaping from religion') has been a challenge acknowledged by leading Iranian Shi'ite clerics (ibid.).

5 The asylum claims of Iranian converts to Christianity have posed a challenge to courts in Europe and beyond. At least in the past, judges have denied the authenticity of claimants' conversions by arguing in a pseudo-theological way. Resulting in controversial court rulings, the conundrum has occasionally attracted the attention of the media (cf. Kastner 2017, Schaverien 2019). A volume edited by Lena Rose and Ebru Öztürk with the title *Asylum and Conversion from Islam to Christianity in Europe*, forthcoming from Bloomsbury Academic, will deal with this issue at greater detail.

6 The UK-based NGO Article18, for example, uses the term to 'to denote either converts or ethnic Christians ministering to converts, as opposed to regular members of the "recognised" Armenian and Assyrian minorities in Iran' (Article18b 2022: 1).

7 They may also be, and it is important to mention this, neither from a Christian nor a Muslim background but from a Jewish, Zoroastrian or other religious background. A prominent example for a Jewish convert to Christianity is the former Anglican Bishop of Iran, the Jewish-born Iraj Mottahedeh (b. 1932). My personal interlocutor Daryā, who attended the Evangelical Church of St. Peter in Tehran during the 1980s, told me that the main pastor in those days was a Zoroastrian-born convert. She suggested that his background occasionally made it difficult for him to fully relate to the needs and concerns of the Muslim-born converts active in the church, herself being one of them (interview with Daryā, 2021).

8 Examples are the magazines *Māhnāmeh-ye Kelisā* (Church Monthly) and *Payām-e Kelisā* (Message of the Church), published by the Jamāʿat-e Rabbāni churches, as well as *Nāmeh-ye Mohabat* (Love Letter) and *Nur-e ʿĀlam* (Light of the World) by the Anglican Diocese. It is difficult to acquire copies of these magazines today.

9 Supplemented by the online archive of *Kalameh* magazine.

Chapter 1

1 One should add that such reports vary in scrutiny. The reports I draw upon in this book have thoroughly disclosed their methodology and used a wide range of data. The 2013 report of the International Campaign for Human Rights in Iran (ICHRI), for instance, is based upon thirty-one interviews with Iranian Christians, almost all of which were members of house churches inside Iran. The Iran Human Rights Documentation Center's (IHRDC 2021) report, along with five interviews with personal witnesses, has drawn upon documents issued by non-governmental organizations, academic articles and books, religious resources (e.g. the rulings of Shi'ite clerics on the issue of apostasy), government documents and media reports.

2 Among their distinct minority rights are, for example, the permission to run schools which teach the Neo-Aramaic and Armenian languages as well as Christian religious education. Regarding their religious practices, Iranian Assyrians and Armenians may carry out Christian services in the recognized churches using the communities' respective languages. Moreover, Iranian Armenians run a gated compound in Northern Tehran (the 'Ararat Complex') that is exempt from the Islamic moral code and operates restaurants, sports facilities and a church. Like the other recognized religious minorities, namely Zoroastrians and Jews, Iranian Assyrians and Armenians are represented in Iranian parliament with their own MPs. All this notwithstanding, Iranian Assyrians and Armenians find themselves regularly marginalized in daily life and are actively barred from staffing high-ranking governmental positions (cf. Barry 2020).

3 Another key target was the Jewish minority of Iran. Protestant missionaries working among Iranian Jews were often European Jewish converts to Christianity such as the Bavarian-born Anglican Joseph Wolff (1795–1862). For a detailed documentation of the Western missions among the Jews of Iran, see Flynn (2017: 757–934) and Waterfield (1973: 112–23).

4 It bears mentioning that, as described by Becker (2015), the designation 'Assyrian' here, as well as earlier in this chapter, strictly speaking is an anachronism. The emergence of Assyrian nationalism, linking the Christian population in question to the ancient Assyrian people, only dates to the early twentieth century. While the pre-nationalist self-designation was 'Syrian', the etic term used was 'Nestorian', alluding to the Christological teachings promoted by Nestorius (386–450) and rejected by the Council of Ephesos in 431. This designation however, albeit well established, has often been used pejoratively; Becker therefore always uses the term within quotation marks.

5 There were a number of further Protestant groups that have carried out missionary activities in Iran between the eighteenth and twentieth centuries, among them Moravians, Lutherans, Baptists and Adventists. It is, however, the American

Presbyterian and the Anglican missions which have had the most significant impact.

6 An example is the three-part series 'An Outstanding Christian Personality: Henry Martyn (1781–1812)', authored by 'Isā Dibāj, which appeared in 2003 issues of *Kalameh* (Dibāj 2003d, 2003e, 2003c). For a biography of Martyn, see Flynn (2017: 134–66).

7 The letter reads:

> I do not clearly gather from you whether at this moment there is much actual conversion from Mohammedanism to Christianity going on in Persia. The record you give of what has been done in former years is stimulating and useful, but I am constantly met with the statement that no visible result follows from the devoted work which is being done by yourself and others in Persia now. (Cited in Rzepka 2017: 68)

8 Many missionaries considered themselves liberators of the local women, both Muslim and non-Muslim. In the words of Jasamin Rostam-Kolayi, Iranian women were perceived of being 'in need of rescue from the darkness and barbarity of Islam, represented by child marriage, temporary marriage, and polygamy' (Rostam-Kolayi 2008: 216). The late Qajar ruler Nāseroddin Shah himself visited the Tehran Girls' School in the early 1890s. His ambiguous stance towards the enterprise is documented by his famous later remark, in which he disapprovingly averred that the school's pupils 'were being taught to wear high shoes with long shirts' (Rostam-Kolayi 2008: 220). Waterfield refers to the same episode but cites the Shah as lamenting 'high shoes and long *skirts*' (Waterfield 1973: 135, italics added).

9 Only in 1935, Reza Shah Pahlavi issued a decree demanding his country to be internationally referred to as 'Iran' rather than 'Persia'. The Anglican Diocese followed this request and changed its name accordingly. Generally, in English, the terms 'Iranian' and 'Persian' tend to be used interchangeably where in Persian one would exclusively find the ethnonym *Irāni*.

10 Schuler, as we can ascertain from Waterfield's book, was an American Presbyterian missionary and doctor who, together with his wife, arrived in the northern Iranian city of Rasht in 1902 to establish a hospital (Waterfield 1973: 139).

11 Thomas specifically recounts a visit to Urmia in the company of the Iranian Armenian pastor Edward Hovsepiān with the goal of founding a new church in the city. When he and Hovsepiān were finally allowed to preach in an Assyrian church, they were initially confronted with opposition by the crowd which expected them to preach in Aramaic. Later, they established a Pentecostal church in the city which was attended by different ethnic groups (cf. Thomas and Dibāj 2010).

12 Kordestāni's life has been documented in the Persian-language book *Beloved Physician: The Life Story of Dr. Sa'id Khān Kordestāni* (Rasuli and Allen 1986). He

himself was converted by a certain pastor Yuhannā who, as we can read in the book, travelled from Urmia to Sanandaj (Iranian Kurdistan) 'to spread the religion of Christianity in this religious and radical (*mote'asseb*) city' (ibid.: 10). Yuhannā there hired Kordestāni as his Persian tutor and engaged him in religious debates eventually bringing about Kordestāni's conversion. The story of Sa'id Kordestāni thus presents us with an early example of overt transethnic mission by, judging from his name and his departure from Urmia, an Iranian Assyrian Protestant.

13 Especially among Evangelical Christians, the idea of conversion is little pronounced. Instead, individuals recounting their 'testimonies of faith', that is, their personal trajectories leading them to the embracing of Evangelical Christianity, tend to use terms like 'giving one's life/heart to Jesus', 'doing repentance', 'accepting Christ as one's saviour' or, especially in the Pentecostal context, 'experiencing one's second birth in Christ' to refer to the moment that one from an outside perspective may call the 'conversion'. As this book endeavours to make ample space for primary accounts, the expressions described will occasionally surface throughout the ensuing chapters.

14 Dehqāni-Tafti himself reported the banning of the church's magazine *Nur-e 'Ālam* (Light of the World) in the 1970s. In his own words, the magazine was banned because 'Qom was uneasy about it' (Dehqani-Tafti 1981: 34). The Iranian city of Qom is the main centre of Shi'ite learning and home to influential members of the clergy.

15 From 1988 to 1998, outspoken opponents of the Islamic Republic's government, among them the last prime minister of Pahlavi Iran Shāpur Bakhtiār, the nationalist politician Dāriush Foruhar and the Iranian Kurdish activist 'Abdorrahmān Qāsemlu were assassinated. Their killings were finally blamed on 'rogue elements' in the Iranian Ministry of Intelligence (cf. Ansari 2019: 361–2; cf. Axworthy 2013: 344–8). Whether the extrajudicial killings of Iranian Protestant pastors were committed in the same context remains a matter of speculation, as do much of the serial killings' details.

16 A most egregious example are the 1988 mass killings of members of the Islamist-Marxist *Mojāhedin-e Khalq* organization. The case of Hassan Yusefi-Eshkavari offers an example of an Islamic reformist cleric who was indicted for apostasy. Yusefi-Eshkavari fled Iran in 2005. As for Iranian Christians, next to the cases of Hoseyn Sudmand and Mehdi Dibāj, more recently the pastor Yusef Nāderkhāni has been imprisoned and charged with apostasy. He previously led a 400-people congregation in Northern Iran, belonging to the non-trinitarian Church of Iran (ICHRI 2013: 33–4). Typically, the charge of apostasy is only one among several charges. Iranian judges, when raising the issue of apostasy, tend to draw upon the fatwa of Ayatollah Ruhollāh Khomeini who ruled that the punishment for a male apostate is death (IHRDC 2014: 9).

17 As the IHRDC points out, the closure of Assyrian and Armenian Protestant churches offering services in Persian has also deprived those members of the ethnic Christian minorities of their right to worship in public who are not proficient in Armenian and Neo-Aramaic (IHRDC 2021: 19). It can be assumed that their number is very low.

18 The Iranian Assyrian pastor Victor Bet-Tamraz, for instance, who formerly served as the head pastor at a Tehran Assyrian Pentecostal church offering services in Persian, spent sixty-five days in solitary confinement after his arrest during a Christmas celebration in 2014 (IHRDC 2021: 22). When a Tehran court issued long-term prison sentences against him and his wife Shāmirān ʿIssavi, they left Iran in 2020.

19 Other examples include two elderly Catholic nuns who after decades in Iran were denied a visa renewal in 2021. The Catholic presence in Iran now is diminished to two Chaldean archdioceses, one Armenian Catholic diocese and a Latin archdiocese which is currently vacant as its newly appointed priest, the Belgian Dominique Mathieu, is awaiting the granting of his visa (Vatican News 2021).

20 Article18 mention a recent bail amounting to 600 million tomans (around US$ 22,000); previous bails have been as high as $220,000 (Article18 2022b: 3). The ongoing clamp down on Iranian Christians therefore also in a way is a lucrative business for Iranian authorities. On a related note, raids to house churches often include the confiscation of 'anything that they [the security forces] found to be related to Christian activities, including cell phones, books, cars, and homes' (IHRDC 2021: 24).

21 In the Islamic Republic of Iran, ethnic Christians as well as Jews possess the right to produce and consume alcohol for religious purposes while Muslims are strictly forbidden from doing so. In reality, many Muslims consume alcohol in the private sphere as well; they often purchase it from Iranian Armenians who are active on the black market for alcohol (cf. Barry 2019: 227).

22 The other groups mentioned by Chehabi for the same category were Yazidis, Sikhs, non-believers and Azalis, although he acknowledged that it was difficult to ascertain whether Azalis still existed in Iran.

23 Representatives of the Persian-speaking Christian community in Iran both in past and in present have been politically active to achieve a legal recognition of the entity 'Persian-speaking Christians'. The most noteworthy endeavour in the recent past has been put forward by Behruz Sādeq Khānjāni (b. 1978), a pastor at the non-trinitarian Church of Iran. His initiative, which demanded the granting of a MP representing Persian-speaking Christians, was rejected in 2010 (IHRDC 2021: 38). After he was imprisoned several times, Khānjāni left Iran in 2012.

24 More information can be obtained on the organization's website: https://222 ministries.org/our-vision/ (accessed 15 February 2022).

25 At the time of writing, the countries were Germany, Austria, Armenia, Belgium, Turkey, Sweden, Finland and the Netherlands. An updated list of churches associated with the Persian Christian Community Church can be accessed at https://kelisayejame.org/%d8%b4%d8%b9%d8%a8-%d9%85%d8%a7/ (accessed 15 February 2022).
26 The self-description of the mission of Elam Ministries can be found at https://www.elam.com/page/elams-mission (accessed 15 February 2022).
27 In 2017, a pastor trained at the Assemblies of God's Southeastern University founded the Mozhdeh Theological Centre (*Kānun-e Elāhiyāt-e Mozhdeh*), see https://www.mojdehtheology.org/ (accessed 15 February 2022). Moreover, the Iranian Christian satellite TV channel *Shabakeh7* runs a training programme named *Dāneshgāh7* (Haft University), see https://daneshgah7.com/login/index.php (accessed 15 February 2022).
28 Dehqāni-Tafti mentions Iranian Pentecostals only when discussing the assassination of Iranian Christians after the 1979 Revolution (cf. Dehqani-Tafti 2000: 218–32).

Chapter 2

1 Outside the field of nationalism studies, the 1990s as well witnessed the rebuttal of the previously accepted secularization thesis which considered the decline of religion an inevitable by-product of modernization. See Berger (1999) and Casanova (1994).
2 As early as in 2003, Talal Asad reasoned that 'for both liberals and the extreme right the representation of "Europe" takes the form of a narrative, one of whose effects is to exclude Islam' (Asad 2003: 165). See also a 2013 special issue of the *Journal of Muslims in Europe* on 'Europe with or without Muslims – Narratives of Exclusion and Inclusion' (cf. Larsson and Spielhaus 2013).
3 Academic works often cite the 1966 article 'The African Diaspora – or the African Abroad' by George Shepperson as the pioneering work applying the concept of diaspora to the African context (cf. Shepperson 1966). More recently, Dufoix has pointed to earlier usages of the term for the African example (cf. Dufoix 2008: 11–13; Dufoix 2016).
4 Further attempts to structure the academic debate on 'diaspora' include Anand (2003); Mayer (2005); Mishra (2006) and Tölölyan (1996).
5 Tellingly, the Persian-language Wikipedia entry of the English lemma 'diaspora' is entitled *javāme' dur az vatan* (communities away from the homeland), a translation explicitly including the notion of the 'homeland'. The Iranian diaspora is usually referred to as *Irāni-hā-ye khārej* (Iranians abroad) or *Irāni-hā dar mohājerat*

(Iranians in emigration). A borrowing of the term diaspora as *diāspurā* is very rarely used.

6 The question of whether a certain amount of time has to pass for a diaspora to come into existence has concerned scholars from the very beginning of Diaspora Studies. Marienstras in 1989 vaguely stated that 'time has to pass' in order to know 'whether it is really a diaspora' (1989: 125). Cohen considers temporality a tool in the delineation of diaspora, remarking sarcastically that 'one does not announce the formation of the diaspora the moment the representatives of a people first alight from a boat or aircraft at Ellis Island, London Heathrow or Chatrapati Shivaji (Bombay)' (Cohen 2008: 16). A more concrete suggestion is made by Kim D. Butler who writes that at least two generations had to pass to justify the term 'diaspora' (Butler 2001: 192). This proposal, in my view, is arbitrary. I agree with Sökefeld who pointed out that 'there can be a temporal gap between migration or dispersal and the development of a transnational imagination of community', but added that 'it is also clear that such deferral of the formation of diaspora is not a necessary condition' (Sökefeld 2006: 275). In the Iranian case, the 1979 Revolution accelerated the emergence of a diasporic consciousness among those who were exiled as a consequence of the event.

Chapter 3

1 '*Vā! Ya'ni rafti Ermani shode'i?*'; 'Isā Dibāj here mimics an Esfahāni accent in Persian by altering the standard term *Armani* to *Ermani*.
2 As pointed out by Barry in his exceptional study of Iranian Armenian life in contemporary Tehran, it is especially young Iranian Armenians who struggle with calling themselves 'Iranian', while members of the previous generation may still possess a vivid memory of a higher degree of social inclusion in pre-revolutionary Iran (Barry 2019: 10). Resorting to rigid segregation, young Armenians now can even be heard to speak with an Armenian accent in Persian again, a phenomenon atypical for the previous generation (ibid.: 218).
3 Hyphenated in the original Persian.
4 For a discussion of conceptualizations of contextual theology, see Pears (2010: 7–49). Bevans's main work in the field was first published in 1992 under the title *Models of Contextual Theology* (cf. Bevans 2002).
5 Available sources only indicate the *hejri* years (1257–1333). Qazzāq Irvāni's date birth could therefore also be 1879 and his year of passing 1955.
6 On a similar note, Shaked mentions that some Hadiths make positive references to the festival of Nowruz. This includes an episode citing the Prophet Muhammad

as having exclaimed, 'If only every day was Nowruz!', after he was presented with sweets on the occasion of the festival (Shaked 1991: 91).

7   A bibliography of relevant works about the historical aspects of Nowruz is offered by Shaked (1991: 88).

8   References to the verse, though sometimes cursory in nature, were found at Ārshām-Far (2020: m. 21:14), Bāghestāni (2009a: 2, 2016: m. 28:21); 'Erfān (2017: m. 6:05); Heydari (2018a: m. 13:57, 2019: m. 55:30); Hovsepiān-Mehr and Hovsepiān-Mehr (2020: m. 41:14); Khezri (2007: 4); Mortazavi (2003a: 2); Qoli-Zādeh (2019: m. 2:56); Sāleh (2020b: m. 16:28); Sepehr (2012: m. 14:12) and Shari'at (2020: m. 27:17).

9   An example is Rev. 21.5, 'And he who was seated on the throne said, "Behold, I am making all things new"', which Mozhdeh Shirvāniān features as the calligraphic centrepiece of her colourful, floral video backdrop (Shirvāniān 2018), same verse cited in Bāghestāni (2008: 2).

10 An example is Mohammad Jalil Sepehr's 2012 Nowruz message where he refers to spiritual Nowruz as '*Nowruz-e rowhāni*' (Sepehr 2012: m. 5:59).

11 Ağuiçenoğlu has observed a similar tendency among Turkish Evangelicals who, avoiding the loan terms *paskalya* and *noel*, use the terms *diriliş bayramı* (resurrection feast) and *doğuş bayramı* (birth feast) to, respectively, denote Easter and Christmas (Ağuiçenoğlu 2016: 4).

12 The cited episode is one of the very few instances in which the Armenian ethnicity of a pastor is mentioned. Usually, Iranian Armenian pastors speak as Iranians to fellow Iranians.

13 Zahrā Sālāri in her list does not mention the exact verses; I myself could not safely ascertain which verse in Isa. 51 could be intended.

14 Verse likewise could not be ascertained.

15 In examples 1 and 2, the term *sarvar-e salāmati* seems to have referred to what in example 3 is listed as *sarvar-e solh*, the 'Prince of Peace'. It is clear from the deliberations following the mentioning of *sarvar-e salāmati* that *salāmati* here in fact is used as 'health', as is usually the case in colloquial Persian.

16 This can be gathered from several Nowruz recordings during which pastors have pointed out the high number of newcomers in the congregation. Generally, also outside of Nowruz, Iranian exile churches – like other churches – have a habit of asking newcomers at their service to identify themselves by raising their hand or standing up.

17 Quotes the original Latin *natalis solis invicti*.

18 Dibāj's account partially relies on hypotheses circulating among historians. The so-called 'History of Religions hypothesis' indeed holds that the 25th of December was chosen 'to act as a counter-attraction' to festivals like that of Sol Invictus (Bradshaw 2020: 8). Similar to Dibāj, proponents of this theory point to the

symbolical links made between the figure of Christ and the supposedly preceding pagan festivals (ibid.: 9). More recently, however, the hypothesis' credibility has been put into doubt (ibid.: 10). Moreover, neither Bradshaw nor the historian Hans Hillerbrand in their accounts make any reference to Iran, Mithraism or the Yaldā Night; in the words of Hillerbrand, 'the precise origin of assigning December 25 as the birth date of Jesus is unclear' (Hillerbrand 2021). Thus, Dibāj's account benefits from the shrouded history of the dating of Christmas.

Chapter 4

1 The poem, woven into a Persian rug, adorns a meeting room at the UN headquarters in New York. More recently, the poem has even entered pop culture as the British pop band Coldplay featured a track named 'Bani Ādam' on their 2019 album *Everyday Life*.
2 Like in the case of Irvāni, I could only retrieve the *hejri* date (1360). Avarsaji's birth year in the Gregorian calendar may as well be 1982.
3 Cited in Dehqāni-Tafti (1956: 9).
4 Matthew 11, 28 (English Standard Version).
5 Cited in Dehqāni-Tafti (1956: 12).
6 The poem I will cite further down, for instance, in April 2021 was viewed over 21,000 times – this is an exceptionally high number among videos from the Iranian Christian milieu.
7 In the case of poems sent in from Iran, this may be because of safety reasons.
8 In the English Standard Version the verses read:

> There shall not be found among you anyone who burns his son or his daughter as an offering, anyone who practices divination or tells fortunes or interprets omens, or a sorcerer or a charmer or a medium or a necromancer or one who inquires of the dead …

9 The term *Tāziān* denotes Arabs in a derogatory way and is especially prominent in Iranian nationalist discourses.
10 The term *beshārat* has a strong Christian tone to it. It is often used synonymously with the 'good news of the Gospel'; it is, moreover, related to the words *tabshir* (proselytyzing, spreading of the good news) and *mobashsher* (Christian missionary).
11 The Shah's eulogy goes as follows:

> O Cyrus, great King, King of Kings, Emperor of the Achaemenians, monarch of the land of Iran. I, the Shahanshah of Iran, offer thee salutations from myself and from our nation. We are here to acclaim Cyrus, the Great, the immortal of Iran, the founder of the most ancient

empire of the World; to praise Cyrus, the extraordinary emancipator of History; and to declare that he was one of the most noble sons of the Humanity. Cyrus, we gather today around the tomb in which you eternally rest to tell you: Rest in Peace, for we are well awake and we will always be alert in order to preserve your proud legacy. We promise to preserve forever the traditions of humanism and goodwill, with which you founded the Persian Empire: traditions which made our people be the carrier of message transmitted everywhere, professing fraternity and truth. (Cited in Ansari 2012: 110)

12 Cf. video footage of the gatherings available online, for example: https://flashvideo.rferl.org/Videoroot/Pangeavideo/2016/10/e/ea/ea84adaa-1c81-47b5-87a4-fab1f8971c1e.mp4 (accessed 7 May 2021).

13 Slogans have, for instance, included: 'We are Aryans, we don't worship Arabs' (*Mā Āryāyi hastim, 'Arab nemiparastim!*) and 'They say that everything is from God, but any misfortune is from the Arabs!' (*Hamash migan dast-e Khodāst, har chi balāst az 'Arabāst!*) (Ja'fari 2016).

14 *Mash shodeh* and *Masih* ultimately both mean 'anointed'. The title *Masih* of course is usually reserved for Jesus Christ.

15 Mentions of the Cyrus prophecy include Heydari (2018b: m. 29:20); Parsa (2018: 50); Sālāri, Sālāri and Navā'i (2016: m. 2:34:16); Shabānlāri (2019b: m. 12:52); Shari'at and Ebrāhimiān (2018: m. 9:06); Shariat (2020: 181); Zargari and Zargari (2014: m. 15:20). Zargari dates the prophecy to 200 years before Cyrus's birth, Pārsā to 140 years.

16 This number is contested; Edward Hovsepiān-Mehr, for instance, claims Cyrus is mentioned eleven times (Hovsepiān-Mehr 2008).

17 The term 'Christ' of course derives from the Greek term *Christos*, a translation of the word 'Messiah'. It is therefore not taken for granted that Shari'at here alludes to *Jesus* Christ. Yet, it can fairly be assumed that the readers' immediate association with the term is Jesus himself.

18 Zargari here alludes to the above-quoted eulogy of Mohammad Rezā Shah to Cyrus the Great, the first words of which ('Cyrus, sleep, for we are awake!') are well-known to many Iranians up to the present day.

19 In a source I have used for a different project, Pastor Lāzāros Yeqnazar proudly referred to Habakkuk's burial in Iran and displayed a photo of the tomb (Yeqnazar 2020: m. 1:03:23).

20 Similarly, *Kalameh* for a certain period featured a women's page entitled 'Woman's Viewpoint' (*Didgāh-e Zan*). The gendered title was eventually removed and the page 'integrated into the whole of the magazine' due to its 'ample reception among *male* readers' (Yeqnazar 2007: 3, italics added).

21 Rostampur and Amirizādeh were released after eight months in November 2009. They now live in the United States and have written a book about the time of their imprisonment (Rostampour and Amirizadeh 2014).
22 Dāneshvar in her article mentions that she is referring to what in English is called 'astrology'. The term *tāle'-bini* nevertheless can as well be translated as 'soothsaying', or may at least conjure up pertaining associations (cf. Emami 2006: 587).
23 Pastor Edward Hovsepiān-Mehr, the now UK-based brother of the deceased Hāyk Hovsepiān, has made use of the same term for the Magi in a 2008 article (Hovsepiān-Mehr 2008).
24 Talebi's contribution also engages with the spatial separation of graves. In Iranian cemeteries, one often finds a distinct section dedicated to the 'state martyrs'; this is while the 'dissident martyrs' are banned from cemeteries and at best are allotted an anonymous spot for their burial. This practice was also applied to, for instance, Pastor Hoseyn Sudmand's burial.
25 Likewise, a 2007 obituary in *Tabdil* mentions that the famous pop singer Mahasti (1946–2007) had embraced Christianity and received baptism before her death (Tabdil 2007a).

Chapter 5

1 The question of the extent and nature of the European impact on Iranian nationalism continues to be contested in pertaining academic works. Vaziri's (1993) account implies a thorough copying of European discourses by the pioneering intellectuals of Iranian nationalism. Tavakoli-Targhi, concerned with an earlier period, presented a sophisticated critique of the Orientalist narrative, highlighting the impact pre-modern Persianate intellectuals had on the first generation of Orientalists (Tavakoli-Targhi 2001). Conscious of the issue's complexity, Zia-Ebrahimi proposed a middle way by stressing the 'hybridization' of European Orientalist discourses among Persianate thinkers (Zia-Ebrahimi 2016). This does not save him from being labelled 'relentlessly Eurocentric' by Mana Kia in her recent book *Persianate Selves: Memories of Place and Origin before Nationalism* (Kia 2020: 206). What is beyond discussion is that, as Ansari pointed out, 'the dominant narratives (along with the conceptual vocabulary)' in Iranian nationalism have been defined by 'a European intellectual tradition' (Ansari 2012: 3).
2 Gholami himself acknowledged the awkward sound of the term 'non-Islamiosity' and its derived adjective 'non-islamious' by admitting that his coinage was 'perhaps not the most linguistically appealing or easily pronounced of words' (Gholami 2016: 5). Gholami developed the term in parallel with 'non-religiosity' and therefore opted to add the suffix '-iosity' to 'Islam'.

3 It is worth noting that, despite its popularization through the Runnymede Trust, the term 'Islamophobia' itself dates back far earlier. Where and how exactly it was used for the first time is subject to an ongoing debate in the field: Fernando Bravo López has convincingly argued that the term originates in the academic work of early twentieth-century French colonialist anthropologists (cf. Bravo López 2011). Interestingly, they used the term to criticize French colonialist officials for what they as academics considered an unjustified negative fixation on Islam. Allen's (2010) monograph, which for good reasons has been criticized as 'a very UK-centered account' (Bangstad 2014), offers further genealogies.

4 Edward Said in a 1985 piece already pointed out that Islamophobia 'has historically gone hand in hand with, has stemmed from the same source, has been nourished at the same stream as anti-Semitism' as is evident from the work of Orientalists like Renan (Said 1985: 99). The entangled history of Islamophobia and anti-Semitism also is the subject of Reza Zia-Ebrahimi's book *Antisémitisme et Islamophobie: Une Histoire Croisée* (Zia-Ebrahimi 2021). Meanwhile, the analytical limits and merits of a comparison between the two phenomena have been discussed by, among others, Bunzl (2007); Gidley and Renton (2017) and Klug (2014). Again, Hafez (2016) has offered an overview of the field.

5 It is this episode from his book that, tellingly, has been used by Evangelical media outlets to also apply the image of a 'former radical' to Shari'at: the German webpage 'livenet.de', for instance, in 2020 featured an article on Shari'at entitled 'Militant Muslim becomes "Billy Graham of Iran"' (Schmidt 2020).

6 Reza Zia-Ebrahimi has devoted some critical attention to the accusation according to which the Islamic conquerors of Persia had inflicted arsons on libraries. It is likely that this motif has been nourished by the projection of episodes of European and Christian history to Iranian history in Orientalist writings (Zia-Ebrahimi 2016: 91). In any case, the accusation 'does not stand up to examination' (ibid.: 115).

7 The verb *do'ā kardan* also is the usual word used by Persian-speaking Christians to refer to their prayers, alongside *shafā'at kardan*, which goes more into the direction of a prayer of intercession. The term *namāz* does not find any applicability in the Iranian Christian context. It specifically refers to the Islamic ritual prayer. On a related note, an article in a 2008 issue of *Tabdil* has featured an article asking 'What is the *Namāz* of Christians?' The article specifies that 'in Biblical Christianity, there is no such ritual under the name of *Namāz*' (Tabdil 2008a: 3). A Christian did not pray 'out of compulsion or fear of God'.

8 This emphasis often is also used to point to inner-Iranian ethnic diversity which many Iranian Christian exile churches, although maintaining Persian as the unquestioned dominant language, try to accommodate. Hormoz Shari'at, on the occasion of Nowruz 1397 (2018) explained:

God is a God of diversity (*tanavvoʻ*). God has created the Iranian nation in a way that we are different from each other. There are Kurds, Turks, Persians (*fārs*), Arabs – all kinds of ethnic groups, and God is a God who says: it was *me* who created you in diversity. (Shariʻat and Ebrāhimiān 2018: m. 16:52–17:22).

Endeavours to do justice to this diversity include the invitation to pray in one's native languages, worship songs in languages other than Persian and dance performances in regional attire during the service; see Kelisā-ye Jāmeʻe Fārsi-Zabānān (2020: m. 24:26–26:09); Sālāri, Sālāri and Navāʼi (2016: m. 2:11:03–2:25:35); Shariʻat and Ebrāhimiān (2016: m. 2:49, 2020: m. 52:50) and Zargari and Zargari (2018a: m. 53:16–59:08).

9 Derived from the Arabic root *dh-h-b*, the term *madhhab* in Arabic denotes a legal school of thought in Islam. In Persian, however, the term *mazhab* is used synonymously with *din* and simply means '(a) religion'. Accordingly, the derived adjective *mazhabi* denotes a religious individual (unlike *dini*).

10 See, for instance, the 2012 YouTube hit 'Why I Hate Religion, But Love Jesus', viewed 35 million times in early August 2021 (Bethke 2012).

11 The usage of *hazrat* is not limited to the Islamic context. Bahais, for instance, use the same title when talking about Bahāʼollāh or ʻAbdolbahāʼ, two central figures in the Bahai tradition.

12 The term *akhund* is usually used derogatively.

13 *Rowzeh* or *rowzeh-khāni* in the Shiʻite tradition denotes the mournful recitation of homilies recounting the tragic events of Karbalā in a literary fashion.

14 A most striking example of this tendency is a sermon by Peymān Shabānlāri in which he uses the phrase 'that religion that currently exists in Iran' (*un mazhab-e feʻli keh dar Irān hast*) (Shabānlāri 2019b: m. 33:06).

15 As Dehqāni-Tafti's books are published in both Persian and English, I have not included them into the category of English-language books published by Iranian pastors. They do not specifically speak to a non-Iranian audience, unlike the books discussed earlier in this chapter.

Chapter 6

1 The term *tabʻid*, unlike *ghorbat*, implies exile as a punishment, that is, the banishment of someone to a foreign place.

2 The opening lines of the *Masnavi* read:

Hearken to the reed-flute, how it complains / Lamenting its banishment from its home: / Ever since they tore me from my osier bed, / My plaintive notes have moved men and women to tears. / I burst my breast, striving to give vent to sighs, / And to express the pangs of my yearning for my home. / He who abides far away from his home / Is ever longing for the day he shall return. (Whinfeld 2001: 3)

3 Chehabi, moreover, describes the utilization of the 'Mosaic myth' in other contexts. Examples include the evacuation of Ethiopian Jews to Israel in the 1980s, framed as 'Operation Moses', as well as the Black Civil Rights Movement in the United States. In the Islamist context, representatives of the Muslim Brotherhood have used the image of Pharaoh to vilify Egyptian presidents Nasser and Sadat (cf. Chehabi 2010).
4 The two songs were 'Amenu Israel' from the 2006 album *Lekha Eli* and 'Isha Yafa' from the 2011 album *Mitgaagea*.
5 The song, among others, has been performed by the worship team of *ElamTV*, available at https://www.youtube.com/watch?v=5xDWh0FVgAM (accessed 14 December 2021).
6 Especially popular is the version by Messianic worship artist Paul Wilbur, released in his 1999 album *Levántate Jerusalén*.
7 The Persian Christian adaptation, entitled 'With Every Step I Draw Near to You' (*Har Qadam beh Suyat Āyam*), can be found at https://www.youtube.com/watch?v=yKED222RDz4 (accessed 14 December 2021). The original version by Avraham Fried appeared as a single in 2019, both in Hebrew and in Yiddish.
8 The term was, for example, used by Hovsepiān-Mehr and Hovsepiān-Mehr (2020: m. 41:09); Kelisā-ye 222 Kāyseri (2019: m. 11:07); Shariʿat and Ebrāhimiān (2020: m. 48:01); Tabari (2018: m. 1:46); Zargari and Zargari (2018a: m. 43:39).
9 The verse reads the Prophet Daniel stating: 'The prince of the kingdom of Persia withstood me twenty-one days, but Michael, one of the chief princes, came to help me, for I was left there with the kings of Persia' (English Standard Version). Hormoz Shariʿat as well identifies Islam as the 'Prince of Persia' (Shariat 2020: 184).
10 The slogan mentioned by Zargari first surfaced with the 2017 mass protests against the Iranian government, referred to as the *Dey-Māh* Protests. It usually goes '*Mā eshtebāh kardim keh Enqelāb kardim!*' – 'We committed a mistake in supporting the Revolution!'

Conclusion

1 That said, Iraqi Kurdistan during the past decade has witnessed the creation of an infrastructure that allows for large-scale conversions to Zoroastrianism (cf. Szanto 2018). Closely resembling the Iranian context, such conversions are experienced as a return to the 'original' religion of Kurds and constitutes an immediate reaction to the horrors experienced through the terrorism of ISIS (cf. ibid.). Szanto points

out that the Zoroastrianism construed by the individuals involved is very much an 'invented tradition' (ibid.: 97), although practitioners themselves vehemently reject this label (cf. ibid.: 105). A similar development is equally conceivable in the Iranian context, even if it would need to take place in exile, given the restrictions in the Islamic Republic.
2 Sociologist Pierre Hecker has used this phrase in his research on young atheists in Turkey (cf. Hecker 2021). It goes back to Turkish reformist theologian Necdet Subaşı.
3 *Al-Islām huwa al-ḥall*, slogan of the Egyptian Muslim Brotherhood.

Bibliography

Primary material

Monographs

Ansari, Mike (2016), *Heart4Iran: The Forbidden Stories*, n.p.: CreateSpace Independent Publishing Platform.
Dehqāni-Tafti, Hassan B. (1956), *Chun Mahzun vali Shādemān: Sharh-e Hāl va Ash'ār-e Jalil Qazzāq Irvāni*, Esfahān: Nur-e Jahān.
Dehqani-Tafti, Hassan B. (1981), *The Hard Awakening*, New York: Seabury Press.
Dehqani-Tafti, Hassan B. (1990), *Christ and Christianity in Persian Poetry*, Basingstoke: Sohrab Books.
Dehqāni-Tafti, Hassan B. (1993), *Masih va Masihiyyat nazd-e Irāniān: Dar She'r-e Fārsi – Dowrān-e Sabk-e Kohan*, Basingstoke: Sohrab Books.
Dehqāni-Tafti, Hassan B. (1994), *Masih va Masihiyyat nazd-e Irāniān: Dar Nazm o Nasr o Honar-e Mo'āser*, Basingstoke: Sohrab Books.
Dehqani-Tafti, Hassan B. (2000), *The Unfolding Design of My World: A Pilgrim in Exile*, Norwich: Canterbury Press.
Markaz-e Āmār-e Irān (2018), *Natāyej-e Kolli-ye Sarshomāri-ye 'Omumi-ye Nofus o Maskan-e 1395-e Koll-e Keshvar*, Tehran: Nashriyyāt-e Markaz-e Āmār-e Irān.
Mirkiāyi, Mehdi (2015), *Āsude'ash Nagozārid: Doktor Mostafā Chamrān*, Tehran: Sāzemān-e Tablighāt-e Eslāmi.
Namdar, Flor (2017), *Liebe statt Furcht: Muslimin. Atheistin. Pastorin: Mein Langer Weg in die Freiheit*, Aßlar: Gerth Medien.
Parsa, Ramin (2018), *From Ashes to Glory: The Story of a Former Muslim from Iran*, n.p.: Westbow Press.
Rasuli, Jay M., and C. H. Allen (1986), *Tabib-e Mahbub: Sharh-e Zendegi-ye Sa'id Khān Kordestāni*, Ann Arbor: Iranian Christians International.
Rostampour, Maryam, and M. Amirizadeh (2014), *Captive in Iran: A Remarkable True Story of Hope and Triumph amid the Horror of Tehran's Brutal Evin Prison*, n.p.: Tyndale House Publishers.
Safa, Reza F. (1996), *Inside Islam: Exposing and Reaching the World of Islam*, Orlando, FL: Creation House.
Safa, Reza F. (2006), *The Coming Fall of Islam in Iran*, Lake Mary, FL: FrontLine.
Shariat, Hormoz (2020), *Iran's Great Awakening: How God Is Using a Muslim Convert to Spark Revival*, Melissa, TX: Iran Alive Ministries.

Shayesteh, Daniel (2012), *The House I Left Behind: A Journey from Islam to Christ*, Sydney: Talesh Books.

Vaziri, Bozorgmehr (n.d.), *Hāfez va Masih: Āyā Hāfez Masihi Bud?*, Houston, TX: Kelisā-ye Mehr-e Masih.

Magazine articles

Āseriān, Robert (2004), 'Masihiyyat va Farhang', *Kalameh: Majalleh-ye Imān o Farhang-e Masihi-ye Irāni*, 10 (39): 12–13, 17.

Āseriān, Robert (2005), 'Erā'eh-ye Ketāb-Moqaddas dar Chārchub-e Farhangi', *Kalameh: Majalleh-ye Imān o Farhang-e Masihi-ye Irāni*, 11 (41): 32–3, 37.

Āseriān, Robert (2015), 'Ma'nā-ye Zendegi', *Shāgerd: Fasl-nāmeh-ye Jahānbini-ye Masihi*, 1 (1): 8–11.

Āseriān, Robert (2017), 'Ta'ammoli beyn-e Do Sokut', *Shāgerd: Fasl-nāmeh-ye Jahānbini-ye Masihi*, 2 (5): 27–32.

Āseriān, Robert, M. Borji, M. Fātehi, S. Khāchikiān and S. Tavassoli (2015), 'Sokhan-e Aghāzin: Qadami barāye Khedmati Tāzeh', *Shāgerd: Fasl-nāmeh-ye Jahānbini-ye Masihi*, 1 (1): 2–3.

Bāghestāni, Elnātān (2008), 'Sar-Maqāleh', *Māhnāmeh-ye Tabdil*, 3 (29): 2.

Bāghestāni, Elnātān (2009a), 'Sar-Maqāleh', *Māhnāmeh-ye Tabdil*, 4 (41): 2.

Bāghestāni, Elnātān (2009b), 'Sar-Maqāleh', *Māhnāmeh-ye Tabdil*, 4 (48): 2.

Dāneshvar, Maryam (2006), 'Āyā Moghān Tāle'-bin Budand?', *Kalameh: Majalleh-ye Imān o Farhang-e Masihi-ye Irāni*, 12 (48): 24–5.

Dehqāni-Tafti, Hassan B. (2007), 'Sheykh Sa'di va Polus-e Rasul', *Kalameh: Majalleh-ye Imān o Farhang-e Masihi-ye Irāni*, 13 (51): 21.

Dibāj, 'Isā (2003a), 'Masihiyyat va Nowruz-e Bāstān', *Kalameh: Majalleh-ye Imān o Farhang-e Masihi-ye Irāni*, 9 (33): 14, 36.

Dibāj, 'Isā (2003b), 'Panāhandegi va Imān-e Masihi', *Kalameh: Majalleh-ye Imān o Farhang-e Masihi-ye Irāni*, 9 (34): 14, 37.

Dibāj, 'Isā (2003c), 'Shakhsiyyat-e Barjasteh-ye Masihi: Henri Mārtin (1781–1812)', *Kalameh: Majalleh-ye Imān o Farhang-e Masihi-ye Irāni*, 9 (36): 30–1, 36.

Dibāj, 'Isā (2003d), 'Shakhsiyyat-e Barjasteh-ye Masihi: Henri Mārtin (1781–1812)', *Kalameh: Majalleh-ye Imān o Farhang-e Masihi-ye Irāni*, 9 (34): 31–3.

Dibāj, 'Isā (2003e), 'Shakhsiyyat-e Barjasteh-ye Masihi: Henri Mārtin (1781–1812)', *Kalameh: Majalleh-ye Imān o Farhang-e Masihi-ye Irāni*, 9 (35): 31–3.

Dibāj, 'Isā (2004a), 'Krismas: Padide'i Gharbi yā Irāni?', *Kalameh: Majalleh-ye Imān o Farhang-e Masihi-ye Irāni*. Available online: https://www.kalameh.com/article/%DA%A9%D8%B1%DB%8C%D8%B3%D9%85%D8%B3-%D9%BE%D8%AF%DB%8C%D8%AF%D9%87%E2%80%8C%D8%A7%DB%8C-%D8%BA%D8%B1%D8%A8%DB%8C-%DB%8C%D8%A7-%D8%A7%DB%8C%D8%B1%D8%A7%D9%86%DB%8C%D8%9F (accessed 8 March 2021).

Dibāj, 'Isā (2004b), 'Moruri bar Zendegi-ye Shohadā-ye Kelisā-ye Irān: Bakhsh-e Avval', *Kalameh: Majalleh-ye Imān o Farhang-e Masihi-ye Irāni*, 10 (40). Available online: https://www.kalameh.com/article/%D9%85%D8%B1%D9%88%D8%B1%DB%8C-%D8%A8%D8%B1-%D8%B2%D9%86%D8%AF%DA%AF%DB%8C-%D8%B4%D9%87%D8%AF%D8%A7%DB%8C-%DA%A9%D9%84%DB%8C%D8%B3%D8%A7%DB%8C-%D8%A7%DB%8C%D8%B1%D8%A7%D9%86 (accessed 12 November 2021).

Dibāj, 'Isā (2005a), 'Dard-e Ghorbat', *Kalameh: Majalleh-ye Imān o Farhang-e Masihi-ye Irāni*, 11 (44): 12–13, 45.

Dibāj, 'Isā (2005b), 'Moruri bar Zendegi-ye Shohadā-ye Kelisā-ye Irān: Bakhsh-e Dovvom', *Kalameh: Majalleh-ye Imān o Farhang-e Masihi-ye Irāni*, 11 (41): 6–9.

Dibāj, 'Isā (2009a), 'Khāneh-Tekāni-ye Kalameh', *Kalameh: Majalleh-ye Imān o Farhang-e Masihi-ye Irāni*, 15 (57): 2–3.

Dibāj, 'Isā (2009b), 'Salib bar Gerdan-e Nedā', *Kalameh: Majalleh-ye Imān o Farhang-e Masihi-ye Irāni*, 15 (58): 7.

Dibāj, 'Isā (2011), 'Zendegi-Nāmeh-ye Set Yeqnazar', *Kalameh: Majalleh-ye Imān o Farhang-e Masihi-ye Irāni*. Available online: https://www.kalameh.com/article/%D8%B2%D9%86%D8%AF%DA%AF%DB%8C%E2%80%8C%E2%80%8C%D9%86%D8%A7%D9%85%DB%80-%D8%A8%D8%B1%D8%A7%D8%AF%D8%B1-%D8%B3%D9%90%D8%AA-%DB%8C%D9%82%D9%86%D8%B8%D8%B1 (accessed 29 January 2022).

Fātehi, Mehrdād (2004), 'Dar Ebtedā Kalameh Nabud!: Sar-Maqāleh', *Kalameh: Majalleh-ye Imān o Farhang-e Masihi-ye Irāni*, 10 (37): 3–4.

Hāyrāpetiān, Leon, and 'I. Dibāj (2010), 'Pā-ye Sohbat-e Chehreh-hā-ye Barjasteh-ye Kelisā-ye Irān', *Kalameh: Majalleh-ye Imān o Farhang-e Masihi-ye Irāni*, 10 (61): 12–5.

Hovsepiān, Tākush, and 'I. Dibāj (2007), 'Mosāhebeh bā Khāhar Tākush Hovsepiān, Hamsar-e Osqof-e Shahid Hāyk Hovsepiān', *Kalameh: Majalleh-ye Imān o Farhang-e Masihi-ye Irāni*, 13 (51): 10–12, 43.

Hovsepiān-Mehr, Edward (2008), 'Juyandegān-e Haqiqat', *Kalameh: Majalleh-ye Imān o Farhang-e Masihi-ye Irāni*. Available online: https://www.kalameh.com/article/%D8%AC%D9%88%DB%8C%D9%86%D8%AF%DA%AF%D8%A7%D9%86-%D8%AD%D9%82%DB%8C%D9%82%D8%AA (accessed 26 May 2021).

Kalameh (2003), 'Sarzamin-e Esrā'il az Didgāhi Digar', *Kalameh: Majalleh-ye Imān o Farhang-e Masihi-ye Irāni*, 9 (34): 34–5.

Kalameh (2004), 'Nāmeh-hā-ye Shomā: Shokufāyi-ye Qariheh-ye Shā'eri', *Kalameh: Majalleh-ye Imān o Farhang-e Masihi-ye Irāni*, 10 (39): 11.

Kalameh (2005), 'Āshti-ye Masihiyyat va Farhang-e Irāni', *Kalameh: Majalleh-ye Imān o Farhang-e Masihi-ye Irāni*, 11 (41): 14.

Kalameh (2006), 'Haft Sin-e Alqāb-e Masih', *Kalameh: Majalleh-ye Imān o Farhang-e Masihi-ye Irāni*, 12 (45): 50.

Khezri, Khosrow (2007), 'Peyghām-e Nowruzi', *Kalameh: Majalleh-ye Imān o Farhang-e Masihi-ye Irāni*, 13 (49): 3–5.
Mortazavi, Hesām (2003a), 'Negāhi Do Bāreh beh Khod: Sar-Maqāleh', *Kalameh: Majalleh-ye Imān o Farhang-e Masihi-ye Irāni*, 9 (33): 2.
Mortazavi, Hesām (2003b), 'Sar-Maqāleh: Hozuri-ye Shahādat-dahandeh', *Kalameh: Majalleh-ye Imān o Farhang-e Masihi-ye Irāni*, 9 (35): 2.
Rāh-e Salib (2016a), 'Ester: Malakeh-ye Pādeshāh-e Pārs', *Rāh-e Salib: Avvalin Māhnāmeh-ye Irāniān-e Masihi-ye Holand*, 5 (17): 7.
Rāh-e Salib (2016b), 'Khodāvand Korush, Pādeshāh-e Pārs rā Mash Kard', *Rāh-e Salib: Avvalin Māhnāmeh-ye Irāniān-e Masihi-ye Holand*, 5 (17): 19.
Rowshan-Zamir, Rezā (2003), 'Kākh-neshini Miān-e Kukh-neshinān', *Kalameh: Majalleh-ye Imān o Farhang-e Masihi-ye Irāni*, 9 (36): 2.
Sepehr, Mohammad J. (2008), 'Birun Kardan-e Sabzeh-ye 'Eyd dar Sizdah Bedar', *Māhnāmeh-ye Tabdil*, 3 (30): 4–5.
Sepehr, Mohammad J. (2009), 'Nowruzetān dar Ghorbat Mobārak Bād', *Māhnāmeh-ye Tabdil*, 4 (41): 8.
Sepehr, Mohammad J. (2010), 'Ketāb-e 'Eshq va Andisheh va yā Fāl va Estekhāreh???', *Māhnāmeh-ye Tabdil*, 5 (59): 3.
Sepehr, Mohammad J., and 'I. Dibāj (2009), 'Mosāhebeh bā Keshish Mohammad Sepehr', *Kalameh: Majalleh-ye Imān o Farhang-e Masihi-ye Irāni*, 15 (60): 10–13, 40.
Shāgerd (1394 [2015]), 'Mo'arrefi-ye Ketāb', *Shāgerd: Fasl-nāmeh-ye Jahānbini-ye Masihi*, 1 (1): 26–7.
Shirvāniān, Mozhdeh (2006), '"Pishgoftār-e" Āyandeh-ye Masihiyyat-e Pārsi-zabān', *Kalameh: Majalleh-ye Imān o Farhang-e Masihi-ye Irāni*, 12 (48): 2.
Smyrna (2018a), 'Man yek Zan Hastam … Ester', *Smyrna: Majalleh-ye Farhang o Honar-e Masihi* (26): 38–41.
Smyrna (2018b), 'Masihiyyat dar Irān', *Smyrna: Majalleh-ye Farhang o Honar-e Masihi* (29): 30–3.
Tabdil (2006a), 'Hāfez-e Shirāzi', *Māhnāmeh-ye Tabdil*, 2 (13): 4.
Tabdil (2006b), 'Yaldā', *Māhnāmeh-ye Tabdil*, 2 (14): 1.
Tabdil (2007a), 'Bānu Mahasti dar Imān-e beh Masih beh Khāb Raft', *Māhnāmeh-ye Tabdil*, 2 (21): 5.
Tabdil (2007b), 'Dānyāl-e Nabi', *Māhnāmeh-ye Tabdil*, 2 (15): 9.
Tabdil (2007c), 'Mājerā-ye 'Adad-e Haft', *Māhnāmeh-ye Tabdil*, 2 (18): 10.
Tabdil (2008a), 'Namāz-e Masihiān Cheguneh Ast?', *Māhnāmeh-ye Tabdil*, 4 (36): 3.
Tabdil (2008b), 'Norooz, Persian New Year of 2567 (1387)', *Māhnāmeh-ye Tabdil*, 3 (29): 12.
Tabdil (2008c), 'Pishguyi dar bāreh-ye 'Ilām', *Māhnāmeh-ye Tabdil*, 3 (32): 10.
Tabdil (2008d), 'Pishguyi dar bāreh-ye 'Ilām', *Māhnāmeh-ye Tabdil*, 3 (29): 10.
Tabdil (2008e), 'Pishguyi dar bāreh-ye 'Ilām', *Māhnāmeh-ye Tabdil*, 3 (30): 10.
Tabdil (2008f), 'Pishguyi dar bāreh-ye 'Ilām', *Māhnāmeh-ye Tabdil*, 3 (28): 10.
Tabdil (2008g), 'Pishguyi dar bāreh-ye 'Ilām', *Māhnāmeh-ye Tabdil*, 3 (31): 10.

Tabdil (2008h), 'Pishguyi dar bāreh-ye 'Ilām', *Māhnāmeh-ye Tabdil*, 3 (27): 10.
Tabdil (2009), "Adad-e Haft", *Māhnāmeh-ye Tabdil*, 5 (50): 3.
Thomas, Dāvud, and 'I. Dibāj (2010), 'Pā-ye Sohbat-e Chehreh-hā-ye Barjasteh-ye Kelisā-ye Irān: Mosāhebeh bā Keshish Dāvud Thomas', *Kalameh: Majalleh-ye Imān o Farhang-e Masihi-ye Irāni*, 16 (63): 10–3.
Yeqnazar, Samuel (2003), 'Irān dar Naqsheh-ye Nejāt-e Qowm-e Khodā', *Kalameh: Majalleh-ye Imān o Farhang-e Masihi-ye Irāni*, 9 (34): 2.
Yeqnazar, Samuel (2004), 'Dar Āstāneh-ye Sāl-e Now-e Irāni', *Kalameh: Majalleh-ye Imān o Farhang-e Masihi-ye Irāni*. Available online: https://www.kalameh.com/article/%D8%AF%D8%B1-%D8%A2%D8%B3%D8%AA%D8%A7%D9%86%DB%80-%D8%B3%D8%A7%D9%84-%D9%86%D9%88-%D8%A7%DB%8C%D8%B1%D8%A7%D9%86%DB%8C%E2%80%8C (accessed 25 February 2021).
Yeqnazar, Samuel (2007), 'Panjāhomin Shomāreh-ye "Kalameh"', *Kalameh: Majalleh-ye Imān o Farhang-e Masihi-ye Irāni*, 13 (50): 2–3.

Online videos

Amini, Mohammad M. (2020), *Marāsem-e Nowruz 1399*, Apeldoorn: Kelisā-ye Korush/Kores Kerk. Available online: https://www.youtube.com/watch?v=gu6qWlZlfgE; https://www.youtube.com/watch?v=dGzv9SUYz_A; https://www.youtube.com/watch?v=Jdsl-TKShEg; https://www.youtube.com/watch?v=-hJVVso3JiE (four parts; accessed 22 March 2020).
Ārshām-Far, Mehdi (2020), *Har Ruzetān Nowruz dar 'Isā-ye Masih*, Stockholm: Kelisā-ye Fārsi-Zabān-e Estokholm. Available online: https://www.youtube.com/watch?v=jbAxDBDxAY4 (accessed 22 June 2020).
Avarsaji, Hanif (2016), *She'r-e Zibāyi az Hanif dar Vasf-e 'Isā Masih*, Sunnyvale: Kelisā-ye Irāniān-e Sāniveyl. Available online: https://www.youtube.com/watch?v=4qWw6NKFXE8 (accessed 24 March 2021).
Avarsaji, Hanif, A. Hovsepiān and J. Hovsepiān (2019), *Molāqāt: Shahādat-e Zendegi-ye Hanif Avarsaji*, London: SAT7 PARS. Available online: https://www.youtube.com/watch?v=a65qFmQELHY (accessed 23 March 2021).
Avarsaji, Hanif, and H. Shari'at (2018), *Man o Shomā: Mosāhebeh-ye Zibā bā Barādar Hanif*, Dallas: Shabakeh 7. Available online: https://www.youtube.com/watch?v=lWcZGWTN048 (accessed 23 March 2021).
Bābākhāni, Verzh (2019), *Payām-e Nowruzi-ye Sāl-e 1398: Zendegi-ye Shādāb-tar va Tāzeh va Sabz*, Almere: Kelisā-ye 222 Ālmireh. Available online: https://www.youtube.com/watch?v=3L9f5sGfl3Q (accessed 5 December 2019).
Bāghestāni, Elnātān (2016), *Jashn-e Nowruz-e Kelisā-ye Safirān-e Masih 1391*, Los Angeles: Kelisā-ye Safirān-e Masih. Available online: https://www.youtube.com/watch?v=2E4Fkrq_ksQ (accessed 2 September 2019).
Bethke, Jefferson (2012), *Why I Hate Religion, But Love Jesus*. Available online: https://www.youtube.com/watch?v=1IAhDGYlpqY (accessed 3 August 2021).

ʿErfān, Māni (2014), *Payām-e Nowruzi-ye Sāl-e 1393*, Dickinson: Kelisā-ye Hayāt-e Now. Available online: https://www.youtube.com/watch?v=otnYgbbBqeA (accessed 22 March 2020).

ʿErfān, Māni (2017), *Sāl-e Now va Nowruz bar Shomā Mobārak Bād*, Dickinson: Kelisā-ye Hayāt-e Now. Available online: https://www.youtube.com/watch?v=S1kdEXk7ipY (accessed 22 March 2020).

Habibi, Asghar (2018), *Nowruz-e 1397 dar Kelisā-ye Pārsi-Zabānān-e Sidney*, Sydney: Kelisā-ye Pārsi-Zabānān-e Sidney. Available online: https://www.youtube.com/watch?v=NyAYL97xKuo (accessed 16 April 2020).

Hāyrāpetiān, Gevik (2018), *Nowruz va Qiām-e Masih*, Venlo: Kelisā-ye 222 Fenlu. Available online: https://www.youtube.com/watch?v=GeeCHaMwrQU (accessed 26 September 2020).

Heydari, Rasul (2014), *Fāl va Fālgiri*, West Hills: Kelisā-ye Parastandegān-e Masih/Persian Worshipers of Christ Church. Available online: https://www.youtube.com/watch?v=KHKCu44td3o (accessed 16 March 2021).

Heydari, Rasul (2018a), *Jashn-e Nowruzi-ye Kelisā-ye Parastandegān-e Masih*, West Hills: Kelisā-ye Parastandegān-e Masih/Persian Worshipers of Christ Church. Available online: https://www.youtube.com/watch?v=14eTGkJGSlQ (accessed 3 September 2019).

Heydari, Rasul (2018b), *Jashn-e Nowruzi-ye Kelisā-ye Parastandegān-e Masih*, West Hills: Kelisā-ye Parastandegān-e Masih/Persian Worshipers of Christ Church. Available online: https://www.youtube.com/watch?v=fuscAkw4FWw (accessed 3 September 2019).

Heydari, Rasul (2019), *Jashn-e Nowruzi-ye Kelisā-ye Parastandegān-e Masih 1398*, West Hills: Kelisā-ye Parastandegān-e Masih/Persian Worshipers of Christ Church. Available online: https://www.youtube.com/watch?v=912JtJv9MnE (accessed 16 April 2020).

Heydari, Rasul, and K. Melāmed (2018), *Karmel Melamed Interviews Iranian Pastor Rasoul Heidari*, Los Angeles: Karmel Melamed. Available online: https://www.youtube.com/watch?v=aUoBUTMPJKY (accessed 11 December 2021).

Hovsepiān, Hāyk (2017), *Majusiān-e Irāni dar Josteju-ye ʿIsā*, Glendale: Hovsepian Ministries. Available online: https://www.youtube.com/watch?v=MHCPKm7P0so (accessed 16 September 2019).

Hovsepiān, Joseph (2014), *Marāsem-e Bistomin Sālgerd-e Shahādat-e Keshish Hāyk Hovsepiān*, Glendale: Hovsepian Ministries. Available online: https://www.youtube.com/watch?v=0XFEl5Hbha4&t=5168s (accessed 13 November 2021).

Hovsepiān-Mehr, Hovān, and E. Hovsepiān-Mehr (2020), *Marāsem-e Nowruz-e 2020: Khodāvand-e Man Bartar Ast*, London: North London Iranian Church. Available online: https://www.youtube.com/watch?v=Xys6EUIJNqA (accessed 29 April 2020).

IranWire (2022), *The Persecution of Christians in Iran*, n.p. Available online: https://www.youtube.com/watch?v=_jU0XEkXtu0 (accessed 15 February 2022).

Kelisā-ye 222 Kāyseri (2019), *Peyghām-e Kelisā-ye Irāniān-e Kāyseri beh Monāsebat-e 'Eyd-e Nowruz*, Kayseri: Kelisā-ye 222 Kāiseri. Available online: https://www.youtube.com/watch?v=k2ssZA9tzUA (accessed 3 September 2019).

Kelisā-ye Jāme'e Fārsi-Zabānān (2020), *Vizheh Barnāmeh-ye Nowruz 1399*, Venlo: Kelisā-ye Jāme'e Fārsi-Zabānān/Persian Christian Community Church. Available online: https://www.youtube.com/watch?v=DVYIuo2xVJY (accessed 22 March 2020).

Keshish-Ābnus, Edvin, J. Shamun and F. Ansāri (2014), *Pezhvāk: Fālgiri, Do'ā-nevisi va Kaf-bini dar Masihiyyat*, Chesapeake: Mohabat TV. Available online: https://www.youtube.com/watch?v=Lfp6ig7YLbo (accessed 18 March 2021).

Navā'i, Kāmil (2009), *Masihiyyat Chist?*, Dallas: Shabakeh 7. Available online: https://www.youtube.com/watch?v=kWstndA6zEk (accessed 3 August 2021).

Navā'i, Kāmil (2015), *Barnāmeh-ye Kāmel-e Nowruzi-ye Kelisā-ye Irāniān*, Sunnyvale: Kelisā-ye Irāniān-e Sāniveyl. Available online: https://www.youtube.com/watch?v=-bLoFrmMx-U (accessed 2 September 2019).

Navā'i, Kāmil (2019), *Nahsi rā Bedar Kon*, Sunnyvale: Kelisā-ye Irāniān-e Sāniveyl. Available online: https://www.youtube.com/watch?v=6xDfb6OjDAk (accessed 2 April 2021).

Philadelphia Elam Church (2015), *Marāsem-e Jashn-e 'Eyd-e Qiām va Nowruz-e Kelisā-ye Esmirnā*, Göteburg: Philadelphia Elam Church. Available online: https://www.youtube.com/watch?v=CdcRdq8qVmk (accessed 2 September 2019).

Qoli-Zādeh, Andreas (2019), *Payām Nowruz-e Shabān-e Andreas Qoli-Zādeh*, Afyon: Afyon Moravian Church. Available online: https://www.youtube.com/watch?v=S-IUI5yG9m8 (accessed 20 August 2020).

Safā, Rezā (2019), *Sāl-e 2019: Āyā Emsāl Sāl-e Qezāvat-e Dowlat-e Sharir-e Eslāmi-ye Irān Hast?*, Irvine: TBN Nejat Television. Available online: https://www.youtube.com/watch?v=wZRTpy-p_7s (accessed 8 December 2021).

Safāriān, Patrick (2020), *Shab-e Yaldā*, Los Angeles: Kelisā-ye Irāniān-e Lus Ānjeles/Iranian Church of Los Angeles (ICLA). Available online: https://www.youtube.com/watch?v=GGkiwdW6Otw (accessed 23 December 2020).

Sālāri, Hoseyn, Z. Sālāri and K. Navā'i (2016), *Barnāmeh-ye Nowruzi-ye Kelisā-ye Irāniān*, Sunnyvale: Kelisā-ye Irāniān-e Sāniveyl. Available online: https://www.youtube.com/watch?v=7uKmkIYnzis (accessed 2 September 2019).

Sāleh, Edvin (2015), *Payām-e Masih dar Haft-Sin-e Bāstāni*, Toronto: Kelisā-ye Bar Sakhreh. Available online: https://www.youtube.com/watch?v=uaB1JlJIDZ0 (accessed 22 March 2020).

Sāleh, Edvin (2018), *Tafāvot beyn-e Eslām va Masihiyyat*, Toronto: Kelisā-ye Bar Sakhreh. Available online: https://www.youtube.com/watch?v=NljO01OC1ak (accessed 3 August 2021).

Sāleh, Edvin (2020a), *Barnāmeh-ye Man o Shomā Vizheh-ye Yaldā*, Toronto: Kelisā-ye Bar Sakhreh. Available online: https://www.youtube.com/watch?v=WnkJiRrH_PM (accessed 19 December 2020).

Sāleh, Edvin (2020b), *Haft Sin yā Haft Sini*, Toronto: Kelisā-ye Bar Sakhreh. Available online: https://www.youtube.com/watch?v=FqT0b065FtU (accessed 30 March 2020).

Sāleh, Edvin (2020c), *Kelisā-ye Shomā: Vizheh Barnāmeh-ye 1399*, Toronto: Kelisā-ye Bar Sakhreh. Available online: https://www.youtube.com/watch?v=Tu25XlCO6-g (accessed 22 March 2020).

Sāleh, Edvin (2020d), *Payām-e Nowruzi-ye Doktor-e Edvin Sāleh beh Monsāsebat-e Nowruz 1399*, Toronto: Kelisā-ye Bar Sakhreh. Available online: https://www.youtube.com/watch?v=hpgmBVwCeac (accessed 22 March 2020).

Sāleh, Fred (2016), *Payām-e Nowruzi-ye Shabān-e Fred Sāleh*, Toronto: Kelisā-ye Bar Sakhreh. Available online: https://www.youtube.com/watch?v=k_3xJHyS3wA (accessed 20 August 2020).

Sepehr, Mohammad J. (2012), *Nowruz bā Keshish-e Sepehr*, Southern California: Mohabat TV. Available online: https://www.youtube.com/watch?v=G5XuMQs9skE (accessed 22 June 2020).

Shabānlāri, Peymān (2017), *Payām-e Nowruz-e Kelisā-ye Navid-e Rahāyi: Sokhani bā To Hamvatan*, Amsterdam: Kelisā-ye Navid-e Rahāyi. Available online: https://www.youtube.com/watch?v=ZS-blfbnCcg (accessed 2 September 2019).

Shabānlāri, Peymān (2019a), *Payām-e Kutāh: Krismas va Yaldā*, Amsterdam: Kelisā-ye Navid-e Rahāyi. Available online: https://www.youtube.com/watch?v=sA3LrivYkqI (accessed 25 September 2019).

Shabānlāri, Peymān (2019b), *Payām-e Nowruz: Nowruz Neshāne'i az Feyz-e Khodā*, Amsterdam: Kelisā-ye Navid-e Rahāyi. Available online: https://www.youtube.com/watch?v=aTIITEXLZWM (accessed 16 April 2020).

Shabānlāri, Peymān (2021a), *Payām-e Kutāh: Dalil-e Asli-ye Ruyi Āvardan beh Fālgiri va Khorāfāt*, Amsterdam: Kelisā-ye Navid-e Rahāyi. Available online: https://www.youtube.com/watch?v=FfweuVy3Xrg (accessed 18 March 2021).

Shabānlāri, Peymān (2021b), *Payām-e Kutāh: Dalil-e Dovvom-e Ruyi Āvardan beh Fālgiri va Khorāfāt*, Amsterdam: Kelisā-ye Navid-e Rahāyi. Available online: https://www.youtube.com/watch?v=os3OUdRsw7g (accessed 18 March 2021).

Shariʻat, Hormoz (2016), *Vizheh Barnāmeh-ye Shab-e Yaldā*, Dallas: Shabakeh 7. Available online: https://www.youtube.com/watch?v=6sfNmX_S2fE (accessed 25 September 2019).

Shariʻat, Hormoz (2017), *Vizheh Barnāmeh-ye Shab-e Yaldā*, Dallas: Shabakeh 7. Available online: https://www.youtube.com/watch?v=nChEJCGnHL0&feature=youtu.be (accessed 4 March 2020).

Shariʻat, Hormoz (2018), *Mash-e Kurosh bar Irān*, Dallas: Shabakeh 7. Available online: https://www.youtube.com/watch?v=53pJAYWNtpk (accessed 16 September 2019).

Shariʻat, Hormoz (2019), *Az Fālgiri Āzād Shodam*, Dallas: Shabakeh 7. Available online: https://www.youtube.com/watch?v=9JQuqVoCwWc (accessed 18 March 2021).

Shariʿat, Hormoz (2020), *Vizheh Barnāmeh-ye Nowruzi-ye Kelisā-ye Haft*, Dallas: Shabakeh 7. Available online: https://www.youtube.com/watch?v=ldM_SjZZIpM (accessed 22 March 2020).

Shariʿat, Hormoz, and M. Ebrāhimiān (2014), *Barnāmeh-ye Makhsus-e Shab-e Yaldā*, Dallas: Shabakeh 7. Available online: https://www.youtube.com/watch?v=7yLtOWWjupI&t=37s (accessed 4 March 2020).

Shariʿat, Hormoz, and M. Ebrāhimiān (2015), *Vizheh Barnāmeh-ye Shab-e Yaldā 1394*, Dallas: Shabakeh 7. Available online: https://www.youtube.com/watch?v=qO3YN-u02Hc (accessed 26 September 2019).

Shariʿat, Hormoz, and M. Ebrāhimiān (2016), *Vizheh Barnāmeh-ye Jashn-e Nowruzi-ye Sāl-e 1395*, Dallas: Shabakeh 7. Available online: https://www.youtube.com/watch?v=ErkaSXFvkYQ (accessed 2 September 2019).

Shariʿat, Hormoz, and M. Ebrāhimiān (2018), *Barnāmeh-ye Vizheh-ye Nowruzi-ye 1397 bā Khānevādeh-ye Haft*, Dallas: Shabakeh 7. Available online: https://youtu.be/FP6vVeiShdc (accessed 3 September 2019).

Shariʿat, Hormoz, and M. Ebrāhimiān (2020), *Vizheh Barnāmeh-ye Jashn-e Nowruzi-ye 1399*, Dallas: Shabakeh 7. Available online: https://www.youtube.com/watch?v=CEa1_UMZTEU (accessed 22 March 2020).

Shirvāniān, Mozhdeh (2018), *Payām-e Tabrik-e Barnāmeh-ye Donyā-ye Zan beh Monsāsebat-e Nowruz va ʿEyd-e Qiām*, London: Elam TV. Available online: https://www.youtube.com/watch?v=haIY986zQjQ (accessed 25 September 2020).

Tabari, Māziār (2018), *Nowruz-e Bāstāni*, Bremen: Kelisā-ye Ruh-e Khodā. Available online: https://www.youtube.com/watch?v=haIY986zQjQ (accessed 25 September 2020).

Yeqnaẓar, Lāzāros (2020), *Dar Hāshiyeh-ye Nowruzi Kamrang, Bahāri Dardmand, Omid-e Mā beh Khodā*, London: Kelisā-ye Jāmeʿe Fārsi-Zabānān. Available online: https://www.youtube.com/watch?v=_9ZHPerZ3SQ (accessed 25 September 2020).

Zargari, Siāmak, and R. Zargari (2014), *Mowʿezeh-ye Nowruz-e 93: Kurosh keh beh Imān Dāsht?*, Essen: Kelisā-ye ʿIlām-e Zendeh/Elam Alive Ministries. Available online: https://www.youtube.com/watch?v=ECdIUIP3N3g (accessed 2 April 2020).

Zargari, Siāmak, and R. Zargari (2017a), *Irān, ey Sarzamin-e m'Mehrabāni keh Aknun Del-e To Por az Dard Shodeh, Masih To rā Shafā Dahad*, Essen: Kelisā-ye ʿIlām-e Zendeh/Elam Alive Ministries. Available online: https://www.youtube.com/watch?v=d6utaz0bdYc (accessed 16 September 2019).

Zargari, Siāmak, and R. Zargari (2017b), *Jalaseh-ye ʿEbādati-ye Parasteshi-ye Nowruz-e 96*, Essen: Kelisā-ye ʿIlām-e Zendeh/Elam Alive Ministries. Available online: https://www.youtube.com/watch?v=Y8ZXkvPkVrs (accessed 13 July 2020).

Zargari, Siāmak, and R. Zargari (2018a), *Marāsem-e Vizheh-ye ʿEyd-e Nowruz-e 2577*, Essen: Kelisā-ye ʿIlām-e Zendeh/Elam Alive Ministries. Available online: https://www.youtube.com/watch?v=Ywio-xiqOw0 (accessed 2 September 2019).

Zargari, Siāmak, and R. Zargari (2018b), *Peyghām-e Nabovvati barāye Irān*, Essen: Kelisā-ye ʿIlām-e Zendeh/Elam Alive Ministries. Available online: https://www.youtube.com/watch?v=YN-AnjrwtMA (accessed 16 September 2019).

Zargari, Siāmak, and R. Zargari (2019), *Marāsem-e Vizheh-ye Nowruz-e Kelisā-ye ʿIlām-e Zendeh*, Essen: Kelisā-ye ʿIlām-e Zendeh/Elam Alive Ministries. Available online: https://www.youtube.com/watch?v=G7w1rwpczHI (accessed 2 September 2019).

Zargari, Siāmak, and R. Zargari (2020), *Marāsem-e Vizheh-ye Nowruz-e Sāl-e 2579*, Essen: Kelisā-ye ʿIlām-e Zendeh/Elam Alive Ministries. Available online: https://www.youtube.com/watch?v=E9JC1wmH3JY (accessed 4 May 2020).

Anonymous interviews

Amir, 2021, UK
Ānāis, 2021, UK
Daryā, 2021, Germany
Henrik, 2021, UK
Mahlā, 2021, Germany (via Zoom)
Martin, 2022, Germany (via Zoom)
Peymān, 2021, UK

Documentaries and movies

Dibāj, ʿIsā, and M. Shirvāniān (2005), *Bahā-ye Mohabbat: Mosāhebeh bā Osqof Hasan Dehqāni-Tafti*, Godalming: Elam Ministries.

Hovsepiān, Joseph (2003), *Āhang-e Ghorbat*, Los Angeles: JFA Productions.

Hovsepiān, Joseph, and A. Hovsepiān (2007), *Faryādi az Irān*, Los Angeles: JFA Productions.

Podcasts

Āseriān, Robert, and T. Nettleton (2020), *IRAN: From Atheist to Persecuted Pastor*, Bartlesville: The Voice of the Martyrs Radio.

Radiomarz (2019), *Armani-hā*, n.p.

Clerical statements

Khāmeneʾi, Seyyed ʿ. (n.d.), 'Ajvebeh-ol-esteftāʾāt: Velādat-hā va Aʿyād', KHAMENEI.IR. Available online: https://farsi.khamenei.ir/treatise-content?id=132 (accessed 10 February 2021).

Khāmene'i, Seyyed ʿ. (2010), 'Bayyānāt dar Ejtemāʿe Bozorg-e Mardom-e Qom'. Available online: https://www.leader.ir/fa/speech/7363 (accessed 10 February 2022).
Makārem-Shirāzi, Nāser (n.d.), 'Hokm-e Bargozāri-ye Sonnat-e Irāni-ye Shab-e Yaldā'. Available online: https://makarem.ir/main.aspx?typeinfo=21&lid=0&catid=46496&mid=259746 (accessed 10 February 2021).

Translated poetry

Davis, Dick (2012), '"For Years My Heart Asked of Me": Ghazal 143'. Available online: https://blogs.harvard.edu/sulaymanibnqiddees/2012/08/15/hafez-for-years-my-heart-asked-of-me-ghazal-143/ (accessed 26 March 2021).
Thackston, Wheeler M. (2008), *The Gulistan (Rose Garden) of Saʿdi: Bilingual English and Persian Version with Vocabulary*, Maryland: Ibex Publishers.
Whinfeld, Edward H. (2001), *Masnavi i Maʾnavi: Teachings of Rumi*, Iowa: Omphaloskepsis.

Secondary material

Monographs

Abrahamian, Ervand (1999), *Tortured Confessions: Prisons and Public Recantations in Modern Iran*, Berkeley: University of California Press.
Abrahamian, Ervand (2008), *A History of Modern Iran*, Cambridge: Cambridge University Press.
Aghaie, Kamran S. (2004), *The Martyrs of Karbala: Shi'i Symbols and Rituals in Modern Iran*, Seattle: University of Washington Press.
Allen, Chris (2010), *Islamophobia*, Farnham: Ashgate Books.
Amanat, Abbas (2017), *Iran: A Modern History*, New Haven: Yale University Press.
Anderson, Benedict (1983), *Imagined Communities: Reflections on the Origin and Spread of Nationalism*, London: Verso.
Ansari, Ali M. (2012), *The Politics of Nationalism in Modern Iran*, Cambridge: Cambridge University Press.
Ansari, Ali M. (2019), *Modern Iran Since 1797: Reform and Revolution*, New York: Routledge.
Armstrong, John A. (1982), *Nations before Nationalism*, Chapel Hill: University of North Carolina Press.
Asad, Talal (1993), *Genealogies of Religion: Discipline and Reasons of Power in Christianity and Islam*, Baltimore: Johns Hopkins University Press.
Asad, Talal (2003), *Formations of the Secular: Christianity, Islam, Modernity*, Stanford: Stanford University Press.

Axworthy, Michael (2008), *Iran: Empire of the Mind: A History from Zoroaster to the Present Day*, London: Penguin.

Axworthy, Michael (2013), *Revolutionary Iran: A History of the Islamic Republic*, New York: Oxford University Press.

Barry, James (2019), *Armenian Christians in Iran: Ethnicity, Religion, and Identity in the Islamic Republic*, Cambridge: Cambridge University Press.

Baumann, Martin (2003), *Alte Götter in neuer Heimat: Religionswissenschaftliche Analyse zu Diaspora am Beispiel von Hindus auf Trinidad*, Marburg: Diagonal-Verl.

Becker, Adam H. (2015), *Revival and Awakening: American Evangelical Missionaries in Iran and the Origins of Assyrian Nationalism*, Chicago: University of Chicago Press.

Bevans, Stephen B. (2002), *Models of Contextual Theology*, Maryknoll: Orbis Books.

Billig, Michael (1995), *Banal Nationalism*, London: Sage Publications.

Boyer, Paul (1992), *When Time Shall Be No More: Prophecy Belief in Modern American Culture*, Cambridge: Harvard University Press.

Bradley, Mark (2008), *Iran and Christianity: Historical Identity and Present Relevance*, London: Continuum.

Bradley, Mark (2014), *Too Many to Jail: The Story of Iran's New Christians*, Oxford: Monarch Books.

Breuilly, John (1993), *Nationalism and the State*, Manchester: Manchester University Press.

Bunzl, Matti (2007), *Anti-Semitism and Islamophobia: Hatreds Old and New in Europe*, Chicago: Prickly Paradigm Press.

Casanova, José (1994), *Public Religions in the Modern World*, Chicago: University of Chicago Press.

Chehabi, Houchang E. (2010), *Li Kulli Fir'awn Musa: The Myth of Moses and Pharaoh in the Iranian Revolution in Comparative Perspective*, Waltham: Brandeis University.

Chidester, David (1996), *Savage Systems: Colonialism and Comparative Religion in Southern Africa*, Charlottesville: University Press of Virginia.

Clark, Victoria (2007), *Allies for Armageddon: The Rise of Christian Zionism*, New Haven: Yale University Press.

Cohen, Robin (1997), *Global Diasporas: An Introduction*, Seattle: University of Washington Press.

Cohen, Robin (2008), *Global Diasporas (2. ed.): An Introduction*, London: Routledge.

Dressler, Markus (2015), *Writing Religion: The Making of Turkish Alevi Islam*, Oxford: Oxford University Press.

Dubuisson, Daniel (2007), *The Western Construction of Religion: Myths, Knowledge, and Ideology*, Baltimore: Johns Hopkins University Press.

Dufoix, Stéphane (2008), *Diasporas*, Berkeley: University of California Press.

Dufoix, Stéphane (2016), *The Dispersion: A History of the Word Diaspora*, Leiden: BRILL.

Fischer, Michael M. J. (1980), *Iran: From Religious Dispute to Revolution*, Wisconsin: University of Wisconsin Press.

Fitzgerald, Timothy (2003), *The Ideology of Religious Studies*, New York: Oxford University Press.

Flynn, Thomas S. (2017), *The Western Christian Presence in the Russias and Qajar Persia, c.1760–c.1870*, Leiden: BRILL.

Funke, Christian (2017), *Ästhetik, Politik und Schiitische Repräsentationen im Zeitgenössischen Iran*, Leiden: BRILL.

Gellner, Ernest (1983), *Nations and Nationalism*, Ithaca: Cornell University Press.

Gholami, Reza (2016), *Secularism and Identity: Non-Islamiosity in the Iranian Diaspora*, London: Taylor and Francis.

Gidley, Ben, and J. Renton (2017), *Antisemitism and Islamophobia in Europe: A Shared Story?*, London: Palgrave Macmillan.

Hastings, Adrian (1997), *The Construction of Nationhood: Ethnicity, Religion and Nationalism*, Cambridge: Cambridge University Press.

Hayes, Carlton J. H. (1960), *Nationalism: A Religion*, New York: Macmillan Company.

Hopkins, Philip O. (2020), *American Missionaries in Iran during the 1960s and 1970s*, Cham: Springer International Publishing.

Juergensmeyer, Mark (1993), *The New Cold War? Religious Nationalism Confronts the Secular State*, Los Angeles: University of California Press.

Khosravi, Shahram (2008), *Young and Defiant in Tehran*, Philadelphia: University of Pennsylvania Press.

Kia, Mana (2020), *Persianate Selves: Memories of Place and Origin before Nationalism*, Stanford: Stanford University Press.

King, Richard (2009), *Orientalism and Religion: Postcolonial Theory, India and 'the Mystic East'*, London: Routledge.

Krannich, Conrad (2020), *Recht Macht Religion: Eine Untersuchung über Taufe und Asylverfahren*, Göttingen: V&R unipress.

Liberatore, Giulia (2017), *Somali, Muslim, British: Striving in Securitized Britain*, London: Bloomsbury Academic.

Maleki, Ammar, and P. Tamimi Arab (2020), *Iranians' Attitudes toward Religion: A 2020 Survey Report*, Tilburg: GAMAAN.

Marashi, Afshin (2020), *Exile and the Nation: The Parsi Community of India and the Making of Modern Iran*, Austin: University of Texas Press.

Masuzawa, Tomoko (2007), *The Invention of World Religions: Or, How European Universalism Was Preserved in the Language of Pluralism*, Chicago: University of Chicago Press.

Mayer, Ruth (2005), *Diaspora: Eine Kritische Begriffsbestimmung*, Bielefeld: Transcript.

McCutcheon, Russell T. (1997), *Manufacturing Religion: The Discourse on Sui Generis Religion and the Politics of Nostalgia*, New York: Oxford University Press.

Mishra, Sudesh (2006), *Diaspora Criticism*, Edinburgh: Edinburgh University Press.

Naficy, Hamid (1993), *The Making of Exile Cultures: Iranian Television in Los Angeles*, Minneapolis: University of Minnesota Press.

Nongbri, Brent (2013), *Before Religion: A History of a Modern Concept*, New Haven: Yale University Press.
Pears, Angie (2010), *Doing Contextual Theology*, London: Routledge.
Ringer, Monica M. (2011), *Pious Citizens: Reforming Zoroastrianism in India and Iran*, Syracuse: Syracuse University Press.
Runnymede Trust (1997), *Islamophobia: A Challenge for Us All*, London: The Runnymede Trust Commission on British Muslims and Islamophobia.
Rzepka, Marcin (2017), *Prayer and Protest: The Protestant Communities in Revolutionary Iran*, Krakow: Unum Press.
Said, Edward W. (2001), *Reflections on Exile and Other Literary and Cultural Essays*, London: Granta Books.
Sanasarian, Eliz (2004), *Religious Minorities in Iran*, Cambridge: Cambridge University Press.
Sharpe, Eric J. (1986), *Comparative Religion: A History*, La Salle: Open Court.
Shooman, Yasemin (2014), '… *weil ihre Kultur so ist': Narrative des Antimuslimischen Rassismus*, Bielefeld: transcript Verlag.
Smith, Anthony D. (1986), *The Ethnic Origins of Nations*, Oxford: Blackwell.
Smith, Anthony D. (2003), *Chosen Peoples: Sacred Sources of National Identity*, New York: Oxford University Press.
Smith, Anthony D. (2009), *Ethno-symbolism and Nationalism: A Cultural Approach*, London: Routledge.
Smith, Jonathan Z. (1978), *Map Is Not Territory: Studies in the History of Religions*, Chicago: University of Chicago Press.
Smith, Jonathan Z. (1987), *To Take Place: Toward Theory in Ritual*, Chicago: University of Chicago Press.
Spector, Stephen (2009), *Evangelicals and Israel: The Story of American Christian Zionism*, Oxford: Oxford University Press.
Spellman, Kathryn (2004), *Religion and Nation: Iranian Local and Transnational Networks in Britain*, New York: Berghahn Books.
Steele, Robert (2021), *The Shah's Imperial Celebrations of 1971: Nationalism, Culture and Politics in Late Pahlavi Iran*, London: I.B. Tauris.
Tavakoli-Targhi, Mohamad (2001), *Refashioning Iran: Orientalism, Occidentalism and Historiography*, Basingstoke: Palgrave.
Tweed, Thomas A. (1997), *Our Lady of the Exile: Diasporic Religion at a Cuban Catholic Shrine in Miami*, Oxford: Oxford University Press.
Vahman, Fereydun (2019), *175 Years of Persecution: A History of the Babis & Baha'is of Iran*, London: Oneworld Publications.
Van der Veer, Peter (1994), *Religious Nationalism: Hindus and Muslims in India*, Los Angeles: University of California Press.
Van der Veer, Peter (2013), *The Modern Spirit of Asia: The Spiritual and the Secular in China and India*, Princeton: Princeton University Press.

Van Gorder, A. C. (2010), *Christianity in Persia and the Status of Non-Muslims in Iran*, Lanham: Lexington Books.

Vaziri, Mostafa (1993), *Iran as Imagined Nation: The Construction of National Identity*, New York: Paragon House.

Vejdani, Farzin (2015), *Making History in Iran: Education, Nationalism, and Print Culture*, Stanford: Stanford University Press.

Waterfield, Robin E. (1973), *Christians in Persia: Assyrians, Armenians, Roman Catholics and Protestants*, London: Allen and Unwin.

Zia-Ebrahimi, Reza (2016), *The Emergence of Iranian Nationalism: Race and the Politics of Dislocation*, New York: Columbia University Press.

Zia-Ebrahimi, Reza (2021), *Antisémitisme et Islamophobie: Une Histoire Croisée*, Amsterdam: Èditions Amsterdam.

Edited volumes

Ağuiçenoğlu, Hüseyin (2016), 'Die Konversion Türkischsprachiger Personen in Deutschland zum Christentum. Eine Nicht-Denominationale Gruppe: İsa Mesih İmanlıları', in J. Zimmermann, C. Herzog and R. Motika (eds), *Osmanische Welten: Quellen und Fallstudien: Festschrift für Michael Ursinus*, 1–31, Bamberg: University of Bamberg Press.

Amanat, Abbas (2005), 'Mujtahids and Missionaries: Shi'i Responses to Christian Polemics in the Early Qajar Period', in R. Gleave (ed.), *Religion and Society in Qajar Iran*, 247–69, London: Routledge.

Anderson, Allan (2010), 'Varieties, Taxonomies, and Definitions', in M. Bergunder, A. F. Droogers, C. van der Laan, C. M. Robeck and A. Anderson (eds), *Studying Global Pentecostalism: Theories and Methods*, 13–29, Berkeley: University of California Press.

Balibar, Etienne (1991), 'Is There a 'Neo-Racism'?', in E. Balibar and I. Wallerstein (eds), *Race, Nation, Class: Ambiguous Identities*, 17–28, London: Verso.

Bayraklı, Enes, F. Hafez and L. Faytre (2019), 'Making Sense of Islamophobia in Muslim Societies', in E. Bayraklı and F. Hafez (eds), *Islamophobia in Muslim Majority Societies*, 5–20, London: Routledge.

Berger, Peter L. (ed.) (1999), *The Desecularization of the World: Resurgent Religion and World Politics: The Resurgence of Religion in World Politics*, Washington DC: Ethics and Public Policy Center.

Bergunder, Michael, A. F. Droogers, C. van der Laan, C. M. Robeck and A. Anderson (eds) (2010), *Studying Global Pentecostalism: Theories and Methods*, Berkeley: University of California Press.

Bozorgmehr, Mehdi, and E. Ketchman (2018), 'Adult Children of Professional and Entrepreneurial Immigrants: Second-Generation Iranians in the United States', in M. Mostafavi-Mobasher (ed.), *The Iranian Diaspora: Challenges, Negotiations and Transformations*, 25–49, Austin: University of Texas Press.

Bradshaw, Paul F. (2020), 'The Dating of Christmas: The Early Church', in T. Larsen (ed.), *The Oxford Handbook of Christmas*, Oxford: Oxford University Press.

Dressler, Markus, and A.-P. S. Mandair (2011a), 'Introduction: Modernity, Religion-Making, and the Postsecular', in M. Dressler and A.-P. S. Mandair (eds), *Secularism and Religion-Making*, 3–36, New York: Oxford University Press.

Dressler, Markus, and A.-P. S. Mandair (eds) (2011b), *Secularism and Religion-Making*, New York: Oxford University Press.

Hall, Stuart (1990), 'Cultural Identity and Diaspora', in J. Rutherford (ed.), *Identity: Community, Culture, Difference*, 222–37, London: Lawrence and Wishart.

Hecker, Pierre (2021), 'Tired of Religion: Atheism and Non-belief in 'New Turkey', in P. Hecker, I. Furman and K. Akyıldız (eds), *The Politics of Culture in Contemporary Turkey*, 68–88, Edinburgh: Edinburgh University Press.

Hobsbawm, Eric J., and T. O. Ranger (eds) (1983), *The Invention of Tradition*, Cambridge: Cambridge University Press.

Lachenicht, Susanne (ed.) (2007), *Religious Refugees in Europe, Asia and North America: (6th–21st century)*, Hamburg: Lit.

Lean, Nathan C. (2019), 'The Debate over the Utility and Precision of the Term "Islamophobia"', in I. Zempi and I. Awan (eds), *The Routledge International Handbook of Islamophobia*, 11–17, London: Routledge.

Liberatore, Giulia, and L. Fesenmeyer (2019), 'Diaspora and Religion: Connecting and Disconnecting', in R. Cohen and C. Fischer (eds), *Routledge Handbook of Diaspora Studies*, 233–40, London: Routledge.

Malek, Amy (2015), 'Displaced, Re-rooted, Transnational: Considerations in Theory and Practice of Being an Iranian Outside Iran', in R. Mohabbat-Kar (ed.), *Identity and Exile: The Iranian Diaspora between Solidarity and Difference*, 24–31, Berlin: Heinrich Böll Foundation.

Marashi, Afshin (2009), 'The Nation's Poet: Ferdowsi and the Iranian National Imagination', in T. Atabaki (ed.), *Iran in the 20th Century: Historiography and Political Culture*, 93–112, London: I.B. Tauris.

Marienstras, Richard (1989), 'On the Notion of Diaspora', in G. Chaliand and T. Berrett (eds), *Minority Peoples in the Age of Nation-States*, 119–25, London: Pluto Press.

Özyürek, Esra (2012), 'Christian and Turkish: Secularist Fears of a Converted Nation', in B. Turam (ed.), *Secular State and Religious Society: Two Forces in Play in Turkey*, 95–120, Basingstoke: Palgrave Macmillan.

Rudolph, Susanne H. (2018), 'Introduction: Religion, States, and Transnational Civil Society', in S. H. Rudolph and J. P. Piscatori (eds), *Transnational Religion and Fading States*, 1–23, New York: Routledge.

Schrode, Paula (2008), 'Das Türkische Nevruz-Fest: Erfindungen einer Tradition', in H. Anetshofer, I. Baldauf and C. Ebert (eds), *Über Gereimtes und Ungereimtes Diesseits und Jenseits der Turcia: Festschrift für Sigrid Kleinmichel*, 111–35, Schöneiche bei Berlin: scrîpvaz.

Shaked, Shaul (1991), 'Aspekte von Noruz, dem Iranischen Neujahrsfest', in J. Assmann (ed.), *Das Fest und das Heilige: Religiöse Kontrapunkte zur Alltagswelt*, 88–104, Gütersloh: Gütersloher Verlagshaus Gerd Mohn.

Skey, Michael, and M. Antonsich (eds) (2017), *Everyday Nationhood: Theorising Culture, Identity and Belonging after Banal Nationalism*, London: Palgrave Macmillan.

Smart, Ninian (1987), 'The Importance of Diasporas', in S. Shaked, G. Stroumsa and A. Shulman (eds), *Gilgul: Essays on Transformation, Revolution and Permanence in the History of Religions*, 288–97, Leiden: Brill.

Smith, Jonathan Z. (1998), 'Religion, Religions, Religious', in M. Taylor (ed.), *Critical Terms for Religious Studies*, 269–84, Chicago: University of Chicago Press.

van der Veer, Peter, and H. Lehmann (eds) (1999), *Nation and Religion: Perspectives on Europe and Asia*, Princeton: Princeton University Press.

Vásquez, Manuel (2010), 'Diasporas and Religion', in K. Knott and S. McLoughlin (eds), *Diasporas: Concepts, Intersections, Identities*, 128–33, London: Zed.

Vertovec, Steven (2004), 'Religion and Diaspora', in P. Antes, A. W. Geertz and R. R. Warne (eds), *Textual, Comparative, Sociological, and Cognitive Approaches*, 275–304, Berlin: De Gruyter.

Zempi, Irene, and I. Awan (2019), 'Introduction', in I. Zempi and I. Awan (eds), *The Routledge International Handbook of Islamophobia*, 1–8, London: Routledge.

Journal articles

Akcapar, Sebnem K. (2006), 'Conversion as a Migration Strategy in a Transit Country: Iranian Shiites Becoming Christians in Turkey', *International Migration Review*, 40 (4): 817–53.

Anand, Dibyesh (2003), 'A Contemporary Story of 'Diaspora': The Tibetan Version', *Diaspora: A Journal of Transnational Studies*, 12 (2): 211–29.

Anthias, Floya (1998), 'Evaluating 'Diaspora': Beyond Ethnicity?', *Sociology*, 32 (3): 557–80.

Bangstad, Sindre (2014), 'Review of Chris Allen, Islamophobia', *Contemporary Islam*, 8 (1): 69–74.

Baumann, Martin (2000), 'Diaspora: Genealogies of Semantics and Transcultural Comparison', *Numen*, 47 (3): 313–37.

Bravo López, Fernando (2011), 'Towards a Definition of Islamophobia: Approximations of the Early Twentieth Century', *Ethnic and Racial Studies*, 4 (34): 556–73.

Brubaker, Rogers (2005), 'The 'Diaspora' Diaspora', *Ethnic and Racial Studies*, 28 (1): 1–19.

Butler, Kim D. (2001), 'Defining Diaspora, Refining a Discourse', *Diaspora: A Journal of Transnational Studies*, 10 (2): 189–219.

Carpenedo, Manoela (2021), 'Christian Zionist Religiouscapes in Brazil: Understanding Judaizing Practices and Zionist Inclinations in Brazilian Charismatic Evangelicalism', *Social Compass*, 68 (2): 204–17.

Casale, Giancarlo (2007), 'The Ethnic Composition of Ottoman Ship Crews and the "Rumi Challenge" to Portuguese Identity', *Medieval Encounters*, 13 (1): 122–44.

Darwish, Linda (2018), '"When Your Heart Is Touched, It's Not a Decision": A Narrative Analysis of Iranian Muslim Conversion to Christianity', *Studies in Religion/Sciences Religieuses*, 47 (1): 1–33.

Dressler, Markus (2022), 'Tracing the Nationalisation of Millet in the Late Ottoman Period: A Conceptual History Approach', *Die Welt des Islams*, 62 (3–4): 360–88.

Ferdowsi, Ali (2008), 'The "Emblem of the Manifestation of the Iranian Spirit": Hafiz and the Rise of the National Cult of Persian Poetry', *Iranian Studies*, 41 (5): 667–91.

Foster, Lawrence (1984), 'Career Apostates: Reflections on the Works of Jerald and Sandra Tanner', *Dialogue: A Journal of Mormon Thought*, 17 (2): 35–60.

Fox, Jon E., and C. Miller-Idriss (2008), 'Everyday Nationhood', *Ethnicities*, 8 (4): 536–63.

Friedland, Roger (2001), 'Religious Nationalism and the Problem of Collective Representation', *Annual Review of Sociology*, 27 (1): 125–52.

Garner, Steve, and S. Selod (2015), 'The Racialization of Muslims: Empirical Studies of Islamophobia', *Critical Sociology*, 41 (1): 9–19.

Glick Schiller, Nina, L. Basch and C. Blanc-Szanton (1992), 'Towards a Transnationalization of Migration: Race, Class, Ethnicity and Nationalism Reconsidered', *The Annals of the New York Academy of Sciences*, 645: 1–24.

Hafez, Farid (2016), 'Comparing Anti-Semitism and Islamophobia: The State of the Field', *Islamophobia Studies Journal*, 3 (2): 16–34.

Hafez, Farid (2018), 'Schools of Thought in Islamophobia Studies: Prejudice, Racism, and Decoloniality', *Islamophobia Studies Journal*, 2 (4): 210–25.

Hall, Stuart (1989), 'Rassismus als Ideologischer Diskurs', *Das Argument* (178): 913–22.

Johnson, Paul C. (2012), 'Religion and Diaspora', *Religion and Society*, 3 (1): 95–114.

Kéri, Szabolcs, and C. Sleiman (2017), 'Religious Conversion to Christianity in Muslim Refugees in Europe', *Archive for the Psychology of Religion/Archiv für Religionspychologie*, 39 (1): 1–14.

Klug, Brian (2014), 'The Limits of Analogy: Comparing Islamophobia and Antisemitism', *Patterns of Prejudice*, 48 (5): 442–59.

Larsson, Göran (2016), '"Most Muslims Are Like You and I, but 'Real' Muslims …": Ex-Muslims and Anti-Muslim Sentiments', *Journal of Muslims in Europe* (5): 205–23.

Larsson, Göran, and R. Spielhaus (2013), 'Narratives of Inclusion and Exclusion: Islam and Muslims as a Subject of European Studies', *Journal of Muslims in Europe*, 2 (2): 105–13.

Marti, Gerardo (2016), '"I Was a Muslim, but Now I Am a Christian": Preaching, Legitimation, and Identity Management in a Southern Evangelical Church', *Journal for the Scientific Study of Religion*, 55 (2): 250–70.

McAuliffe, Cameron (2007), 'A Home Far Away?: Religious Identity and Transnational Relations in the Iranian Diaspora', *Global Networks*, 7 (3): 307–27.

Miller, Duane A. (2015), 'Power, Personalities and Politics', *Mission Studies*, 32 (1): 66–86.
Reed, Randall (2012), 'Of Prophets and Propaganda: An Exploration of Modern Christian Dispensationalism Using the Work of Martin Riesebrodt', *Journal for the Scientific Study of Religion*, 51 (3): 468–81.
Ricks, Thomas M. (2011), 'Alborz College of Tehran, Dr. Samuel Martin Jordan and the American Faculty: Twentieth-Century Presbyterian Mission Education and Modernism in Iran (Persia)', *Iranian Studies*, 44 (5): 627–46.
Rostam-Kolayi, Jasamin (2008), 'From Evangelizing to Modernizing Iranians: The American Presbyterian Mission and its Iranian Students', *Iranian Studies*, 41 (2): 213–39.
Rzepka, Marcin (2019), 'To Make Christianity More Iranian: Studying the Conversions to Christianity in Iran in the Early Pahlavi Period', *Studia Litteraria Universitatis Iagellonicae Cracoviensis*, special issue: 209–18.
Safran, William (1991), 'Diasporas in Modern Societies: Myths of Homeland and Return', *Diaspora: A Journal of Transnational Studies*, 1 (1): 83–99.
Said, Edward (1985), 'Orientalism Reconsidered', *Cultural Critique*, 1: 89–107.
Shepperson, George (1966), 'The African Diaspora – or the African Abroad', *African*, 1 (2): 76–93.
Skenderovic, Damir, and C. Späti (2019), 'From Orientalism to Islamophobia: Reflections, Confirmations, and Reservations', *ReOrient – The Journal of Critical Muslim Studies*, 2 (4): 130–43.
Smith, Christopher C. (2014), '"Ex-Muslims," Bible Prophecy, and Islamophobia: Rhetoric and Reality in the Narratives of Walid Shoebat', *Islamophobia Studies Journal*, 2 (2): 76–93.
Sökefeld, Martin (2006), 'Mobilizing in Transnational Space: A Social Movement Approach to the Formation of Diaspora', *Global Networks*, 6 (3): 265–84.
Soysal, Yasemin N. (2000), 'Citizenship and Identity: Living in Diasporas in Post-War Europe?', *Ethnic and Racial Studies*, 23 (1): 1–15.
Szanto, Edith (2018), '"Zoroaster was a Kurd!": Neo-Zoroastrianism among Iraqi Kurds', *Iran and the Caucasus*, 22: 96–110.
Talebi, Shahla (2012), 'From the Light of the Eyes to the Eyes of the Power: State and Dissident Martyrs in Post-Revolutionary Iran', *Visual Anthropology*, 25 (1–2): 120–47.
Tölölyan, Khachig (1996), 'Rethinking Diaspora(s): Stateless Power in the Transnational Moment', *Diaspora: A Journal of Transnational Studies*, 5 (1): 3–36.
Vertovec, Steven (1997), 'Three Meanings of "Diaspora," Exemplified among South Asian Religions', *Diaspora: A Journal of Transnational Studies*, 6 (3): 277–99.
Zirinsky, Michael P. (1993), 'Render Therefore unto Caesar the Things Which Are Caesar's: American Presbyterian Educators and Reza Shah', *Iranian Studies*, 26 (3–4): 337–56.

Encyclopaedia entries

Boyce, Mary (2016), 'NOWRUZ i. In the Pre-Islamic Period', *Encyclopaedia Iranica*. Available online: https://iranicaonline.org/articles/nowruz-i (accessed 13 February 2021).

Cristoforetti, Simone (2009), 'NOWRUZ iii. In the Iranian Calendar', *Encyclopaedia Iranica*. Available online: https://iranicaonline.org/articles/nowruz-iii (accessed 1 March 2021).

Dandamayev, Muhammad A. (1993), 'CYRUS iii. Cyrus II The Great', *Encyclopaedia Iranica*. Available online: https://iranicaonline.org/articles/cyrus-iiI (accessed 5 May 2021).

Dandamayev, Muhammad A. (2000), 'MAGI', *Encyclopaedia Iranica*. Available online: https://www.iranicaonline.org/articles/magi (accessed 24 May 2021).

Hillerbrand, Hans J. (2021), 'Christmas', *Encyclopaedia Britannica*. Available online: https://www.britannica.com/topic/Christmas (accessed 29 March 2022).

Kasheff, Manouchehr, and A.-A. Saʿīdī Sīrjānī (1990), 'ČAHĀRŠANBA-SŪRĪ', *Encyclopaedia Iranica*. Available online: https://iranicaonline.org/articles/caharsanba-suri (accessed 27 February 2021).

Netzer, Amnon (1993), 'DĀNĪĀL-E NABĪ i. In the Biblical and Popular Traditions', *Encyclopaedia Iranica*. Available online: https://iranicaonline.org/articles/danial-e-nabi#pt1 (accessed 20 May 2021).

Netzer, Amnon (1998), 'ESTHER AND MORDECHAI', *Encyclopaedia Iranica*. Available online: https://iranicaonline.org/articles/esther-and-mordechai (accessed 20 May 2021).

Omidsalar, Mahmoud (1990), 'ČELLA i. In Persian Folklore', *Encyclopaedia Iranica*. Available online: https://iranicaonline.org/articles/cella-term-referring-to-any-forty-day-period#pt1 (accessed 8 March 2021).

Omidsalar, Mahmoud (1995), 'DIVINATION', *Encyclopaedia Iranica*. Available online: https://iranicaonline.org/articles/divination.

Schmidt, Stephen A. (2016), 'URSHAN, ANDREŌS BAR DĀWĪD', *Encyclopaedia Iranica*. Available online: https://iranicaonline.org/articles/urshan-andrew (accessed 29 January 2022).

Shapur Shahbazi, Alireza (2002), 'HAFT SIN', *Encyclopaedia Iranica*. Available online: https://iranicaonline.org/articles/haft-sin (accessed 22 February 2021).

Shapur Shahbazi, Alireza (2009), 'NOWRUZ ii. In the Islamic Period', *Encyclopaedia Iranica*. Available online: https://iranicaonline.org/articles/nowruz-ii (accessed 11 February 2021).

Soroudi, Sorour (2002), 'ḤABAQUQ, TOMB OF', *Encyclopaedia Iranica*. Available online: https://iranicaonline.org/articles/habaquq-tomb-of- (accessed 20 May 2021).

Strothmann, Rudolf, and M. Djebli (2012), 'Taḳiyya', *Encyclopaedia of Islam*. Available online: https://referenceworks.brillonline.com/entries/encyclopaedia-of-islam-2/takiyya-SIM_7341?s.num=0&s.rows=20&s.mode=DEFAULT&s.f.s2_parent=encyclopaedia-of-islam-2&s.start=0&s.q=takiyya (accessed 27 July 2021).

Vallat, François (2011), 'ELAM i. The History of Elam', *Encyclopaedia Iranica*. Available online: https://www.iranicaonline.org/articles/elam-i (accessed 20 December 2021).

NGO reports

Article18 (2022a), 'Iranian Christian Prisoners List'. Available online: https://articleeighteen.com/prisoners-list/ (accessed 11 February 2022).

Article18 (2022b), 'Rights Violations against Christians in Iran: Annual Report'. Available online: https://articleeighteen.com/wp-content/uploads/2022/01/Annual Report-2021-1.pdf (accessed 12 February 2022).

ICHRI (2013), *The Cost of Faith: Persecution of Christian Protestants and Converts in Iran*, New York: International Campaign for Human Rights in Iran.

IHRDC (2014), *Apostasy in the Islamic Republic of Iran*, New Haven: Iran Human Rights Documentation Center.

IHRDC (2021), *Living in the Shadows of Oppression: The Situation of Christian Converts in Iran*, New Haven: Iran Human Rights Documentation Center.

News items

Bolhari, Ruzbeh (2010), 'Mowzeʿe Rahbar ʿayleh-e Chahārshanbeh-suri: Bahsi Siāsi dar Qāleb-e Esteftā", Radio Farda. Available online: https://www.radiofarda.com/a/f35_IRI_Leader_on_CharshanbeSuri/1983788.html (accessed 10 February 2021).

Jaʿfari, Sorush (2016), 'Enteqād az Tajammoʿ dar Ārāmgāh-e Korush: Cheh Kasi Kutāhi Kardeh keh Afrād-e Inguneh Jamʿ Shodand?', Euronews. Available online: https://per.euronews.com/2016/10/30/reax-to-thousands-of-iranians-gather-in-pasargadae-tomb-of-cyrus (accessed 7 May 2021).

Kastner, Bernd (2017), 'Ungläubige Behörde', Süddeutsche Zeitung. Available online: https://www.sueddeutsche.de/politik/asyl-unglaeubige-behoerde-1.3416151 (accessed 22 March 2022).

Mohammadi, Majid (2018), 'Tahlil-e Shoʿār-hā-ye Harekat-e Eʿterāzi-ye Dey-Māh 1396-e Irān', BBC Persian. Available online: https://www.bbc.com/persian/blog-viewpoints-42620668 (accessed 7 May 2021).

Schaverien, Anna (2019), 'Rejecting Asylum Claim, U.K. Quotes Bible to Say Christianity Is Not 'Peaceful', *The New York Times*. Available online: https://www.nytimes.com/2019/03/21/world/europe/britain-asylum-seeker-christianity.html (accessed 22 March 2022).

Schmidt, Rebekka (2020), 'Militanter Muslim Wird "Billy Graham des Iran"', livenet.de. Available online: https://www.livenet.de/themen/glaube/theologie_philosophie_religion/islam/368014-militanter_muslim_wird_billy_graham_des_iran.html (accessed 6 September 2021).

Sharq (2011), 'Enteqāl-e Marāsem az Takht-e Jamshid beh Saʻd-Ābād', *Sharq*, 21 March. Available online: https://www.magiran.com/article/2259716 (accessed 19 December 2023).

Shojāʻi, Mitrā (2011), 'Az Takhrib-e Takht-e Jamshid tā Bargozāri-ye Nowruz dar Ān', DW Persian. Available online: https://p.dw.com/p/R86J (accessed 10 February 2021).

Vatican News (2021), 'Iran Expels Italian Nun Who Has Spent Her Life for the Poor of the Country'. Available online: https://www.vaticannews.va/en/church/news/2021-06/iran-italian-nun-berti-denied-visa-renewal-expelled.html (accessed 11 February 2022).

Online videos

Amanat, Abbas (2018), 'Abbas Amanat: Iran's Relationship with the Jewish People', New York: Carnegie Council for Ethics in International Affairs. Available online: https://www.youtube.com/watch?v=-xW_l0nedUI (accessed 11 December 2021).

Chehabi, Houchang E. (2013), 'The Legal Aspects of Religious Diversity in Iran'. London: SOAS University of London. Available online: https://www.youtube.com/watch?v=raPWh9XcPr8&t=61s (accessed 14 February 2022).

Marashi, Afshin (2017), 'Return of the King: Cyrus the Great and the Iranian National Imagination', Oklahoma: University of Oklahoma. Available online: https://www.youtube.com/watch?v=P1gqPULW1AI (accessed 5 May 2021).

Dictionaries

Emami, Karim (2006), *Farhang Moaser: Persian-English Dictionary*, Tehran: Farhang Moaser Publishers.

Index

Note: *Italicized* and **bold** pages refer to figures and tables respectively. Endnotes are indicated by the page number followed by 'n' and the endnote number e.g., 201 n.1 refers to endnote 1 on page 201.

Achaemenids 64, 76, 91, 116–19, 125, 128, 135
Ahmadinezhād, M. 23–4, 65, 119
American Presbyterians mission 11–12
Anglican churches 11–12
Anglican Diocese of Iran 14, 20, 189
anti-Muslim racism 140, 141
Apostasy (*ertedād*) 21, 24–5, 197 n. 1
Apostle Paul 60
Arabs 1, 13, 63, 79, 115, 119, 138–40, 148–53, 160, 173, 179, 204 n. 9, 205 n. 13
Armenian Apostolic Church 10
Artaxerxes I (Ardashir) 116, 124
Aryans 13
Āseriān, R. 60, 101, 133
Ashura 63, 93
Avarsaji, H. 98
   poetry of 107–10

Bahais 24, 27, 57, 184, 196 n. 3, 208 n. 11
baptism 70
Bardiya (King) 76
Bābākhāni, V. 157
Beautiful World *(Jahān-e Zibā)* (poem) *111*
Bevans, S. B. 59
Bāghestāni, E. 69, 76, 123, 152
Bible 1, 8, 16, 17, 21, 24, 44, 70, 80, 93–5, 101–3, 116, 122, 123, 128, 135, 136, 164, 191
   Haft Sin of 76
   Iranians in 116–17
biblical Israelites 170–6
birth of Christ 90–2, 107, 112
Blessed is the One (Ey Khosh ān Kas) (poem) 105
Book of Kings (Ferdowsi) 76, 118, 150
Bozorgmehr, M. 184

Castro Revolution 51
Chaldean Catholic Church 10
Christian converts 4, 27
Christian Zionism 24, 172–6
Christmas 73
   Iranian origins of 90–2
   Yaldā, meanings of 92–3
Chronicles, biblical books of 118
Churchill, W. 146
Church Missionary Society (CMS) 11
Covid-19 pandemic 5–6
culturalism 140, 147
cultural racism 140
Cyrus the Great (King) 6, 76, 116, 135, 150, 191
   calendar 120–1
   icon of Iranianness 117–19
   messiah for Iranian people 120–4
Cyrus the Great Day 119, 140

Darius the Great (King) 76, 124, 125
Dehqāni-Tafti, H. 9, 14, 19, 20, 55, 58, *61*, 94, 98, 104, 132, 160, 189
   poetry works of 99–100
diaspora
   concepts of 46–9
   nationalism 53
   nation and 2
   religion 49–52
Dibāj, I. 133
Dibāj, M. 21, 56, 58, 79, 83, 91, 132, 165
dislocative nationalism 13, 139
double foreignness of Christianity 55–8

Easter 72–4, 174
Elam Ministries 29, 33, 59, *81*, *111*, *162*, 177, 187

Elam Prophecy 8, 176–8, 182, 183, 187, 192
ethnic Christians 10–11
ethnicity 40, 48, 50, 55
ethno-symbolism 39–42
Evangelical Christianity 3, 137, 193, 199
Ezra, biblical books of 118

fālgiri, practice of 113–16
fāl, practice of 113–16
Fātehi, M. 59

'German-Muslim' identity 43, 44
ghorbat 161, 163
  by divine will 165–7
  from heavenly homeland 164–5
  Nowruz in 167–70
  Yaldā in 167–70
Gospel 60, 69, 70, 104, 129, 181
Graham, B. 16

Hadith 99
Hāfez (poet) 102–3, 115–16
Haft Sin table 68, 74, 102, 191
  with Bible 76, 80
  history of 75
  Iranian Christian interpretations of 79
  meanings 82
  origin of custom 77
Har Ruzetān Nowruz 71–2
Hāyrāpetiān, G. 71, 79, 87, 88
Hāyrāpetiān, L. 16
Hebrew 45, 173–5, 177, 209 n. 7
Heydari, R. 71, 173
Hezbollāhis 18
Holy Spirit 15, 34, 71, 86, 87, 98, 108, 112, 152, 167, 190
house churches 10, 22–3
Hovsepiān, E. 16, 22, 129, 163, 167
Hovsepiān, H. 17, 127, 132, 161
Hovsepiān, J. 161

ICnetTV 30, 72, 77, 85, 169
indigenization, quest for 13–15
Iran
  double foreignness of Christianity 55–8
  ethnic Christian minorities 10–11
  nationhood 55–8
  Pentecostalism in 15–17
  pre-Islamic 62–5, 75, 119, 138–40
  Western Protestant missions 11–12
Iranian Armenians 4, 5, 10, 14, 16, 21, 33, 127, 185
Iranian Assyrians 10, 14, 16, 26, 28, 56, 127
Iranian Christian exile churches 2, 4, 6–9, 34, 53, 189
  mapping of 28–31
Iranian Christians
  academic research on 2–4
  definition 4–5
Iranian Evangelicals 4
Iranian Protestantism 189
Iranian Protestants 4, 20, 32, 33, 57
  killings of pastors 22
Iranian Qajar Empire 11, 104
Iranian Revolutionary Guard Corps (IRGC) 23, 152
Iran-Iraq war 130, 144, 152
Irvāni, J. Q. 61, 98
  poetry of 104–7
Isaiah, biblical books of 118, 122
ISIS, atrocities by 146
Islam
  depictions of 145–7
  Islamophobia 140–1
  Mazhab vs. Christianity 153–7
  non-Islamiosity 138–40
Islamic Society *(Anjoman-e Eslāmi)* 18
Islamic Studies 2–4
Islamism 9, 17–19, 138, 140, 148, 159, 171–2, 187, 193, 209 n. 3
Islamophobia
  concept of 140–1, 146
  non-Islamiosity as linchpin of 148–50

Jamā'at-e Rabbāni Church 14, 17, 18, 21, 22, 26, 29, 33, 56, 58, 60, 62, 76, 133, 167
Jerusalem 45, 52, 100, 117
Jewish 43
  diaspora, conceptualization of 44
  symbols, appropriation of 172–6

Khalkhāli, S. 64
Khezri, K. 83, 84
Khāmene'i, 'A. 23–5, 66
Khāneh-Tekāni 75, 82, 83, 85

Khātami, M. 119
Khomeini, R. 20, 149, 160, 172,
    199 n. 16

Magi 127–9
Makārem-Shirāzi, M. 64
Martyn, H. 11
martyrs 6, 8, 22, 130, 132
'Martyrs of the Iranian Church,' portraits
    of 130-2, 161
  biographies of 130–133
*Masnavi of the Prodigal Son (Masnavi-ye
    Pesar-e Gomshodeh)* (poem) 105
Mazhab 153–7
Mikā'eliān, T. 132
*Mohabat*TV 30, 114, 115
Mohammad Rezā Shah Pahlavi ('the
    Shah') 19–20, 64–5, 117–19, 121, 145,
    172, 204 n. 11, 205 n. 18
Mojāhedin-e Khalq organization 21,
    199 n. 16
Mortazavi, H. 73, 186
'Mosaic myth,' deployment of 172
Moshiri, F. 74
'Muslim ban,' in United States 43,
    148
Muslim-born converts 5, 8, 25, 137,
    158, 190
Muslims *see also* Islam
  career apostates 142–5, 192
  crown witnesses 142–5, 192
  depictions of 147–8

Namdar, F. 74
nationalism
  definition of 38
  vs. nationhood 38–9
  political aspects of 38
nationalization, of Persian-speaking
    Christianity 31–5, 189
nationhood
  religious affiliation 42–3
  vs. nationalism 38–9
'Nature Day' *(Ruz-e Tabi'at)* 87
Navā'i, K. 83, 86, 88, 155
Neo-Aramaic language 15
'Nestorian' Christians 42
New Testament 11, 60, 68, 84, 94, 100,
    103, 116, 152, 191
  Iranians in 126–7

1979 Revolution 9, 15, 56, 62, 64, 65, 93,
    151, 160, 189
  during Iran-Iraq war 130
  during Persian-speaking churches 17
  Iranian Protestant communities 19
non-ethnic Christians 4
'non-Islamiosity'
  concept of 138–140
  as linchpin of Islamophobia 148–50
Nowruz (festival) 1, 6, 8, 31, 110, 116, 150,
    152, 154, 157, 165, 174, 185, 190, 191
  customs 82–6
  and Easter 72–4
  in *ghorbat* 167–70
  Haft Sin table 75–82
  ideological contestation of 63–8
  in Turkey 66–7

Old Testament 103, 116, 117, 123, 125,
    126, 170
oppression 9, 167, 171, 172, 184
Ottoman Empire 42

PARS Theological Centre 29–30, 59–
    60, 133
Pentecost, event of 129
Pentecostalism
  ambiguity 17–19
  history of 15–17
pentecostalization, of Persian-speaking
    Christianity 31–5
'perennialist' approach 39
Persian Christian Community Church 29
'Persian National Hymn' 61
Persian-speaking Christians 5, 8, 9,
    14, 25, 27
  concept of 27
  nationalization of 31–5
  1979 Revolution 17–22
  pentecostalization of 31–5
Persepolis 52, 64–5, 119, 178, 192
Pharaoh, tyranny of 171–2
poetry 6, 8
  among Iranian Christians 97–8
  Hāfez 102–3
  Hanif Avarsaji 107–10
  Hassan Dehqāni-Tafti, works of 99–100
  of Jalil Qazzāq Irvāni 104–7
  as prayer and worship 110–13
  wisdom in 101–2

post-revolutionary violence 19–22
Presbyterian Mission 12
Prophet Daniel 116, 125–6, 129, 135
Prophet Muhammad 63, 120, 146
Protestant Churches 7, 14, 21, 32, 33
Pārsā, R. 122, 124, 125, 143–52, 158, 159, 173
public churches 25–8

Qajar Iran 42
Qoli-Zādeh, A. 86
Queen Esther 116, 124–6, 135
Quran 1, 24, 75, 99, 114, 149, 151

Rafsanjāni, 'A. 119
Red Wednesday *(Chahārshanbeh-Suri)* 63, 65, 66, 74, 75, 85, 86, 113
religion
  'compartmentalization' of 50
  and diaspora 44–53
  religion-making 50
  secularism 39–42
religious individualism 3
repentance, necessity of 181–2
Rezā Shah Pahlavi 12, 198 n. 9
Roman Catholic missionaries 11
Rowhāni, H. 119

Safā, R. 143, 144, 146, 147, 149, 158, 171, 172
Safāriān, P. 93
Said, E. 164
SamaTV 30
SAT7 PARS 107
Schuler, H. C. 13
secularism 39–42
Sepehr, M. J. 87, 88, 115
Shabakeh7 (Network7) (TV channel) 30, 69, 84, 89, 92, 94, 98, 101, 107, 112, 143, 158, 168, 169, 178, 186
Shabānlāri, P. 77, 93, 94, 115, 156
Shah 'Abbās 10
Shari'at, H. 1, 59, 84, 92, 108, 123, 129, 143, 145, 171, 172, 181–3
Shayesteh, D. 94, 102, 120, 121, 143–9, 151, 152
Shi'ite Islam
  Arab Allah *vs.* Christian God of diversity 151–3
  vs. joyful Christianity 157–8
  martyrdom in 130
  Mazhab vs. Christianity 153–7
Shirvāniān, M. 74, 127–8
Shāyesteh, D. 102, 121
Sizdah Bedar 63, 86–9
Sāleh, E. 72, 77, 78, 85, 93, 156, 169
Sālāri, Z. 185
Solar Hejri Calendar 120, 121
spiritual awakening 3
Stileman, C. H. 13
Sudmand, H. 132

Tagore, R. 97
taqiyyeh, concept of 148
TBN Nejat TV 30, 143
Thomas, D. 14, 167
The Tune of Nostalgia is *Āhang-e Ghorbat* (movie) 161, *162*, 165
Turkey 2, 5, 23, 29, 44, 59, 66, 67, 86, 189, 193
'Turkish Christian' identity 43, 44

Urshan, A. D. 15

'the West' 44, 58, 190
Western Protestant 4, 9
  American Presbyterians 11–12
  Anglicans 11–12
  missionary 189

Xerxes I (King) 116, 124, 125

Yaldā (festival) 8, 116, 191
  in *ghorbat* 167–70
Yaldā Night *(Shab-e Yaldā)* 89–92
  Christian meanings of 92–3
Yeqnazar, L. 21, 29
Yeqnazar, S. 16, 17

Zargari, R. 70, 79, 84, 122, 124, 153, 179–83
Zargari, S. 103, 124, 153, 158
'Zoroastrian' festival 63–4, 75, 99, 127, 128, 191
Zoroastrianism, Iranians 91, 128, 193

www.ingramcontent.com/pod-product-compliance
Lightning Source LLC
Chambersburg PA
CBHW071827300426
16CB00009B/1468